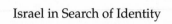

Israel in Search of Identity

ISRAEL
IN SEARCH OF IDENTITY

Reading the Formative Years

NISSIM REJWAN

University Press of Florida

Gainesville · Tallahassee · Tampa · Boca Raton
Pensacola · Orlando · Miami · Jacksonville

04 03 02 01 00 99 6 5 4 3 2 1

Library of Congress Cataloging-in-Publication Data

Rejwan, Nissim.
Israel in search of identity: reading the formative years / Nissim
Rejwan.
p. cm.
ISBN 0-8130-1664-9 (cloth: alk paper)
1. Jews—Israel—Identity. 2. Zionism—Philosophy. 3. Israel—Ethnic
relations. 4. Arab-Israeli conflict. 5. Nationalism—Arab countries.
I. Title.
DS143.R35 1999

305.892'4'05694—dc21 98-53889

The University Press of Florida is the scholarly publishing agency
for the State University System of Florida, comprising Florida
A&M University, Florida Atlantic University, Florida International
University, Florida State University, University of Central Florida,
University of Florida, University of North Florida, University of
South Florida, and University of West Florida.

University Press of Florida
15 Northwest 15th Street
Gainesville, FL 32611
http://www.upf.com

The sight of human affairs deserve admiration and pity. They are worthy of respect, too. And he is not insensible who pays them the undemonstrative tribute of a sigh which is not a sob, and of a smile which is not a grin.

JOSEPH CONRAD, *A Personal Record*

CONTENTS

PREFACE

Some people may fear what the morrow will bring,
but I am afraid of what happened yesterday.

Old Arab saying

Fifty years after its establishment, Israel continues to face the same basic problems and challenges it faced at its birth. These can be summed up under three interrelated headings: Israel's being accepted by its Arab neighbors; its succeeding in meaningfully integrating itself into its habitat; and the accommodation of its non-Jewish citizens by integrating them into Israeli society and polity. These three objectives are in turn closely related to Israel's intra-ethnic problem—the integration into its sociopolitical and economic fabric of that part of its Jewish population called variously Sephardic, Oriental, or Middle Eastern–North African.

In *Israel in Search of Identity*, an attempt is made to trace the roots of these and related problems back to the historical, cultural, religious, and intellectual backgrounds of those pioneers and founding fathers who had embraced the Zionist doctrine and subsequently set the tone for the new state ideologically and culturally as well as socially and politically. After probing these roots and their origins in the political cultures and the ethnic-nationalist ideologies of the pan-movements of nineteenth-century Eastern and Central Europe, ways and means are considered in which present-day Israelis can reappraise their attitudes and their possible future place in the Middle Eastern community of nations.

Part 1, "A Problem and Its Roots," opens with an introductory chapter in which Zionism's "Arab Doctrine" is historically and critically analyzed. An attempt is made here to show how the early Zionists' whole concept of "Arab" and of the Arab nationalist movement was a mirror image of their own perception of themselves, of their community, and of their movement—and that, consequently, the doctrine could not work.

Chapters 2 and 3 are devoted to an examination of the concepts of "nation" and "nationality" in both Zionist and pan-Arab perceptions. The idea of an ethnic Jewish nationality is analyzed in the context of the question "Who is a Jew?" This is followed by a critical reading of the basic concepts of the Zionist ideology as they are reflected in the writings of Theodore Herzl, Peretz Smolenskin, Leo Pinsker, Ahad Ha-Am, and others.

Chapters 4 and 5—comprising part 2, "Prospects"—focus on the book's central theme: Israel's continuing search for identity—national, religious, and cultural. The subject of Jewish identity is examined in the light of what the author perceives as the three major identities that the Jews in their various environs acquired through the ages—the Middle Eastern/Sephardic, the European/Ashkenazic, and the West European/North American.

The meaning and the significance of the term "Jewish" as it is used in Israel today are probed critically, the author's contention being that Judaism and "Jewish consciousness," as they are taught, preached, and practiced by the basically secularist state apparatus, have been largely emptied of their contents. State-synagogue relations and their impact on Israeli society are treated in some detail.

The role of the Middle Eastern half of Israel's Jewish population is examined in chapter 5, "Israel as an Open Society." The argument is set forth that Israel cannot reasonably expect to integrate in an open, pluralist Middle East without itself becoming an open and genuinely pluralist society in which Jew and non-Jew, Ashkenazi and Oriental, orthodox and secularist can feel at home as equal citizens.

Part 3, "Middle Eastern Themes," deals with two related subjects. In chapter 6, "Arab Nationalism and Pan-Arabism," the Arab nationalist movement and its fortunes are examined in the light, among others, of Islam's attitude to the nationality question and of the emergence of a distinct Palestinian identity that seems to repudiate the ethnic foundations of the ideology of pan-Arabism. Chapter 7, "East, West, and Other Vanities," deals with the problem of the future "orientation" of Israeli culture and society and offers an exposé of what the author calls "the myth of Orienstalization." Also scrutinized is the subject of "cultural planning" and the calls made by Western-oriented Israeli academics and intellectuals for a "Western," as against an "Eastern," Israel.

Acknowledgments

Parts of certain chapters in this book appeared over the years in a number of newspapers and periodicals. Their editors and publishers deserve my thanks. Special thanks are due to the directors and to members of the staff of the Harry S. Truman Research Institute for the Advancement of Peace,

Hebrew University of Jerusalem—in which, as a research fellow since 1996, I was able to finish writing the book and preparing it for publication. The congenial atmosphere and generous grants from the institute were of great help. Thanks, too, are due to the Jesse Zel Lurie Fund for helping fund the retyping and editing. And, last but not least, my gratitude goes to Rachel, my wife, who as always patiently bore with me and made it possible for me to devote my time to writing and researching.

PART 1

A Problem and Its Roots

—But do you know what a nation means? Says John Wyse.
—Yes, says Bloom.
—What is it? says John Wyse
—A nation? says Bloom. A nation is the same people living in the same place.

James Joyce, *Ulysses*

1

Assorted Misconceptions

The utopian and ideological elements with which [Herzl] injected the
new Jewish will to political action are only too likely to lead the Jews
out of reality once more—and out of the sphere of political action.

Hannah Arendt

It is generally agreed that the Zionist movement has never had anything
even approaching a coherent "Arab doctrine." However, three persistent
theses are discernible in all Zionist discourse on the subject, scanty and
half-baked as this has always been. These theses clearly run through all
attempts made by the leaders of the Zionist movement in the past and by
official Israeli spokesmen since 1948, to envision the precise conditions in
which Jews and Arabs can live together in peace and amity in the Middle
East. Briefly, these theses are:

1. The national aspirations of the Arabs (their wish to see their civilization revived and themselves "reunited" in a single political entity)
   stand in no opposition to the national aspirations of the Jews.

2. When the Arabs finally manage to get rid of all foreign influence and
   interests, become technologically and culturally "advanced," and
   attain all their national aspirations, they will be far more inclined to
   accept the presence of Israel in their midst. As one observer, writing
   in 1965, put it: "Perhaps rapprochement will become a reality after
   the Arab states achieve their own political maturity, expand their
   own educational patterns, liberalize their entire social structure, and
   realize that a progressive Israel, as a neighbour, can be a boon to their
   own national destiny."[1]

3. The Arabs will reconcile themselves to Israel's existence only when
   they become finally and conclusively convinced that they stand no
   chance of defeating Israel by force.

Today, fifty years after the proclamation of the state of Israel and thirty years after the Six-Day War, the fallacious and rather dangerous nature of these assumptions has become fairly evident. The Six-Day War itself, with the resounding military victory it gave Israel, served finally to shatter the illusion (so fondly nurtured by many Israelis in high places) that force alone and "new facts" would convince the Arabs that it is in their own best interest to accept Israel and reconcile themselves to the existence of another non-Arab state in the Middle East.

Zionism's "Arab Doctrine"

If a show of sufficient force and the creation of new facts were—as Israelis tended to believe over the years—capable of carrying the day with the Arabs, Israelis long ago would have attained the peace they all wish to see prevail. By the early 1970s, Israel already had managed to create as many "new facts" as it was either possible or advisable for it to do—facts that were impressive, visible, and awe-inspiring. And yet, as Israel's then defense minister Moshe Dayan was to realize, these facts did not help. "What greater 'creation of facts' could there be," Dayan asked rhetorically in an address he gave in the summer of 1968, "than the establishment of the state, the concentration of 2.5 [million] Jews there, and the victories in three wars?" Despite this rather intensive "creation of facts," he added, the Arabs persisted in their refusal to sign a peace agreement with Israel. "The facts have been created," he lamented, "but the tension is no less than it was before."[2]

An American observer who visited Israel some two years after the Six-Day War described the situation in even more striking and perceptive terms. Writing from Jerusalem in March 1969, he observed:

> Israel won the war in 1967 and surrendered immediately to a myth. Originally the line of Ben-Gurion, the myth held that once the Arabs have been truly defeated—not just thrown back as in 1948, not just penetrated briefly "with foreign help" as in 1956—but once they had had their cultural and technological vulnerabilities thrust upon them in an utterly painful and total way—then, only then, but finally then would the Arabs abandon their dream of undoing the existence of Israel, and instead make peace.

When Dayan announced, a day or two after the cease-fire in June 1967, that he was "waiting for a telephone to ring" and for leaders of the defeated Arab countries to invite themselves to the negotiating table, he expressed (according to the American journalist) "the belief and confidence of a nation convinced that its travail was nearing an end." "After all," he explained, "was not General Dayan the man most respected among Israelis for his special knowledge of the Arabs? Did not ample Biblical tradition and historical precedent and contemporary analysis all point to the conclusion that out of victory would come peace? Did not the Israelis deserve such a result?"[3]

However, not only did Dayan's telephone fail to ring. Shortly after his statement, Arab kings and heads of state convened in a summit meeting in Khartoum (August 29 to September 1, 1967) to decide on their three famous "no's": no peace with Israel, no negotiations with Israel, and no recognition of Israel. With their largest and best-equipped military machines in ruins, with some of their best territories occupied, with the Suez Canal closed, with Egypt's oil installations and industrial complex west of the canal partly destroyed and exposed to a more thorough destruction by Israeli forces stationed nearby, and with the danger of rendering up to 1 million Canal Zone inhabitants homeless, the Khartoum conferees coolly chose defiance as the only available alternative to what they perceived as capitulation. This earned the Arabs the reputation of being "irrational." The Israeli argument was that, by refusing to join (or at least make peace with) those whom they had failed to "lick," the Arabs had shown themselves to be impervious to reason and logic.

The irony of these assertions is so deep it is almost bottomless. The Arabs are said to be "irrational" creatures who understand only one language—force. However, though it is not entirely clear whether this alleged trait really renders them irrational, it is reasonable to assume that "rational" people would understand languages and devices other than sheer force. Be that as it may, accusing the Arabs of irrationality because they *refused* to bow to force amounted to asking them to be rational through *accepting* the logic of force. In any event, the Arabs refused to do so, and this refusal was not devoid of a certain kind of rationality: for what could be more irrational than mere force?

Two further considerations may have accounted for the Arabs' refusal to bow to the logic of events following the Six-Day War. First, Arabs may well have had concepts of realism and reality different from those accepted by Israelis. For them, it would have been equally and probably even more "unrealistic" and "irrational" to surrender their sense of honor and their dignity than it would have been to ignore willfully the logic of events when that logic contradicted those values. Second, and perhaps even more decisively, the Arabs may well have felt that the stronger Israel proved itself to be, the more dangerous it would be for them in the long run—and therefore the more objectionable and impossible to tolerate as an independent entity in their midst.

The idea that only an utterly superior Israeli might can persuade the Arabs to accept Israel is a fallacy and was to prove counterproductive in more senses than one. For example, it is a fact of history that Egyptian president Anwar al-Sadat's 1977 peace drive came only after the Yom Kippur War of 1973—a war that the Egyptians and Arabs generally perceived as a clear victory for themselves and as conclusive proof that Israel was not invincible militarily.

So much for what can be termed the "only-through-force" thesis. The two remaining precepts of Israeli-Zionist thinking on the Arab question are best considered in unison, since they are identical in their essential thrust. Their fallacious nature, too, is now more evident than it would have been fifty, sixty, or seventy years ago.

To start with, the Arabs have now finally managed to rid themselves of all foreign dominance, and their societies are far more "advanced," their ways of life more modern, their educated classes more numerous, and their political ideologies more "progressive." Yet not only do they go on refusing to accept Israel on its own terms but they now accuse it of such "backward" traits as racism, capitalism and imperialism. Their own advancement—for what it was—has thus in no way helped weaken their opposition to Israel; the contrary tends to be the case.

Far from making them more inclined to accept Israel, in fact, the Arabs' educational and technological attainments are being used for, and are often themselves given impetus by, the wish to defeat Israel. As I. F. Stone once put it:

> Zionist propaganda always spoke of the role that the Jews could play in helping to modernize the Arab world. Unless firm steps are now taken towards a general and generous settlement, this will become true in a sense never intended. The repercussions of the 1948 war set off seismic tremors that brought a wave of nationalist revolutions in Egypt, Syria and Iraq. The repercussions of the [June 1967] defeat will lead a new generation of Arabs to modernize and mobilize for revenge, inspired (like the Jews) by memories of past glory.[4]

It is to be noted that Stone wrote this long before the start of the so-called Islamic revival.

The same can be said about another, earlier Zionist delusion—namely, that the material benefits that Jewish settlement in Palestine would bring the Arabs were bound to make them not only accept the idea of a national home for the Jews there but also rather to welcome it. In *Altneuland* (Old-new land)—a romance that Theodor Herzl published in 1902 depicting conditions in the Holy Land twenty years hence—the founder of political Zionism envisaged no difficulties in that respect. The incoming of the Jews brought nothing but gain for the Arabs—first by their sale of unneeded land to the Jews and also by well-paid work in the draining of swamps (a work to which, by the way, they prove to be better suited than the Jews).

In addition, Herzl's Arabs learned much from the Jews by way of organization, new methods of production, and superior transportation. In one of the central passages of *Altneuland*, indeed, the Muslim-Arab Rashid Bey replies to a Christian nobleman, Mr. Kingscourt, who expresses surprise that Rashid's people do not "look upon these Jews as intruders." The Muslim notable's reply is unequivocal: "'Christian! How strange your speech sounds! Would you regard those as intruders and robbers who don't take anything away from you but give you something? The Jews have enriched us, why should we be angry at them? They live with us like brothers, why should we not love them? We Muslims have always had better relations with the Jews than you Christians'."[5]

Early Murmurs of Dissent

This rosy vision of the future and the ideas on which it was based have long since collapsed completely, although early Zionist optimists continued to insist that Arab resistance to their enterprise was the result of instigation by Arab *efendis* and would-be nationalist leaders. However, as early as the mid-1940s it became abundantly clear that Herzl's idyllic picture of Muslim-Arab attitudes to the Jewish settlers had no relation to reality. "Nowhere in the world," wrote Hans Kohn about the position of the Jews in Palestine some fifty years after the publication of Herzl's blueprint, *The Jewish State*, "was a Jewish community regarded with the hostility, distrust, and fear directed at Jews in Palestine by their neighbours. Nowhere have Jews felt so exposed as in Palestine."

The case of Vladimir Jabotinsky (1880–1940) and his ideas on the Arab question may be considered both the antithesis of and the inescapable logical conclusion to Herzl's amateur brand of Zionism, Kohn suggests.

Jabotinsky, of course, rejected Herzl's vision of the Jewish state as outlined in *Altneuland*. "He was convinced," Kohn writes, "that the Arabs could not be reconciled to Jewish domination of Palestine. Rather, he believed that the same methods must be applied there as in other schemes of European colonization in backward lands."

Like so many of the young men in Central and Eastern Europe after World War I and after the rise of fascism, Kohn adds, Jabotinsky was impressed by the "realism" of toughness. "The old liberal world of the West seemed doomed. New forces, which scornfully rejected humanitarianism or concern for the rights of others, claimed to represent the wave of the future. National egoism alone seemed to guarantee survival in a world which gloried more in biological vitality than in ethical rationality."[6]

It was a measure of that perfect identification of toughness with realism referred to above that Jabotinsky's program and his philosophy became, as early as 1942, the Zionist movement's official policy. In the so-called Biltmore Program of that year, the Zionists called for the establishment of "a Jewish commonwealth integrated in the structure of the new democratic world." Thus, for the first time they proclaimed Zionism's goal as full Jewish statehood in the Holy Land. It was at Biltmore that, to quote Hannah Arendt's telling phrase, "the Jewish minority granted minority rights to the Arab majority."[7]

During the years that preceded the Biltmore Program, several prominent Zionist leaders and thinkers tried (unavailingly, as it happened) to effect some sort of compromise between the basic aspirations of Zionism and the rights of the indigenous inhabitants of Palestine. Ahad Ha-Am (Asher Ginzberg, 1856–1927) warned that the revival of Zion was desirable and practicable only if the Jews did not become like other peoples. He consistently opposed a settlement in Palestine based on overemphasizing the relevance of numbers, power, and speed. "He knew," writes Kohn, "that the means determine the end, and that the way in which the foundations are laid defines the strength of the structure."

Ahad Ha-Am wrote in a Zionist General Council report entitled "The Truth from Palestine," that "The main point, upon which everything depends, is not how much we do but how we do it." The report was written after a visit Ahad Ha-Am made to Palestine in 1891. During this visit, writes Kohn, he was to lay his finger on the real problem, "the problem which, for practical and ethical reasons alike, was the fundamental though neglected problem of Zionism in Palestine—the Arab problem." The trouble was that, to most Zionists, "the land of their forefathers appeared empty, waiting for the return of the dispersed descendants, as if history had stood still for two thousand years."[8]

In "The Truth from Palestine," Ahad Ha-Am warned that the Jewish settlers under no circumstances must arouse the wrath of the native population by ugly actions; rather, they must meet them in a friendly spirit of respect. "Yet what do our brethren do in Palestine? Just the very opposite! Serfs they were in the lands of the Diaspora and suddenly they find themselves in freedom, and this change has awakened in them an inclination to despotism. They treat the Arabs with hostility and cruelty, deprive them of their rights, offend them without cause, and even boast of these deeds; and nobody among us opposes this despicable and dangerous inclination."

"We think," Ahad Ha-Am lamented, "that the Arabs are all savages who live like animals and do not understand what is happening around them." But this was "a great error"—as later events were to prove without any doubt. Twenty years later, indeed, in a letter to a friend in Jaffa dated July 9, 1911, Ahad Ha-Am wrote: "As to the war against the Jews in Palestine, I am a spectator from afar with an aching heart, particularly because of the want of insight and understanding shown on our side to an extreme degree. As a matter of fact, it was evident 20 years ago that the day would come when the Arabs would stand up against us."[9]

Chaim Weizmann, too, was not entirely happy about the turn events were taking—and he too found it impossible to reconcile his essentially liberal, humanist wishes with the increasingly militant tendencies shown by his followers. The difficulty was that, although officially the Zionists always emphasized that the Jews did not come to Palestine to dominate the Arabs and that no Arab should be expelled from the country, their deeds were often at variance with these assurances.

At the meeting of the Zionist General Council in Berlin in August 1930, Weizmann declared that a transformation of Palestine into a Jewish state was impossible "because we could not and would not expel the Arabs." "Moreover," he said, "the Arabs were as good Zionists as we are; they also love their country and they could not be persuaded to hand it over to someone else. Their national awakening has made considerable progress. These were facts which Zionism couldn't afford to ignore." Again, on the eve of the Seventeenth Zionist Congress, which convened in Basle in 1931, Weizmann opposed proclaiming a Jewish state as the aim of Zionism. "The world will construe this demand only in one sense, that we want to acquire a majority in order to drive out the Arabs," he explained.[10]

Robert Weltsch has called Weizmann one of the last proponents of a

Zionism based on the assumption "that the reborn Jewish nation would avoid all those national excesses from which Jews had so much to suffer among other nations." Explaining what he termed "humanist Zionism," Weltsch continued:

Intolerant, brutal, egotistical nationalism would be unacceptable to Jews who had learned to know what it means. The Jewish people which has recovered its national self-consciousness and pride would be sympathetic to other peoples in similar conditions who are striving to recover their national freedom, and from this attitude a mutual understanding could arise which would enable different nationalities to live together and to cooperate for the sake of the well-being of all.[11]

According to Hans Kohn, however, the climate of strident nationalism and fascism after World War I changed the outlook of many Zionists. Kohn quotes a passage from Weizmann's autobiography in which the man who was to become the first president of the state of Israel describes the atmosphere he found prevailing in Palestine in 1944:

Here and there a relaxation of the old traditional Zionist puritan ethics, a touch of militarization, and a weakness for its trappings; here and there something worse—the tragic, futile, un-Jewish resort to terrorism . . . and worst of all, in certain circles, a readiness to compound with the evil, to play politics with it, to condemn and not to condemn it, to treat it not as the thing it was, namely an unmitigated curse to the National Home, but as a phenomenon which might have its advantages.

The "evil," Kohn comments, "was not only 'here and there'; it was rapidly taking root and growing." Military victory, he explains, "created the new state; and, like Sparta or Prussia, on military virtue it remained based. The militarization of life and mind represented not only a break with humanist Zionism, but with the long history of Judaism. The *Zeitgeist,* or at least the *Zeitgeist* of twentieth century Central and Eastern Europe, had won out over the Jewish tradition."[12]

It will be noted, however, that while both Ahad Ha-Am and Weizmann were sincerely and deeply concerned about the situation, while both implied that a revival of Zion was desirable only if the Jews did not become "like other peoples," neither of these two Zionist luminaries could actually offer a practical formula for the revival of Zion *without the Jews' becoming like other peoples.*

This problem, it must be added, led several early Zionist thinkers to change their minds and hearts. In 1919, Hugo Bergmann, a young Jewish philosopher from Prague who was thereafter to settle in Palestine, wrote in a book called *Yavne and Jerusalem* that Palestine might become a Jewish state and yet be an entirely un-Jewish land—un-Jewish to such a degree that the smallest traditional Jewish school in a far-off Polish village would mean more for Judaism than all the new national institutions.

"The trial by fire of the truly Jewish character of our settlement in Palestine will be our relationship to the Arabs," Bergmann wrote. "An agreement with the inhabitants of the land is much more important for us than declarations of all the governments of the world could be. Unfortunately, Zionist public opinion has not yet become conscious of it."[13]

In the same year, Martin Buber, another German-educated Jewish philosopher, demanded that the Zionists should abstain from all political activities except those calculated to create and to maintain an enduring and solid agreement with the Arabs, "an encompassing brotherly solidarity."[14]

Judah L. Magnes, the American rabbi and thinker and president of the Hebrew University, expressed as late as 1947 fears that a Jewish state could be established and maintained, against Arab opposition, only by force of arms. He called for a binational state because, he said, "the Jewish genius for government can be given full play" through such a state. "The day we lick the Arabs," he warned, "that is the day, I think, when we shall be sowing the seeds of an eternal hatred of such dimensions that Jews will not be able to live in that part of the world for centuries to come. . . . We cannot maintain a Jewish state or a bi-national state or a Yishuv in Palestine if the whole surrounding world be our enemies."[15]

Arthur Ruppin and Rabbi Binyamin

However paradoxical it may sound, the fact remains that though the Zionist movement as a whole refrained consistently from facing the Arab question squarely, this problem remained at the center of all serious heart-searchings and -gropings that exercised the minds of certain intellectual adherents of Zionism. However, all those in the Zionist movement who ever seriously pondered the Arab question in the end found themselves either standing in permanent isolation from or in opposition to the movement, or giving up any hope of reconciling their ethical and humanistic sentiments with the demands of building a national home.

Few, at any rate, had the stamina both to articulate this moral conflict and to draw clear and final conclusions from their findings. The majority were either insensitive to the problem or chose to ignore its existence. It must be added here, however, that neither the lack of sensitivity to nor the refusal to acknowledge the significance of the Arab question was accidental; both were due in no small measure to the oversimplified appraisal of the general Jewish situation which Zionism had always offered. This appraisal depicts the Jews everywhere and at all times, actually or potentially, as surrounded by enemies.

This black-and-white version of the Jewish situation, by implicitly obviating all moral or even empirical efforts and scruples, made the realization of Zionism a rather easy proposition. As Hannah Arendt, writing on Herzl's general outlook, puts it:

> His notion of reality as an eternal, unchanging hostile structure—all *goyim* [gentiles] everlastingly against all Jews—made the identification of hard-boiledness with realism plausible because it rendered any empirical analysis of actual political factors seemingly superfluous. All one had to do was to use the "propelling force of antisemitism" which, like "the wave of the future," would bring the Jews into the promised land. . . . If we actually are faced with open or concealed enemies on every side, if the whole world is ultimately against us, then we are lost.[16]

Lost—but simultaneously also redeemed! Living in a world so full of enemies bent on your undoing tends to give you license to act in almost any way you choose in order to defend yourself.

When Arthur Ruppin (1876–1943), one of the best-known and respected of the Zionist leaders of his generation, was appointed director of the Zionist Executive's colonization department in 1919, he was immediately struck by the lack of interest in "the Arab question" shown by his fellow Zionists. After many years of intensive intellectual probing, he decided that it would be extremely difficult "to put Zionism into effect while adhering continuously to the precepts of ordinary ethics."

However, instead of giving up on an enterprise he considered unethical in favor of "ordinary ethics," Ruppin consciously chose to go on with the enterprise. "The Arabs," he wrote rather resignedly during the riots of 1936, "do not agree to our venture. If we want to continue our work in Palestine against their desires, there is no alternative but that lives could be lost. It is our destiny to be in a state of continued warfare with the Arabs. This situation may well be undesirable, but such is the reality."

Thus not only ethical considerations but peace and physical safety, too, were to be sacrificed in order to make it possible "to continue our work in Palestine against the Arabs' desires."[17] Clearly, the rationale for Ruppin's drastic decision must be sought in the conviction that Jewish settlement in Palestine was an act of sheer self-preservation and self-defense against the ever-hostile gentile. The question as to whether this gentile happened to be the Christian anti-Semite of Central and Eastern Europe or the Muslim-Arab inhabitants of the Holy Land was apparently of no consequence.

Ruppin was one of the few early Zionists who had the courage both to look reality in the face and to draw practical personal conclusions from what he saw. A man who was equally intensively exercised by the Arab question—but who drew rather different conclusions—was Yehoshua Radler-Feldman (1880–1957), better known by the pen name Rabbi Binyamin. Rabbi Binyamin came to Palestine from Galicia in 1907 and was very active in Zionist circles, especially in journalism, authorship, and editing. Even before his settling in Palestine, however, he became aware of the scope and seriousness of the Arab problem. Both before and after the establishment of the state he was associated with the Ihud society and for many years was editor of the group's monthly, *Ner*.

In 1953, four years before his death, Rabbi Binyamin wrote an article entitled "For the Sake of the Survival," in which he gave vent to his deep disillusionment and his misgivings about the future:

After the State of Israel was established, I began receiving news about the terrible things perpetrated both during and after the Israeli-Arab war. I did not recognize my own people for the changes which had occurred in their spirit. The acts of brutality were not the worst because those might be explained somehow or other as accidental, or an expression of hysteria, or the sadism of individuals. Far more terrible was the benevolent attitude toward these acts on the part of public opinion. I had never imagined that such could be the spiritual and moral countenance of Israel.

"What separates us from the mass of our people?" asked Rabbi Binyamin, addressing himself to Ihud members. He answered: "It is our attitude toward the Arabs. They consider the Arab as an enemy, some even say an eternal enemy. So speak the candid among them. The less candid speak supposedly about peace, but these are only words. They want a peace of submission, which the Arabs cannot possibly accept. . . . We, however, do not see the Arab as an enemy, not in the past and not today." Rabbi Binyamin continued:

It is a mistake to think that we are dreamers and do not understand reality. No. . . . We are realistic with the Ten Commandments, and they are the wise men without the Ten Commandments. . . . War gave us a state, and war gave the Arabs, beside military defeat and the loss of territory, the problem of refugees. At the same time it also gave them the concern that, when the State of Israel feels strengthened economically and population-wise through immigration, it will attempt sooner or later to invade the neighboring Arab countries. Theirs is a very simple calculation: If the small army of Israel, which had to be developed underground and which hardly possessed any arms, was able to defeat all the Arab armies, then a large organized and disciplined Israeli army, which has now taken women too into its ranks, would surely be able to do it in the future.

True Zionist that he still considered himself to be, Rabbi Binyamin concluded, with apparent anguish:

The Jewish state is dear to us because it could turn into a treasure for its inhabitants and for Jews all over the world. . . . But the first condition for its continued existence is a true peace with the Arab states. What we failed to do before the war we must do now. . . . I am not so foolish as to believe that these words would have any influence on today's rulers of Israel. I have not written this for the sake of polemics either. I wrote it because I believe that it is my duty to say what I think.[18]

It is a measure both of the prophetic character of Rabbi Binyamin's warnings and of the utter ungainliness of the whole situation that his words should sound as topical in 1998 as they did in 1953—while the gist of his appeals and entreaties has rather gained more in urgency by the passage of the years.

"Arabs" and "Palestinians"

There is a sense in which the core of the Zionists' "Arab doctrine" lay in their very understanding of the term "Arab." For them, all Arabs constitute one great nation, bound sooner or later to attain its legitimate dream of being "reunited" in one single pan-Arab state. It may well be argued now that this "pan-" vision of the Arab situation had been adopted by the early Zionists merely because it seemed rather convenient for them politically at the time—especially where the subject of "room" was concerned.

Yet the Zionists' pan-Arab vision was depicted throughout on the highest and most authoritative of levels. In a speech delivered following the riots in Jerusalem in 1920, Weizmann asserted, "The Arabs are not suffering from lack of room. The centers of Arab culture are Damascus, Baghdad and Mecca—and I hope that there a great and flourishing nation will again rise. But Palestine will be the national home of the Jews."

Returning to this same theme a decade later, Weizmann became rather more specific in his prognosis. "We say to the Arabs," he declared, "that they must distinguish between their 'national home' and their rights in Palestine. The 'national home' of the Arabs is in Damascus and Baghdad, and in the religious sense, perhaps, in Mecca and Medina, those great centres of Arab life in which a mighty Arab culture flourished. It flourished in Baghdad and Damascus, not in Jerusalem."[19]

Right from the beginning, then, even before the Arabs themselves could have conceived of so clear and so appealing a pan-Arab vision, the spokesmen of the Zionist movement found themselves stressing the Arab nationalist theme with growing conviction. There was, to be sure, no lack of ambiguity and confusion on this point in the Arab camp, either. Indeed, the obvious discrepancy between the claims of Palestinian Arabs to their native land on one hand, and the generalized claims to Palestine by the Arabs as Arabs on the other, resulted in confusion not only for outsiders but for the Arabs of Palestine themselves. In the end, this confusion was to play a significant role in their subsequent sufferings and undoing.

Yet the impact of outside concepts and actions was to prove crucial in this respect. Common misconceptions concerning the nature of Arab nationality and Arab nationalism became mixed up, quite early in the proceedings, with the general eagerness to find a solution to the Palestine problem. Lord Samuel, who in 1920 to 1925 served as high commissioner for Palestine and whose Zionist sympathies and involvement dated at least from the outbreak of World War I, suggested in 1922 a confederation of Arab states to include Hijaz, Syria, Palestine, Trans-Jordan, Iraq, and possibly Najd. In a letter to the U.S. secretary of state dated December 12, Samuel envisaged the establishment of a council to look after the federation's common interests, such as communications, customs, extradition, culture, and religion.

"More important, however, than any specific functions of the council," Samuel wrote, "would be the fact of its existence. This in itself would give satisfaction to Arab national aspirations. The confederation would be a visible embodiment of Arab unity, and a center round which the movement for Arab revival—which is a very real thing—could rally; it would give leadership and direction to that movement." The Zionists, Samuel added, would welcome such a scheme, as they "would regard the advantage of satisfying the reasonable national aspiration of the Arabs and of securing the cessation of open and persistent Arab opposition to Jewish expansion in Palestine, as far outweighing the possible future risks that would be involved in Palestine becoming a member of a distinctively Arab polity."[20]

Nevertheless, Lord Samuel's proposal was rejected. Less than sixteen years later, the British government was to extend official de facto recognition to the thesis that Palestine "is not merely a local question," and that "just as it interests Zionists all over the world, so also it interests Arabs outside Palestine wherever they may be, and particularly in the contiguous countries," as Lord Samuel himself so clearly explained in a speech in the House of Lords on December 8, 1938. He was, of course, welcoming Britain's decision to convene the Round Table Conference on Palestine, which was to start its deliberations in London in the following month and in which, for the first time in the history of the Palestine problem, the Arab states were recognized officially as parties to the dispute. The Round Table Conference, indeed, marked the beginning of the pan-Arabization of the Palestine question—a process which was to culminate in the establishment of the League of Arab States in 1945 and, ultimately, the ruin of the Palestinians.

Pan-Arabization and After

In the history of the Zionist-Arab dispute, utter confusion always reigned supreme as between the pan-Arab claim to Palestine as "an integral part of the Arab homeland" and the specific claims of the Palestinians (as the indigenous inhabitants of the land) to their own homeland. Strange as it may sound, this confusion seems to have suited all parties concerned, and no serious attempt was ever made—either by Arab nationalist, Jewish settler, or British administrator—to disentangle this particular knot.

As far as the Zionists were concerned, this is what one observer has to say:

> The shifting reference point of Arabdom, from the intolerably intense preoccupation with the arena of Palestine to the endlessly broad sweep of "the Arab people," from Persia to Morocco, in many ways was made to order for Zionist polemics, since it could be said, with obvious legitimacy, that the Zionists were claiming only a small speck of the "Arab" area, and thus were not affecting the Arabs as such, whatever might then have been said about the just claims of Palestinian Arabs themselves.[21]

Whether or not the Zionists took conscious advantage of this state of affairs may now be of only academic interest. There is, however, sufficient evidence to indicate that the Zionists' obvious tendency to espouse the pan-Arab nationalist thesis had deeper roots in their own ideology and way of thinking. For, in addition to the sheer convenience of dealing with a hypothetical "Arab" world in which "there is plenty of room, plenty of water, plenty of air for us all" (as Dr. Weizmann once put it), there was also the understandable attraction for the Zionists of an Arab nationalist movement made roughly in the image of their own ideology and worldview.

Some most striking illustrations of this attitude are to be found in the way the Zionist movement dealt with what was to become its thorniest problem—namely, its relations with the indigenous population. It was Israel Zangwill who first coined the phrase "the land without a people for the people without a land." He was, of course, referring to Palestine, and the people to whom he advocated allotting the empty land were the persecuted, virtually stateless Jews of the Pale of Settlement in Eastern Europe.

However, ever since they discovered that Palestine was not the desolate place that Zangwill depicted, Zionist leaders and ideologues have been trying desperately to convince themselves and the world that there existed no such national, cultural, geographical or legal entity as "the Palestinians"—though, to be sure, there happen to be "Arabs" who live in Palestine. When Weizmann said in Cologne in 1931 that the Arabs' "national home" was in Damascus and Baghdad but not in Jerusalem, he obviously was using a terminology that was entirely unintelligible to the Palestinians.

Hardly anything, in fact, could have been as remote from the thoughts of the Arab inhabitants of Palestine of 1931 as the novel idea of a "national home" for the Arabs. Rightly or wrongly, what these people and their leaders thought they were engaged in was nothing more complicated than defending their own homeland and birthplace—their scant worldly possessions and their plots of land—against what they perceived as systematic, efficient colonization by foreigners and strangers.

Be that as it may, the Zionists' apparent determination to pan-Arabize the Palestine issue continued unabated. David Ben-Gurion, a man whose part in shaping Zionist policies and tactics was to become decisive, has given what must be the most eloquent formulation to this trend. In his book of reminiscences, *Talks with Arab Leaders,* he gives an account of a meeting he had in Jerusalem with George Antonius, the historian of the Arab nationalist movement, himself a native of Palestine. In this meeting, which took place one day in April 1936, Ben-Gurion sought to pursue his efforts at finding a modus vivendi with the Arab nationalist leadership of the day. As was to be expected, Antonius's point of departure in these discussions with Ben-Gurion was that the question at issue was one that concerned the Arabs of Palestine and the Jewish settlers there, and that if a rapprochement was to be reached, both sides would have to make concessions.

Ben-Gurion would have none of this. He told Antonius:

> As a point of departure, the proposition must be accepted that the issue is not one between the Jews of Palestine and the Arabs of Palestine. Within this limited area the conflict is indeed difficult to resolve. Instead, we have to view the Jews as a single world entity, and the Arabs as a single world entity. I sincerely believe that between the national aspirations of the Jewish people and the national aspirations of the Arab people—which latter may not yet be clear and crystallized but which will no doubt become so in due course—there is no inevitable opposition. For we are interested only and solely in this country, while the Arabs are not interested only in this country—so that no matter what happens in this country it will not affect the world status of the Arab people.[22]

During the decades of conflict and turmoil which have elapsed since Ben-Gurion propounded these fervent pan-Arab hopes and sentiments before Antonius, there were times when it looked as though the pan-Arabization of the Palestine issue had become an accomplished fact. In the Israeli press, following the armistice agreements in 1949, the terms "Palestine" and "Palestinians" were safely closeted in quotation marks. Arab nationalists appeared at last to be heeding Weizmann's old advice and began to distinguish between their "national home" and their rights in Palestine. The drive toward the revival of a great and flourishing "Arab nation" seemed to be making considerable headway—though its center was to be neither in Damascus nor in Baghdad, nor even in Mecca or Medina. Those parts of Palestine that remained in Arab hands came to be known as the "West Bank" and the "Gaza Strip" and fell to Jordanian and Egyptian rule, respectively. Furthermore, senior foreign-ministry officials in Jerusalem started adducing historical evidence to show that no such thing as "Palestine" had ever really existed.

This doubtful idyll was not to last for very long, however. For suddenly, on one summer day in 1967 (June 8, to be exact), Palestine came to life again, and the Palestinians made their appearance on the Middle Eastern stage for everyone to see. It then began slowly to emerge that, far from consenting to be submerged into that "single world entity" called the Arabs, far from seeking their "national home" in Damascus, Baghdad, Beirut, or Cairo, the

Palestinians had a sorry tale to tell about their experience of living with their "Arab brethren," among "their own people," and "in their own culture."

Those who lived in the Gaza Strip wasted no love on their Egyptian overlords and protectors; the relatively highly educated, modernized Palestinians of the West Bank turned out to be full of bitter complaints about the arbitrary rule of King Hussein of Jordan and his army of "primitive Beduins." Those who had sought refuge in Lebanon, in Iraq, in Syria, or in one of the oil-rich states of the Arabian Peninsula spoke of an experience that was thoroughly and uniformly unhappy—how they were looked down on, discriminated against, humiliated and treated far more badly than non-Arabs were treated in those lands. Above all, they spoke of their utter failure to "pass" and the ways in which the appellation "Palestinian" pursued them everywhere they went like their own shadows.

Thus, in a way for which only the irony of history and the vanity of human wishes can account, the six days of war in June 1967 brought the Israelis face to face with a state of affairs similar (identical, in fact) to that which had confronted the Jewish *Yishuv* from its earliest days of settlement to the establishment of the state of Israel. There is, indeed, a sense in which the situation had not really undergone any significant changes even after the 1949 armistice agreements and the subsequent annexation by Jordan of the areas that were partly to constitute the Palestinian Arab state provided for by the U.N. partition plan of November 1947.

However, through a variety of agreed-upon lies and make-believe stratagems, the problem of the Palestinians temporarily had been shelved fairly successfully. In fact, when Abdel Karim Qassem (then Iraq's ruler) came out in 1959 with his idea of a "Palestinian entity," it was not its lack of soundness and/or appeal that killed his proposal in the bud but the dismal state of inter-Arab relations, on one hand, and Jordan's determination to hold on to the West Bank, on the other.

The re-emergence of the Palestinians as an independent political factor in the Middle Eastern situation offers only one demonstration, albeit the most striking, of the fallacy of the thesis dealt with above. The whole relatively brief history of Arab-Zionist relations seems to indicate fairly conclusively that no meaningful rapprochement is likely to be reached between the pan-Arabs and the Zionists. The pan-Arab movement, between which and the pan-Jewish movement the Zionists thought no inevitable opposition existed, proved to be the most implacable enemy of Zionist aspirations in Palestine.

The Israeli-Egyptian peace treaty signed in March 1979 was, in fact, made possible mainly because the Egyptians under Anwar al-Sadat's leadership had finally abandoned all pretenses for Egypt to be the champion and the leading light of the pan-Arab movement. However, Sadat's painful trials with his fellow Arabs, opposition to his peace policy throughout the Arab world, the various boycotts and sanctions to which Egypt was subjected, as well as the experiences of the past five decades, all pointed to one principal moral.

The moral to be drawn is that an overall settlement of the Arab-Israeli conflict, when and if it comes, must have at its basis something other than Zionism's "Arab doctrine" as it was propounded nearly a century ago, and which envisaged, among other things, a unified Arab world with which a pan-Jewish state in Palestine would coexist in peace and amity. Such a vision of a future Middle East has already proved to be virtually impossible to materialize.

In truth, the Zionists and the pan-Arabs have too much in common—too great an ideological affinity with each other, the lines of their respective political development are too parallel, and their national aspirations too obviously fixed on the same object—for them to be able to come together or even accept each other's presence. In pure ideological terms, at least, they have been in agreement on almost every issue, with the crucial exception of one: the right of the other side to lead a sovereign political existence in that strip of territory that both consider their homeland, or part thereof. Moreover, in their single-minded preoccupation with their respective status as "world entities," both pan-Arabs and pan-Jews have tended to ignore the existence of the only Arab group with a legitimate claim to part of Palestine—the Palestinians themselves.

It is with these Palestinians—who regardless of their linguistic-cultural affiliation, must be recognized as Palestinians rather than a group of generalized "Arabs"—that Israel ultimately has to deal. To them Israel will have to give satisfaction. Both the pan-Arab approach and the Zionist vision, which imply an uncompromising either-I-or-you stance, are basically self-defeating and can lead only to despair and desperation.

The two positions are also entirely ahistorical. Jews and Muslim Arabs lived side by side through at least fifteen centuries of their history—and they did so in a way that no adherents of any other two faiths have ever managed to do.

Nationalism Tribal and Territorial

The myth of the barbaric horde

Lewis Namier

What can be described as the "pan-approach" to the subject of nationality and national entities—an approach shared in equal measure by Zionists and Arab ethnic nationalists—decrees that the best of all possible sovereign states is one that manages to accommodate members of what the theoreticians of these movements consider a single "nationality."

In this chapter, it is argued that this perception of the nationality issue was the main cause, and remains at the very core, of what has come to be known as the Middle East crisis. Following a brief summary of the subject of nationality in relation to the nature of the modern state, the doctrines of the pan-movements—and of the ethnic nationalist ethos on which they are based—are critically analyzed and laid bare in the last two sections of the chapter.

Nation and State

Writing more than a century ago, Lord Acton concluded an essay on "Nationality" with the assertion that those states are "substantially the most perfect" that include various distinct nationalities without oppressing them. Those states, he added pointedly, in which no mixture of races has occurred are "imperfect," while those in which the effect of such a mixture has disappeared are "decrepit." Acton continued: "A state which is incompetent to satisfy different races condemns itself; a state which labours to neutralize, to absorb, or to expel them destroys its own vitality; a state which does not include them is destitute of the chief basis of self-government."

Acton's analysis of the problems of nationality, on which he based these conclusions, is in every sense as valid today as it was when his essay was written. The reason why he considered the existence of several "nations" under the same state so beneficial was his conviction that such coexistence was the test, as well as the best security, of the freedom of that state. "It is also one of the chief instruments of civilization and, as such, it is the natural and providential order, and indicates a state of greater advancement than the national unity which is the ideal of modern liberalism."

The combination of different "nations" in one state, Acton believed, was as necessary a condition of civilized life as the combination of persons in society. "Inferior races," he wrote, "are raised by living in political union with races intellectually superior. Exhausted and decaying nations are revived by the contact of a younger vitality. Nations in which the elements of organization and the capacity for government have been lost, either through the demoralizing influence of despotism or the disintegrating action of democracy, are restored and educated anew under the discipline of a stronger and less corrupted race." Where political and national boundaries coincide, on the other hand, "society ceases to advance, and nations elapse into a condition corresponding to that of men who renounce intercourse with their fellow men."

Acton believed firmly that the distinction, the separateness, between political and national boundaries "unites mankind not only by the benefits it confers on those who live together, but because it connects society either by a political or a national bond, gives to every people an interest in its neighbours, either because they are under the same government or because they are of the same race, and thus promotes the interests of humanity, of civilization and of religion." Religion, noted Acton, "rejoices at the mixtures of races, as paganism identifies itself with their differences, because truth is universal, and errors various and particular." In the ancient world, he reminded his readers, "idolatry and nationality went together, and the same term is applied in Scripture to both."

Later in his essay, Acton touched on the differences between patriotism and what can best be termed tribal, or ethnic, nationalism. The difference between nationality and the state, he wrote, is exhibited in the nature of patriotic attachment. Our connection with the race is merely natural or physical, while our duties to the political nation are ethical. The former is a community of affections and instincts infinitely important and powerful in savage life, but pertaining more to the animal than to the civilized person; the latter (what Acton calls "the political nation" and by which he means the state) is an authority governing by laws, imposing obligations, and giving a moral sanction to the natural relations of society. In its real political character, patriotism "consists in the development of the instinct of self-preservation into a moral duty which may involve self-sacrifice." The nationality formed by the state—and which identified with that state legally and geographically—is, according to Acton, "the only one to which we owe political duties, . . . the only one which has political rights." The Swiss, for example, are ethnologically either French, Italian, or German; "but no nationality has the slightest claim upon them, except the purely political nationality of Switzerland."

In contrast to Switzerland, there are states that have succeeded neither in absorbing distinct races in a political nationality nor in separating a particular district from a larger nation. The progress of civilization, Acton asserts, deals harshly with this last category of states, which, in order to maintain their integrity, "must attach themselves by confederations, or family alliances, to greater powers, and thus lose something of their independence." Moreover, in a small and homogeneous population, there is hardly room for a natural classification of society or for inner groups of interests that set bounds to sovereign power. "The government and the subjects contend with borrowed weapons. The resources of the one and the aspirations of the other are derived from some external source, and the consequence is that the country becomes the instrument and the scene of contests in which it is not interested."

It is not nationalities, their rights, or their aspirations that Acton deplored but the equation of state and nation. He wrote in a telling dictum:

The greatest adversary of the rights of nationality is the modern theory of nationality. By making the state and the nation commensurate with each other in theory, it reduces practically to a subject condition all other nationalities that may be within the boundary. It cannot admit them to an equality with the ruling nation which constitutes the state, because the state would then cease to be national, which would be a contradiction of the principle of its existence.

According, therefore, to the degree of humanity and civilization in that dominant body which claims all the rights of the community, the inferior races are exterminated, or reduced to servitude, or outlawed, or put in a condition of dependence.

According to Acton, the national theory marked the end of the revolutionary doctrine and its logical exhaustion. He concluded his essay with the following statement:

Nationalism does not aim either at liberty or prosperity, both of which it sacrifices to the imperative necessity of making the nation the mould and measure of the state. Its course will be marked by material as well as moral ruin, in order that a new invention may prevail over the works of God and the interests of mankind. There is no principle of change, no phase of political speculation conceivable [that would be] more comprehensive, more subversive, or more arbitrary than this. It is a confutation of democracy, because it sets limits to the existence of the popular will, and substitutes for it a higher principle. It prevents not only the division, but the extension of the state, and forbids to terminate war by conquest, and to obtain security for peace.[1]

The theory of nationality, which Acton so devastatingly described as the greatest enemy of the rights of nationality, has had its most pernicious and destructive expression in Central and Eastern Europe. There, the view was to prevail that the nation was a kind of Hegelian organism, a soul or a spiritual principle springing from the history and the very nature of humankind. The doctrine insisted that the nation had a common history, a common past which it sought to elevate to the point of worship—although, in reality, that past, for the most part, was merely invented or imagined. This fascination with the past—real or imaginary—was unknown in those countries where nations had been born in an age and under the symbols of reason and liberty, such as England, France, and the United States. In these nations, nationality had acquired a territorial and legal connotation rather than an ethnic-racial one. Hans Kohn has succinctly described the ethnic nationalist's consuming preoccupation with the past and his fascination with his nation's past "memories."

Kohn writes:

The British and American peoples, in their eighteenth century optimism and their trust in common sense, often miss the impact of history because they have short memories. Other nations miss the opportunities of life because they have too long memories and lose themselves in the tragic implications of "destiny." They remember too vividly, almost as a present-day reality, what happened hundreds or even thousands of years ago, embellishing it by national legends and interpreting it by the present alleged national needs.

It is to be noted that Kohn does not dismiss all preoccupation with past events as futile. He concedes:

To cope with present conflicts man must draw understanding from the past, from the deep resources of history; but nothing is more dangerous than the wish to mould mankind into the moulds of the past and to have nations haunted by its ghosts. In the age of nationalism some nations have claimed for themselves a "mission" here on earth: the divine rights of kings were replaced by the divine rights of nations. Messianic dreams with the nation at their centre put the nation into immediate and independent relations with the Absolute.[2]

The result of these and other assorted fancies and delusions has been a veritable gallery of horrors, as anyone acquainted with European history during the period extending roughly from the middle of the nineteenth century to the middle of the twentieth will readily see. Poland's misfortunes up to the end of World War II were partly caused by the identification of the ethnic Poland of the age of nationalism with the seventeenth-century Polish commonwealth in its vast supranational territories. The Bulgarians fought three wars, and lost every one of them, because of their obsession with the dream of San Stefano and of the medieval empire of Tsar Simeon. In Spain, General Franco's followers set their hearts not upon the modernization and liberalization of their country but upon the resurrection of the glories of the Golden Century.

Obviously, a doctrine with so vastly destructive an impact must have drawn on an extremely powerful emotional and intellectual source. In an essay on the German nationalist historian Heinrich von Treitschke, Kohn speaks of "the German inclination to force ideas in the 'free realm of the mind' to their logical and absurd conclusions without regard for the limitations of reality and common sense." He cites Johann Gottlieb Fichte, the philosopher, whose conclusions from his own idea of the divine nature of the nation offer a striking illustration of this kind of logical absurdity. "Only when each people," Fichte was convinced, "left to itself, develops and forms itself in accordance with its own peculiar quality, and only when in every people each individual develops himself in accordance with that common quality, as well as with his own peculiar quality—then, and then only, does the manifestation of divinity appear in its true mirror as it ought to be." Such fancies, obviously, could emanate only from sick, pathologically introverted minds.[3]

The type of mind that gave birth to such creeds has been savaged eloquently by Lewis Namier. He wrote:

The Greek was a "political animal," the German is not. His creations are inorganic and grotesque. . . . They are the work of men with poor human contacts, isolated and tense, who require rigid rules and regulations in their intercourse with fellow-men, and, if forced into gregarious life, fit themselves into it to the point of self-annihilation, but cannot attain the culture of the *agora*. . . . Introversion and divorce from reality produce a colossal, doctrinaire totalitarianism even in the realm of ideas.

However, Namier continues, "so long as the Germans remained *das Volk der Denker*, such peculiarities, at the worst, merely made them comic." But when these introverts were swept into action, "when their inner tensions were translated into a supreme power-drive; when drunk with might they mistook their victories for a triumph of German *Kultur* . . . ; when every accession of power rendered these latecomers more frantically envious of those who possessed the 'unbought grace of life,' while every frustration filled them with venomous rage; the world catastrophe was at hand."[4]

The Nature of Pan-Movements

The catastrophe duly came. It came when, in Central and Eastern Europe, the whole idea of nationality was transformed. More than any European nation, however, it was the Germans who were to empty the territorial state of its communal content and convert it into "sheer dynastic property." As Namier explains, the British and Swiss concepts of nationality as a primarily territorial description was, in Germany, turned literally upside down: It is not the state that creates and determines the nationality, but vice versa—nationality is the basis of the state. While the highest forms of communal life had become the basis of West European nationalisms, it was "the myth of the barbaric horde" that was to be the basis of German and other Central and Eastern European nationalisms.[5]

Kohn makes the same point. "Nationalism in the West," he writes, "was based upon a nationality which was the product of social and political factors; nationalism in Germany did not find its justification in a rational societal conception; it found it in the 'natural' fact of a community held together . . . by traditional ties of kinship and status." German nationalism, Kohn explains, substituted for the legal and rational concept of "citizenship" the infinitely vaguer concept of "folk," which, first discovered by the German humanists, was fully developed by Herder and the German romanticists.

With roots that "seemed to reach into the dark soil of primitive times," says Kohn, that concept "lent itself more easily to the embroideries of imagination and the excitations of emotions." Moreover, the Germans transferred to the field of society and nationalism Rousseau's ethical and cultural antithesis between the primitive and the artificial. "They established a distinction between state and nation; they regarded the state as a mechanical and judicial construction, the artificial product of historical accidents, while they believed the nation to be the work of nature, and therefore something sacred, eternal, organic, carrying a deeper justification than works of men."[6]

"The myth of the barbaric horde" was, of course, the basis of the "pan-movements"—mainly pan-Germanism and pan-Slavism—which, beyond and above their relatively "moderate" calls for such "national" aims as Germanizing Central Europe or Russifying Eastern and Southern Europe, harbored elaborate programs for world conquest and expansion. The leaders and theoreticians of these movements vested themselves with an aura of holiness; they had only to invoke the ghost of "Holy Russia" or the "Holy Roman Empire" to arouse all kinds of superstitions in Slavic or German intellectuals. "Pseudo-mystical nonsense," to quote Hannah Arendt, "enriched by countless and arbitrary historical memories, provided an emotional appeal that seemed to transcend, in depth and breadth, the limitations of nationalism. Out of it, at any rate, grew that kind of nationalist feeling whose violence proved an excellent motor to set mob masses into motion and quite adequate to replace the older national patriotism as an emotional centre."

This new type of ethnic nationalism differs fundamentally from even the most extreme manifestations of Western-type, or territorial, nationalism. Even the nationalist excesses of a Maurras or a Barrés (with their *nationalisme integrale* and all) cannot be compared with the mystical tribalism of Central and Eastern European nationalist doctrines. Neither Maurras nor Barrés, for example, ever held that men of French origin, born and raised in another country and with no knowledge of the French language and French culture, would be "born Frenchmen" thanks to some mysterious qualities of body or soul.

"Only with the 'enlarged tribal consciousness'," Arendt notes, "did that peculiar identification of nationality with one's own soul emerge—that turned-inward pride that is no longer concerned only with public affairs but pervades every phase of private life until, for example, 'the private life of each true Pole . . . is a public life of Polishness'."[7]

The main difference between even the most violent forms of chauvinism and this tribal nationalist fervor is that the one is extroverted, the other introverted. Chauvinism, no matter how wrongheaded and romantic, is at least concerned with visible spiritual and material achievements of the nation. On the other hand, tribal nationalism concentrates on the individual's own soul, which is considered the embodiment of the presumed general national qualities. According to Arendt:

> Chauvinist mystique still points to something that really existed in the past . . . and merely tries to elevate this into a realm beyond human control; tribalism . . . starts from nonexistent, pseudo-mystical elements which it proposes to realize fully in the future. It can be easily recognised by the tremendous arrogance, inherent in its self-concentration, which dares to measure a people, its past and present, by the yardstick of exalted inner qualities and inevitably rejects [that people's] visible existence, traditions, institutions and cultures.

Tribal nationalism, the ideological core of all pan-movements, moreover always insists that its own people is surrounded by "a world of enemies," "one against all." It insists that, as Arendt puts it, "a fundamental difference exists between this people and all others . . . and claims this people to be unique, individual, incompatible with others—and denies theoretically the very possibility of a common mankind long before it is used to destroy the humanity of man."[8]

One of the most instructive aspects of Central and Eastern European tribal nationalisms—and the pan-movements which were their main political expression—was their attitude toward Jews. Kohn has shown how, in their opposition to Western ideas of individual liberty and human equality, these movements were, by definition and necessity, anti-Semitic. As early as 1815, Friedrich Ruhs, a professor of history at the University of Berlin, demanded the exclusion of the Jews from all civil rights and government positions, especially public offices and the army, and asked that "the Hebrew enemy" should wear a special sign on his garment to make him easily recognizable.

In the first half of the nineteenth century, pogroms against the Jews swept many German cities, amid shouts of "Hep, Hep, let the Jew die like a beast!" In these pogroms, students took the lead and organized the mob. Moritz Busch, a German liberal and publicist and Bismark's press agent, conducted a violent campaign against the Jews. Eugen Duhring, a prolific philosopher, in 1881 wrote a book entitled *The Jewish Question as a Racial, Ethical and Cultural Problem*, in which he suggested those same "remedies" that Adolf Hitler was to apply just a little more than a half-century later. Alfred Wagner, a Berlin University economist, joined Adolf Stocker in the leadership of the Christian Socialist Workmen Party, founded in 1878 to organize the proletariat on a strictly monarchist and paternalistic basis against Marxism and bourgeois liberalism, both regarded as inspired and dominated by Jews. These are but a few examples from a seemingly endless list.[9]

In justifying their anti-Semitism, spokesmen of the European pan-movements naturally used various specific charges against the Jews. Hidden connections between the Jews and the Western European nation-states were suddenly discovered; Jews living among nationalities then still under the Hapsburg monarchy or Czarist Russia were claimed to be agents of an oppressive state machine. Schoernerer, the spokesman of Austrian pan-Germanism, early in his career became aware of the connection between the Hapsburg monarchy and the Rothschilds' domination of Austria's railroad system.

As Arendt notes, however, all this by itself would hardly have made Schoernerer announce that "we Pan-Germans regard antisemitism as the mainstay of our national ideology." Nor could anything similar have induced the Pan-Slav Russian writer Rozanov to pretend that "there is no problem in Russian life in which, like a comma, there is not also the question: How to cope with the Jews?" The real clue to the emergence of anti-Semitism as the center of a whole outlook on life and the world, Arendt concludes, lies in the nature of tribalism rather than in political facts or circumstances. "The true significance of the pan-movements' antisemitism was that hatred of the Jews was, for the first time, severed from all actual experience concerning the Jewish people, political, social or economic, and followed only the peculiar logic of an ideology."[10]

Another crucial factor that made anti-Semitism so natural and effective a feature of the pan-movements was that there existed an inherent affinity between these movements' theories about peoples and the rootless existence of the Jewish people itself. The Jews, it seemed, were the one perfect example of a people in the tribal sense, their organization the model that the pan-movements were trying to emulate, their survival and their supposed power the best proof of the validity of tribalism's racial theories. The Jews were, in the view of the tribal nationalists of Central and Eastern Europe, "the example of a people who without any home at all had been able to keep their identity through the centuries and could therefore be cited as proof that no territory was needed to constitute a nationality." In this sense, at least, the pan-German and the pan-Slav ideologues unwittingly became the first theoreticians of pan-Judaism.

If the pan-movements insisted on the secondary importance of the state and the paramount importance of the people, organized in the course of centuries and not necessarily represented in visible institutions, the Jews were a perfect model of a nation without a state and without visible institutions. Arendt adds:

> If tribal nationalities pointed to themselves as the centre of their national pride, if they believed that some mysterious, inherent psychological or physical quality made them the incarnation not of Germany but of Germanism, not of Russia but the Russian soul, they somehow knew ... that the Jewishness of assimilated Jews was exactly the same kind of personal individual embodiment of Judaism and that the peculiar pride of secularized Jews, who had not given up the claim to chosenness, really meant that they believed that they were different and better simply because they happened to be born as Jews, regardless of Jewish achievements and tradition.[11]

Needless to say, this concept of Judaism and of Jewry was a reflection more of the pan-movements' own tribalist doctrines than of the authentic nature of the Jewish religion or the Jewish community. The ethnic nationalists of Central and Eastern Europe read in Judaism and the Jewish tradition what they themselves wanted to read—namely, an added proof that nations were separate natural entities ordained by God and that the best of all possible political worlds would obtain when each of the nations had formed a state of its own.

The view of nationhood that had prevailed in Europe until the end of the eighteenth century was thus altered completely. To the French revolutionaries, a nation meant a number of individuals who had signified their will as to the manner of their government. According to the new doctrine, on the other hand, a nation was a natural division of the human race, endowed by God with its own character which its sons and daughters are duty-bound to preserve pure and inviolable.[12]

Staatsfremde and *Volksfremde*

With his fertile poetic imagination and firm tribalist convictions, the German philosopher J. G. Herder has drawn a remarkable analogy. "The savage," he wrote, "who loves himself, his wife, and child, with quiet joy, and glows with limited activity for his tribe as for his own life, is in my opinion a more real being than that cultivated shadow, who is encaptured with the love of the shades of his whole species, that is of a name." "The savage," Herder elaborated in his own Germanic way, "has room in his hut for every stranger, whom he receives as his brother with calm benevolence, and asks not whence he comes. The deluged heart of the idle cosmopolite is a hut for no one."

On a more theoretical-philosophical level, in his *Ideas towards a Philosophy of the History of Mankind,* Herder maintained that a good state should have "natural" borders—namely, those that coincide with the places inhabited by members of its "nation." "The most natural state," he explains, "is a state composed of a single people with a single national character. . . . A people is a natural growth like a family, only spread more widely. As in all human communities, so in the case of the state, the natural order is the best—that is to say, the order in which everyone fulfils the function for which nature intended him."[13]

Herder's "cultivated shadow"—the detested "idle cosmopolite"—was of course one who could be blind enough to envisage a state in which more than one "nation" lived together. Ironically enough, Herder and other German ideologues of the nation-state condemn the multinational state on the grounds that, beside being "unnatural" and therefore doomed to disintegration, it is "oppressive." Their argument, however, as Elie Kedourie remarks, "is not so much that in such states one element may dominate the others; rather, that they sin against the principle of diversity, for in them the different nations always run the risk of losing their identity, and are not able to fully cultivate their originality."

To lend his point more force, Herder argues that empires such as those of the Ottomans or the Grand Mogul were corrupt states that comprised a multitude of nations, while the states of China, of the Brahmins, and of the Jews were wholesome states. Such a state, even if it perishes, leaves the nation intact, because it has been able—within its own "natural" borders— to withstand intermixture with other nations.[14]

Politically, what this identification of nation with state meant was severe and destructive interference with the proper functions of the state. Hannah Arendt analyzes this aspect of the tribal nationalist doctrine in a simple but highly illuminating manner. In the name of the will of the people, she explains, the state was forced to recognize only "nationals" as citizens, to grant full civil and political rights only to those who belong to the national community by right of origin and fact of birth.

This meant that the state was "partly transformed from an instrument of the law into an instrument of the nation." This "conquest of the state by the nation"—in Arendt's telling phrase—was in the final analysis a direct, if unintended, result of the kind of ideas preached by the French Revolution, mainly in that this revolution combined the declaration of the Rights of Man with the demand for national sovereignty.[15]

Thus, "the same essential rights were at once claimed as the inalienable heritage of all human beings *and* as the specific heritage of specific nations."

The same nation was thus declared to be subject to laws (which supposedly would flow from human rights) *and* sovereign—that is, bound by no universal law and acknowledging nothing superior to itself. The practical outcome of this fundamental contradiction was that "from then on human rights were protected and enforced only as national rights"; the very institutions of a state, whose supreme task was to protect and guarantee a human being's rights as a person, a citizen, and a national, "lost its legal, rational appearance and could be interpreted by the romantics as the nebulous representative of the 'national soul' which through the fact of its existence was supposed to be beyond or above the law." National sovereignty thus "lost its original connotation of freedom of the people and was being surrounded by a pseudo-mystical aura of arbitrariness."[16]

The tribal nationalists' insistence on an almost total separation of nationality from all territorial basis is a negation not only of the status of citizenship and the rights that normally follow from it but also of the very concept of patriotism. Nationalism has often been confused with patriotism, chauvinism, and xenophobia. In its tribal form, however, nationalism has, strictly speaking, nothing to do with any of these attitudes, although it may happen to coincide with one or all of them.

In 1793, a young Jacobin soldier wrote a letter to his mother from the front, proclaiming:[17]

> When *la patrie* calls us for her defence, we should rush to her as I would rush to a good meal. Our life, our goods, and our talents do not belong to us. It is to the nation, to *la patrie*, that everything belongs. I know indeed that you and some other inhabitants of our village do not share these sentiments. You and they are insensible to the cries of this outraged fatherland. But as for me, who have been reared in the liberty of conscience and thought, who have always been a republican in my soul, though obliged to live under a monarch, the principles of love for *la patrie*, for liberty, for the republic, are not only engraved on my heart but they are absorbed in it and they will remain in it so long as that Supreme Being who governs the universe may be pleased to maintain within me the breath of life.[17]

These are fancy, confused, and rather pathetic sentiments, and in their irrational excesses they may sound as crass as the habitual jargon of the pan-movements. Yet the difference between the two rhetorics is fundamental. Patriotism, even chauvinism, in the sense in which they denote affection for one's country or one's group, loyalty to their institutions, and zeal for their safety, are sentiments known in a greater or lesser degree among all kinds of people.

The same is true of xenophobia, which can be defined as the dislike of strangers, outsiders, and the reluctance to admit them into one's own group. However, as Kedourie has pointed out, neither patriotism nor xenophobia depends on a particular anthropology, and neither asserts a particular doctrine of the state or of the individual's relation to it. "Nationalism," Kedourie writes, "does both; it is a comprehensive doctrine which leads to a distinctive style of politics. . . . If confusion exists, it is because nationalist doctrine has annexed these universally held sentiments to the service of a specific anthropology and metaphysic."[18]

It is, therefore, loose and inexact to speak (as is sometimes done) of British and American "nationalism" when describing the thought of those who recommend loyalty to British or American political institutions.

> A British or an American nationalist would have to define the British or the American nation in terms of language, race, or religion, to require that all those who conform to the definition should belong to the British or American state, that all those who do not should cease so to belong, and to demand that all British and American citizens should merge their will in the will of the community. It is at once clear that political thought of this kind is marginal and insignificant in Britain and America, and that those who speak of British or American nationalism do not usually have such views in mind.[19]

In Central and Eastern Europe, on the other hand, political thought of the kind Kedourie refers to was anything but marginal. The pan-movements' successful perversion of the state into an instrument of the nation, and the identification of the citizen with the member of the "nation," may be illustrated by the distinction the pan-Germans used to draw between *Staatsfremde* (aliens of the state) and *Volksfremde* (aliens of the nation). In Austria, the socialist pan-German activists Karl Renner and Otto Bauer went so far as to propose to separate nationality entirely from its territorial basis and to make it a kind of personal status—a proposition that corresponded to a situation in which ethnic groups were dispersed all over the empire without losing any of their national character. "The personal principle," wrote Bauer, "wants to organise nations not as territorial bodies but as mere associations of persons."[20]

According to Hannah Arendt, this rather novel "personal" concept of nationality was to spread among peoples for whom nationality had not yet developed beyond the inarticulateness of ethnic consciousness; whose languages had not yet outgrown the dialect stage, through which all European languages went before they became suited for literary purposes; and to whom, consequently, their national quality appeared to be much more a portable private matter, inherent in their very personality, than a matter of public concern and civilization. Arendt writes:

If they wanted to match the national pride of Western nations, they had no country, no state, no historic achievement to show but could only point to themselves, and that meant, at best, to their language— as though language by itself were already an achievement—at worst, to their Slavic, or Germanic, or God knows what soul. . . . Here were masses who had not the slightest idea of the meaning of *patria* and patriotism, not the vaguest notion of responsibility for a common, limited community.[21]

Prophets as Tribal Chieftains

It was out of this atmosphere of rootlessness that tribal nationalism grew. According to Arendt:

Rootlessness was the true source of that "enlarged tribal consciousness" which actually meant that members of these peoples had no definite home but felt at home wherever other members of their "tribe" happened to live. . . . The hallmark of the pan-movements was that they never even tried to achieve national emancipation, but at once, in their dreams of expansion, transcended the narrow bounds of a national community and proclaimed a folk community that would remain a political factor even if its members were dispersed all over the earth.[22]

The use that the pan-movements made of religion and of the religious sentiment is another aspect of the tribal nationalist's doctrinal frame of mind. Arendt notes:

Nationalism has been frequently described as an emotional surrogate of religion, but only the tribalism of the pan-movements offered a new religious theory and a new concept of holiness. It was the Czar's religious function and position in the Greek Church that led Russian pan-Slavs to the affirmation of the Christian nature of the Russian people, of their being, according to Dostoevski, the "Christopher among the nations" who carry God directly into the affairs of this world. It was because of claims to being "the true divine people of modern times."[23]

Thus, when the peculiar metaphysic of nationalism is used in the interpretation of the human past, history takes on a novel complexion. To quote Kedourie again:

> Men who thought they were acting in order to accomplish the will of God, to make the truth prevail, or to advance the interests of a dynasty, or perhaps simply to defend their own against aggression, are suddenly seen to have been acting in order that the genius of a particular nationality could be manifested and fostered. Abraham was not a man possessed of a vision of the one God, he was really the chieftain of a beduin tribe intent on endowing his horde with a national identity. Moses was not a man inspired by God in order to fulfil and reaffirm his covenant with Israel, he was the national leader rising against colonial oppression. Muhammad may have been the seal of Prophets, but even more important, he was the founder of the Arab nation. Luther was a shining manifestation of Germanism; Hus a precursor of Masaryk.[24]

This historiography is entirely in keeping with the concepts—whether religious, political, or anthropological—of all the pan-movements. These movements, for example, preached the divine origin of their own people as against the Judeo-Christian teaching about the divine origin of humankind. "According to them," Arendt observes, "man, belonging inevitably to some people, received his divine origin only indirectly through membership of a people. The individual, therefore, has his divine value only as long as he belongs to the people singled out for divine origin. He forfeits this whenever he decides to change his nationality, in which case he severs all bonds through which he was endowed with divine origins and falls, as it were, into metaphysical homelessness."[25]

Translated into political terms, the advantage of such a concept of humanity to the nationalists was twofold: First, it made nationality a permanent quality which no longer could be touched by history, no matter what happened to a given people—emigration, conquest, dispersion. The second advantage had an even more immediate impact. For in the absolute contrast between the divine origin of one's own people and all other nondivine peoples, all differences between the individual members of that people disappeared, whether social, economic, or psychological.

As Arendt puts it:

Divine origin changed people into a uniform "chosen" mass of arrogant robots. . . . Politically, it is not important whether God or nature is thought to be the origin of a people; in both cases . . . people are transformed into animal species so that a Russian appears as different from a German as a wolf is from a fox. A "divine people" lives in a world in which it is the born persecutor of all other weaker species, or the born victim of all other stronger species. Only the rules of the animal kingdom can possibly apply to its political destinies.[26]

Lunatic as all this may sound, the attractions of such a version of humanity and human political life are obvious. This brand of nationalism appeals to human beings' tribal instincts, to their passions, and to their prejudices—and to their "nostalgic desire to be relieved from the strain of individual responsibility," which it attempts to replace by a collective or group responsibility. It is apparent that the tribalism of the European pan-movements owed part of its great appeal to its contempt for liberal individualism, the ideals of humankind, and the dignity of human beings as such.

Arendt observes:

No human dignity is left if the individual owes his value only to the fact that he happens to be born a German or a Russian; but there is, in its stead, a new coherence, a sense of mutual reliability among all members of the people which indeed was very apt to assuage the rightful apprehensions of modern men as to what might happen to them if, isolated individuals in an atomized society, they were not protected by sheer numbers and enforced uniform coherence.[27]

That the appeal of tribal isolation was in part due to the instinctive human aversion to sharing in a common human responsibility is aptly illustrated by the following remarks, made by one of the ideologues of pan-Germanism:

We know our own people, its qualities and its shortcomings; mankind we do not know and we refuse to care or to get enthusiastic about it. Where does it begin, where does it end, that which we are supposed to love because it belongs to mankind? Are the decadent or half-bestial Russian peasant of the *mir,* the Negro of East Africa, or the unbearable Jews of Galicia and Rumania all members of mankind? One can believe in the solidarity of the Germanic peoples; whoever is outside this sphere does not matter to us.

The gist of the matter is that—from the point of view of the tribal nationalist—the idea, and ideal, of humanity "has the very serious consequence that in one form or another men must assume responsibility for all crimes committed by men, and that eventually all nations will be forced to answer for the evil committed by all others." Tribalism and racism are highly realistic ways of escaping this responsibility. "Their metaphysical rootlessness, which matched so well the territorial uprootedness of the nationalities it first seized, was equally well suited to the needs of the shifting masses of modern cities and was therefore grasped at once by totalitarians."[28]

Much has been written and said on the subject of nationalism—ethnic, tribal, and territorial. Much of it is beset by confusion, woolly thinking, and prejudice. One prominent and rather damning example is President Woodrow Wilson's celebrated principle of self-determination for peoples. In a scathing comment, Karl Popper terms the principle "well-meant but less well-considered." Popper wonders how anybody with the slightest knowledge of European history, of the shifting and mixing of all kinds of tribes, of the countless waves of peoples who had come forth from their original Asian habitat and split up and mingled when reaching the maze of peninsulas called the European continent "could ever have put forward such an inapplicable principle."

Popper's explanation is as apt as it is simple. Wilson, he asserts, who was a sincere democrat, "fell victim to a movement that sprang from the most reactionary and servile political philosophy that has ever been imposed upon meek and long-suffering mankind." Wilson, in short, fell victim to "his upbringing in the metaphysical political theories of Plato and of Hegel," and to the nationalist movements based upon them.

Popper's verdict on the nation-state is reminiscent of Lord Acton's prophetic utterances of over a century ago:

> The *principle of the national state*, that is to say, the political demand that the territory of every state should coincide with the territory inhabited by one nation, is by no means so self-evident as it seems to appear to many people today. Even if anyone knew what he meant when he spoke of nationality, it would be not at all clear why nationality should be accepted as a fundamental political category, more important for instance than religion, or birth within a certain geographical region, or loyalty to a dynasty, or a political creed like democracy (which forms, one might say, the uniting factor of multi-lingual Switzerland).[29]

Popper goes on to say that, while religion, territory, or political creed can be more or less clearly determined, nobody ever has been able to explain what is meant by a nation in a way that could be used as a basis for practical politics. Of course, he adds, if we say that a nation is a number of people who live or have been born in a certain state, then everything is clear; but this would mean giving up the principle of the national state, which demands that the state should be determined by the nation and not vice versa.

None of the theories, Popper concludes, which maintain that a nation is united by a common origin, or a common language, or a common history, is acceptable or applicable in practice. "The principle of the national state is not only inapplicable but it has never been clearly conceived. It is a myth. It is an irrational, a romantic and utopian dream, a dream of naturalism and of tribal collectivism."[30]

The Jewish Nationality Issue

In the nightmare of the dark
All the dogs of Europe bark,
And the living nations wait,
Each sequestered in its hate.

W. H. Auden

I can think of no better way of introducing this chapter, which deals with various aspects of the Jewish nationality problem, than citing two diametrically opposed views on the subject aired at an interval of more than seven decades.

Writing in the year 1900 in an essay entitled "Nation or Religious Community," the eminent Anglo-Jewish scholar C. G. Montefiore concluded:

> Now, if the saying be accurate that "the roots of the present lie deep in the past," it may well be that the past can throw some light upon the problems of the present. My own small leisure for study has been devoted to the earlier history of the Jewish religion. But this does not put me so utterly out of court in the discussion of the wider and more general problem as might be supposed. For, as I venture to believe, it is the religious factor which must either be the rock against which Jewish nationalism will suffer shipwreck or which must itself be ruined in the fray.[1]

Speaking in Jerusalem on January 1972 at the Twenty-eighth Zionist Congress, Israel's late prime minister Golda Meir formulated the issue in a totally different manner. "There is," she asserted, "no difference between Jewish religion and Jewish nationality. . . . An American can be an Anglican American or a Buddhist American; but I have yet to meet an Anglican Jew or a Buddhist Jew."

By thus reducing the religion of Judaism to the status of nationality and citizenship, Golda Meir came perilously near to vindicating Montefiore's bleak vision of the Jewish religion being ruined in the then-impending "fray." The idea of Jewish nationhood (in the sense, at least, in which this term is used by what we have called the tribal nationalists) has its origins in the ethnic nationalist ideologies which prevailed in Central and Eastern Europe in the nineteenth century. The central thesis propounded in this chapter is that present-day Israeli Jews labor under a hopeless confusion between ethnicity and nationality, nationality and citizenship.

Genesis of a Nonquestion

Who is a Jew? In a memorably funny story, the late American Jewish writer Abraham Cahan once wrote about an Italian barber who falls in love with a Jewish girl from Brooms Street, New York. The barber wants to marry the girl, but her mother would not hear of it. In the end, the mother says the two could be married if the barber converted to Judaism. He does; the mother makes him learn Hebrew and pray every morning with a *yarmulke* on his head. The couple live with the mother-in-law, and the barber doesn't get his breakfast until he has said his prayers. But that isn't the end of it. The girl happens to have a brother named Joe, and Joe doesn't pray before breakfast and still gets his meal. After a while, the barber becomes impatient, and he asks his mother-in-law, "Why doesn't Joe have to pray before breakfast?" The answer comes promptly: "Joe is a Jew. I *know* he's a Jew. *You* got to prove it!"

Who, then, is a Jew? For better or for worse, attempts to answer this question have been legion. One of the simplest is the definition offered by Professor Elia Samuele Artom. "A Jew," Artom maintains, "is he who according to the religion of Israel is obliged to observe the Torah."[2] This of course is something of a non sequitur in that, according to the religion of Israel, a Jew—who in every case is "obliged to observe the Torah"—is a person who either was born to a Jewish mother or is a convert to Judaism.

In slightly different versions—though sometimes crucially different—this definition is accepted by Jews everywhere. The eminent Jewish historian Jacob Talmon, for instance, once suggested that a Jew can be defined as a "person of the Jewish race or religion who has not formally embraced a non-Jewish religion, no matter whether he observes his own or doesn't."[3]

Yet this particular definition, adequate though it may sound, poses a number of problems, especially when we turn from the realm of the individual Jew to the entity called the Jewish people—from the question of "Who is a Jew?" to the more intricate one of "*What* is a Jew?" To give one example of such difficulties (leaving aside the problematics involved in speaking of a Jewish "race"), Talmon's formulation makes it clear that a person who does not belong to the Jewish race can be a Jew; it also seems to suggest—equally rightly—that a confirmed and self-styled atheist also can be a Jew, provided he or she belonged to that race. But then, if religious belief and/or observance ultimately have nothing to do with a person's being and remaining a Jew, why cannot a person "of the Jewish race" be considered a Jew even after he or she has formally embraced a non-Jewish religion?

The question is not as hypothetical as it may sound. Some time in the mid-1950s, a Jewish convert to Catholicism, Oswald Rufeisen (better known as Brother Daniel), went to court in Israel claiming that, being born a Jew, he was eligible to obtain Israeli citizenship under Israel's Law of Return, his conversion to Catholicism notwithstanding. After a great deal of discussion and not a little embarrassment, the Israeli Supreme Court ruled to deny the plaintiff such eligibility. But the court did so on the grounds of the understanding of Jewishness embodied in what was a secular law—admitting, however, that according to Jewish *religious* law, the monk was still a Jew.

As Supreme Court Justice Moshe Silberg, pronouncing the majority opinion, explained:

> The ruling opinion in Jewish law is that an apostate remains a Jew for all purposes save [perhaps] in certain marginal cases which do not affect the general principle. This may be seen from the writings and opinions of leading Talmudic commentators and scholars. . . . In other words, according to Jewish religious law a Jew remains a Jew, for all practical purposes, even though he may deliberately change his religion. But . . . the term "Jew" in the Law of Return does not refer to the "Jew" of Jewish religious law, but to the "Jew" of secular law.[4]

From the point of view of Jewish religious law, then, the question as to who a Jew is, is so simple and so easy to answer that it amounts to a non-question. Proceeding from the elementary premise that it is the undisputed right of a religion, an ideology, a human association, or a club to establish its own definition of itself, we must accept as final Judaism's own definition of itself and of its followers as laid down in Jewish law as we have known it for close on two millennia. According to this definition, a Jew is a person who was born of a Jewish mother or converted to Judaism. Needless to say, too, that when Jewish religious law (*Halakhah*) speaks of conversion (*giyur*), it refers to conversion according to *halakhic* rules. A Jew, therefore, would be defined authoritatively as a person who was born to a Jewish mother or converted to Judaism according to *Halakhah*.

However, while defining a Jewish person is rather simple and easy, difficulties emerge when we try to define the Jews as a collectivity or an entity—a people, a community, a race, a religion. In other words, the question becomes, "What are the Jews?" rather than "Who is a Jew?" To get an idea of these difficulties, some brief remarks about the background of the problem will be in order. The goal set for the movement by the First Zionist Congress, held in Basle in 1897, was "to create for the Jewish people a home in Palestine." The Balfour Declaration, issued two decades later, spoke of the establishment in Palestine of "a National Home" for the Jewish People. The U.N. Partition Plan of 1947 called for the establishment of "a Jewish state" in part of Palestine.

Now a Jewish state (which is how Israel defines itself) has certain ties with, and obligations to, all those who are defined as Jews. The state's founders perceived the first and foremost among these obligations to be granting Jews the right to settle in Israel. This right was codified in the Law of Return of 1950, which provided, in addition to the right to *aliya* (immigration), certain privileges to the Jewish "returnees." While this arrangement appears simple at first, as time passed, difficulties began to arise. Israel's Population Register, like the identity card issued to every Israeli, records an Israeli Jew's nationality (*leom*, in Hebrew) as "Jewish" rather than "Israeli" (non-Jews have the "nationality" rubric in the identity cards marked "Arab" or "Druse").

This procedure, based as it was on the premise of Jewishness being a nationality first and foremost, made it necessary for the Israeli authorities to find a device whereby a person's Jewishness could be verified. At first, the rule was that a newcomer's "nationality" be recorded on the strength of his or her own bona fide declaration or, in the case of minors, in accordance with that of their parents.

In 1958, however, following a controversy involving a cabinet crisis, the Israeli minister of interior issued an administrative ruling decreeing that only persons recognized as Jews by the *Halakhah* could be registered as Jews by nationality. This meant that only a person born to a Jewish mother or *halakhically* converted to Judaism was entitled to the status of immigrant (*oleh*) and, accordingly, entitled to have his or her nationality recorded as "Jewish."

This compromise, which worked fairly smoothly for several years, faced its severest challenge in 1970 when a young army officer by the name of Benjamin Shalit went to court asking that his two sons be registered in the Population Register as Jews despite the fact that their mother was non-Jewish and had no intention of converting to Judaism.

Shalit won. The Supreme Court, sitting for the first time with a bench of nine justices, ruled that the directives issued by the minister of interior in 1958 had no legal backing and that in the absence of any statutory definition of Jewish nationality, Shalit's bona fide declaration concerning his children's nationality must be accepted.

The Shalit children were accordingly duly registered as Jews, but the Supreme Court's decision gave rise to fierce controversy, with the Orthodox circles demanding state legislation providing that a *halakhic* definition of Jewishness be accepted and imposed. After a good deal of squabbling, the government adopted a compromise formula, introducing an amendment to the Law of Return, with two major stipulations: First, it defined a Jew by nationality as a person born to a Jewish mother or converted to Judaism and not having joined another religion; second, it extended the citizenship, housing, taxation, and other benefits to the non-Jewish spouses, children, and grandchildren of Jewish newcomers.

Whether by design or merely by default, however, the amendment introduced in 1970 left a sizable loophole in the law. By failing to define, specify, or qualify the word "conversion," it left the door wide open for the recognition of conversions officiated abroad by Conservative or Reform rabbis.

Two points must be mentioned here in passing: First, the amendment did not affect matters of marriage and divorce, which in Israel are under the sole jurisdiction of the rabbinical courts. Second, on the strength of an unrepealed ordinance dating back to the Mandate period, the amendment did not apply to conversions carried out in Israel.

Nevertheless, the 1970 amendment was criticized severely and bitterly in Orthodox circles both in Israel and abroad, and the National Religious party—which had agreed to the compromise—was denounced by these circles for lending a hand to an arrangement they claimed would imperil the unity of the Jewish people. Orthodox opponents of the amendment argued, quite rightly, that *giyur* as a legal concept in rabbinical Judaism cannot have any but a *halakhic* connotation and that, therefore, it can be performed lawfully only by Orthodox rabbis who follow the strict rules of the *Halakhah* in that respect. However, for reasons too complex to go into here, the Orthodox parties that have been trying to get the *Knesset* to introduce the words "according to the *Halakhah*" to the term "conversion" in the Law of Return, have not managed to do so, even though the National Religious party eventually came to support the move. The repercussions of the Shalit case, as well as the ongoing controversy on the subject of conversion, are discussed in more detail in chapter 5, "Israel as an Open Society," in the section "Marriage, Nationality, and the Law of Return."

Religion and Nationality

The reason why the question, "Who is a Jew?" is asked so frequently in Israel and has caused so much controversy and led to so many cabinet crises is to be sought in spheres other than the religio-theological ones. In essence, the problem is not finding out who a Jew is but rather what the Jews are as a collectivity. At the opening of this chapter, Golda Meir is quoted as saying that she had yet to meet an Anglican Jew or a Buddhist Jew in the same way as she had often met an Anglican American or a Buddhist American.

For reasons best known to herself and to her speech writers, however, the late prime minister of Israel refrained from referring to the far less-dramatic—and fairly common—spectacle of an *American* Jew (or of Jews generally) who, though Jewish by religion, belong to nationalities other than the Israeli one and therefore fail to answer to her peculiar thesis concerning the indivisibility of religion and nationality. She could, for instance, have thought of French, Argentinian, Georgian, British, and Brazilian Jews—all of whom carry passports and identity cards testifying that they belong to nationalities that cannot be termed Jewish by any stretch of the imagination.

The truth, of course, is that in speaking of "nationality," Golda Meir was in fact referring to "ethnicity," "race," or "tribe." On this reading of the term, it would seem, a person of the Jewish faith and of French, Brazilian, or British nationality is a contradiction in terms and thus simply cannot exist—although, strictly speaking, even this cannot be maintained since any person belonging to any ethnic or "racial" group can lawfully and *halakhically* be converted to Judaism.

Moreover, according to this ethnoracial definition of nationality, an Anglican or even a Buddhist Jew is indeed feasible since, if one is born a Jew, one will continue to belong to the Jewish "nationality" regardless of one's religious convictions. In the same way, an atheist Jew is certainly feasible, and Mrs. Meir could not claim she had yet to meet one since she herself and most of her associates, in her party and in the government, could be so described.

Golda Meir's remark, however, should be viewed in its proper context. The Israeli daily, the *Jerusalem Post*, reporting the address from which this remark was taken, noted in parentheses that the prime minister "was apparently referring to the High Court decision earlier in the day to the effect that religion and nationality are inseparable." The High Court's decision in question had been given in the case of a Tel Aviv psychologist, Georges

Tamarin, who had gone to court demanding that the state registrar change the "nationality" classification on his identity card from "Jewish" to "Israeli." The Tel Aviv district court rejected the application on the ground that "an individual cannot establish a nationality by mere talk."

Subsequently, Tamarin took his case to the high court, which, sitting as a court of appeal, again rejected his plea. Press reports of the decision quoted the court as ruling that "to agree to Tamarin's demand could lead to a schism in the Jewish people." They also quoted Supreme Court President Justice Shimon Agranat as saying that "the wish of a handful of Jews to break away from the nation and create a new concept of an Israeli nation was not a legitimate aspiration." The court's decision also said, among other things: "There is no Israeli nation separate from the Jewish people. . . . The Jewish people is composed not only of those residing in Israel but also of Diaspora Jewries."

It is clear that the Supreme Court's verdict in the Tamarin case was a major ideological statement. One Israeli newspaper chose to lead the story with these sentences:

> Does an Israeli nationality (*leom*) exist separately from a Jewish nationality? Is it possible, for instance, that a Jew can come forth and plead: "I am an Israeli by nationality and an atheist by religion?" Tamarin believes it is possible. Through his counsel, Amnon Zichroni, he has argued: "When I immigrated to Israel (in 1949) there existed only a nucleus of an Israeli nation (*leom*) in the process of crystallization. Today, to the best of my understanding, such an Israeli nation already exists." What he intended to argue is that in the course of the years a separation from the Jewish nation has taken place—so that in addition to it a separate Israeli nation has been created. The state's attorney Gabriel Bach argued, however, that no such separation is possible between the two: Jewish nationality and Israeli nationality are one and the same thing.[5]

From this and other reports of the Tamarin case, it becomes abundantly clear that the whole question as to whether an Israeli nationality exists apart from a Jewish nationality really revolves around two crucial points of political terminology and ideology: first, the precise meaning of the Hebrew word *leom* and what it denotes—a nation, a nationality, nationhood, ethnicity and an ethnic group, or "tribe"; and second, the meaning of nationality in Israeli ideological parlance and its relation to citizenship.

The word *leom* first appears in the Hebrew Bible in the plural form: *leomim:* "Let peoples (*'amim*) serve you, and nations (*leomim*) bow down to you" (Gen. 27:29). All the three leading translations of the Bible render the word *leom* as "nation" or "people." As a matter of fact, in the two cases in which the word appears in Genesis, it appears in the plural and as synonymous to "peoples" ("And the Lord said to her: Two nations are in your womb, and two peoples, born of you, shall be divided" [Gen. 25:23]).

In modern usage, too, *leom* has generally denoted either "nation" or "nationality." However, since the Hebrew for "nation" is more generally *ummah*, as in *ha-ummah ha-Yehudit* and *ha-ummot ha-meuhhadot* (the Jewish nation, the United Nations), the word *leom* in recent years has been used to denote "nationality." When Tamarin applied for his *leom* to be changed from "Jewish" to "Israeli," he was therefore plainly referring to the "nationality" classification on his identity card.

This brings us to the meaning of the term "nationality" itself in Israeli political rhetoric. Strange as it may sound, nationality and citizenship in Israel are two entirely different concepts. This stands in contrast to the situation in practically every country in the world, with the notable exception of the Soviet Union and a few other countries of Eastern Europe. In all these countries, nationality and citizenship are not only not two different concepts but are in fact synonymous. A person who is a British citizen is a British national; an American citizen is likewise a national of the United States of America and is of U.S. "nationality."

In Israel—and in the former Soviet Union—the picture is different. In the USSR, one could be a citizen of the Soviet state and a member of any number of "nationalities." In Israel, too, a person can be an Israeli by citizenship and a Jew, an Arab, or a Druse by nationality. (An Arab "national" can be a Muslim or a Christian by religion.) In the Soviet Union, again, one could be a Soviet citizen and a Jew, an Armenian, a Georgian, or a Ukrainian by "nationality." In this sense, of course, nationality becomes equated with ethnicity and ethnic group.

A rather more intricate problem is presented here. Having decided on a separation of the concepts of citizenship and nationality, what then is the relationship between the two? The difficulty here is that, while it is technically true that citizenship and nationality in Israel are two different concepts—and while formally one can be a full-fledged citizen of the state and belong to either the Jewish or the Arab nationality (*leom*), Israel's own definition of itself as a Jewish state makes citizenship and (Jewish) nationality overlap to the point of being interchangeable.

This point can be illuminated by a brief analogy with the situation in the former Soviet Union. While the respective positions in Israel and the Soviet Union were similar in that, strictly speaking, they both make a clear distinction between citizenship and nationality, the USSR did not define itself as a nation-state, or rather a nationality-state, in the sense that Israel does. It is true that Soviet citizens who happened to belong to the Russian "nationality" held top positions and were generally considered a privileged group. Nevertheless, juridically speaking, the Soviet Union never defined itself as a "Russian state."

In contrast, Israel, by simultaneously defining itself as a Jewish state and making a distinction between citizenship and nationality, renders the terms "Israeli" and "Jewish" virtually synonymous. State Attorney Gabriel Bach's insistence that Israeli and Jewish nationalities are one and the same is fully corroborated by the country's ethnic-nationalist ideology and its self-definition as a Jewish state.

Some additional light may be shed on this point by a deeper look at the way in which the Israeli Supreme Court formulated its decision in the Tamarin case. In the course of the lengthy summation of the court's opinion, its president, Justice Agranat, noted that he was prepared to assume that the appellant felt in all good faith that he was nationally an Israeli and not a Jew.

However, he continued, the appellant's claim that he was consequently entitled to have his national grouping registered as "Israeli" instead of "Jewish" would be acceptable only if he could prove that such a nationality (*leom*) did in fact exist. (It is noteworthy that in this particular context the legal correspondent of the English-language *Jerusalem Post* should have chosen to render the word *leom* as "ethnic group"—with the result that Justice Agranat's patently woolly argument sounded quite reasonable, since obviously there is not, nor is there likely to be in the foreseeable future, any such thing as an Israeli ethnicity or ethnic group.)

Clearly, then, what we have here is a total miscomprehension resulting from two completely different usages of the term *leom*. It would have been perfectly understandable had the Israeli lawmaker made it clear that *leom* means, invariably and always, "ethnic group" or "ethnicity." But he did not do so. The state of Israel, as represented in the Tamarin case by State Attorney Bach and as perceived by the Supreme Court, maintains a concept of nationality that is identical in every respect with ethnicity—so that the state itself is clearly identified with one ethnic group regardless of where members of that group happen to dwell.

In keeping with this—and in view of a hopeless confusion in the use of the terms "nationality" and "ethnicity"—non-Jews who are considered citizens of the state cannot be described as Israeli "nationals" even in a purely formal and legalistic sense. Tamarin's fundamental mistake in the case he brought before the Israeli courts was that he himself spoke of *leom* as denoting "nationality," as the term is universally used today (that is, as being identical with "citizenship" rather than with ethnicity) and thus contributing greatly to the rejection of his otherwise well-justified and sensible plea.

Jews as a Family—"The Family of Abraham"

Whether or not the Jews constitute a nationality, or a nation, in the sense in which the founders of Zionism as well as the justices of the Israel Supreme Court in the Tamarin case chose to define the term, is of course part of the continuing debate regarding the Jews' identity as a collectivity.

The question can be put in a simple enough way: Is there a term that would describe with accuracy the category to which the corporate body called Jewry belongs and thus embrace all individual Jews? In the latter half of the 1960s, two American Jewish scholars and rabbis grappled with this question, independently of one another but reaching much the same conclusions. One was Rabbi Jakob Petuchowski, late professor of rabbinics and an authority in Jewish theology; the other was Rabbi Henry Bamberger, of Vassar Temple, Poughkeepsie, New York.

In a book published in 1967, Petuchowski made a systematic attempt to establish a category within which an answer to the question "What are the Jews?" can be placed: race, nation, religion, culture.[6] Similarly, Rabbi Bamberger, in an article printed a year later, again examined the applicability of these same categories to Jewry, adding that of "people."[7]

Neither Petuchowski nor Bamberger could find the answer in the realm of race. For both, the factor that makes Jews Jews cannot be race. Anyone who looks at Jews can see readily that they do not share any consistent physical appearance. Skin, hair color, eyes, height, shape of nose, all the supposed, stereotypical "racial" traits vary widely. Even were this not so, however, the nonracial character of the Jews is demonstrated by the fact alone that it is possible for a Gentile to become a Jew.

Conversions to Judaism go back at least to the time of the Book of Ruth, and they continue to the present day. There have been periods in Jewish history when Jews tended to discourage conversion to their religion. However, there has never been any question that it is possible to convert to Judaism and to be considered a full Jew. Moreover, race is inevitably determined by one's birth. As Petuchowski put it: "It is not possible for the Oriental to convert and become a Negro, or for the Negro to convert and become a Caucasian." Clearly, therefore, the category of race is both inaccurate and misleading when applied to the Jews.

Another category commonly used to describe the Jews is that of nation. Very briefly and rather arbitrarily defined, a nation is a group of people with a common language, a common history, and a common territory. Both Bamberger and Petuchowski find the term inapplicable to the Jews. The common language of the Jews would, of course, be Hebrew. Yet, while Hebrew has always been the language the Jews use for prayer and study, it was, throughout most of Jewish history, certainly not the language of the vast majority of Jewry.

In one sense, again, Jews have a common history. But Jews can say this not because one history has unified them but because they all have chosen to adopt as their own the history of all Jews. Virtually every Jewish child in America learns of the sufferings of the Marranos in Spain, "but the over-whelming majority of American Jews are not the descendants of Marranos or any other Spanish Jews." Jews are not a unified group because they share the Marranos' history; they share that history because they are a unified group. "In the same way," Bamberger adds, "we share the history of the Jews of Yemen, India and Kurdistan. This is an act of the will, not an act of history. We are not what we are because we have a common history; we have a common history because of what we are."

The same type of reservation applies when we speak of a common territory. Bamberger notes:

Through most of our history, we have shared common longings for the Land, not a common land. Today, the land for which we longed is open for us, but most of us have not gone there to live. While the State of Israel may be ours in some sense, in a very real sense it is not ours, because the bulk of Diaspora Jewry would reject the suggestion that it is only through the existence of the State of Israel that we are united.

Petuchowski gives a similar appraisal. He sums up:

There is no such thing as a common Jewish territory, a government to which allegiance is owed by all Jews, or even an everyday language which is common to all Jews. There undoubtedly was such a thing as a Jewish nation in historical antiquity. But that came to an end some twenty centuries ago. And there is the endeavor to create the Jewish nation anew in our time. The State of Israel is engaged in this task. But it has jurisdiction only on its own citizens. Besides, the nation which is coming into being in the State of Israel is an "Israeli," rather than a "Jewish," nation, for Israeli citizenship is by no means restricted to Jews. . . . To assume the existence of a Jewish nation just because the Israelis are trying to create one is a severe case of question-begging.

Even if Israeli citizenship were available to Jews only, the most that could be said about it then would be that *some* Jews, i.e. those living in the State of Israel, constitute a "Jewish nation."

It may, of course, be pointed out—as Salo Baron has done in his essay on "Jewish Ethnicism"—that for Jews religion and nationalism have not been conflicting categories "but an extraordinarily organic wholeness." Yet it all seems to be a question of defining one's terms. Baron himself is aware of this difficulty. "In fact," he writes, "one may legitimately doubt whether these terms genuinely correspond to Jewish reality. . . . Judaism has indeed been more a way of life than a system of beliefs and doctrines."[8]

To this one can reply, however, that while some measure of religious observance always has constituted a part of Jewry's way of life, the attitudes and rites imposed by modern secular nationalism or nationality status cannot be said ever to have formed a part of that way of life. Throughout the ages, the only known characteristics that traditionally have defined a Jew have been belief in the tenets of Judaism and observance of its precepts. This belief and this observance—even when they existed—never gave the Jews the characteristics of a nation, let alone of a nationality.

Finally, with regard to the subject of Jewish nationhood and nationality, Solomon Schechter, a leading modern authority on Judaism, pointed out early in this century:

> Israel is not a nation in the common sense of the word. To the Rabbis, at least, it is not a nation by virtue of race or of certain peculiar political combinations. As Rabbi Saadia expressed it, "Our nation is only a nation by reason of its Torah." The brutal Torah-less nationalism promulgated in certain quarters would have been to the Rabbis just as hateful as the suicidal Torah-less universalism preached in other quarters. And if we could imagine for a moment Israel giving up its allegiance to God, its Torah and its divine institutions, the Rabbis would be the first to sign its death-warrant as a nation.[9]

In contrast to this clear-cut verdict, one may usefully quote David Ben-Gurion's equally blunt statement, which this leading Zionist activist made in reply to an interviewer's query. In the course of a newspaper interview printed in May 1967, Ben-Gurion stated: "If by Judaism you mean religion, then it is true that we have discarded Judaism. But I do not see any calamity in this. The tradition of the *Shulhan 'Arukh* [a compendium of Jewish religious precepts] is today no longer necessary. It was useful to the Jewish people when it was dispersed among the Gentiles; it served as a distinguishing mark."[10]

Do the Jews, then, constitute a religion? Petuchowski maintains that if religion is understood by the analogy, say, of the ecclesiastical framework of Protestantism and Catholicism, then the category of "religion" cannot be the one to which Jewry as a corporate body belongs. "A Protestant who ceases to believe in Protestant dogmas," Petuchowski explains, "and who does not practice the religion in which he was reared, also ceases to be a Protestant."

The same applies to the Catholic. "But it does not apply to the Jews. . . . According to traditional Jewish law, a Jew converted to another faith continues to be a Jew—a bad Jew, or a sinful Jew, but still a Jew. The Covenant which God made with the fathers does not allow for the possibility of 'opting out'."

The term "religion," then, as a category for defining the Jews, is inadequate. "No matter how strongly we feel that the essential component of Jewish existence is religion," writes Bamberger, "we are more than a religious communion. We do cross-adopt history and culture, although the demands of religion would not necessarily include this sharing. The Irish Catholic does not need to adopt the history of Spain or Italy to share his religion with Spaniards or Italians."[11]

There is, as Petuchowski demonstrates, more striking proof that the Jews are more than a religion. The Jewish religionist may well feel that one can only be a good Jew if one professes the Jewish faith, but he does not deny that it is possible to reject belief in God and religious practice and still remain a Jew, albeit a bad one. Can there be a religion that allows atheism within its ranks? But there is a still greater paradox. In speaking of the apostate who has formally accepted another religion, Jewish law states: "Even though he has sinned, he is yet a Jew."

The definition in which Jews are categorized as a "cultural group" is no more felicitous than those involving race, nation, and religion. What people are in the habit of calling "Jewish culture" turns out, in the vast majority of cases, to be nothing more than the culture and folkways of a particular Jewish environment rather than something universally recognized by Jews as their cultural heritage. "*Blintzes* and *gefillte* fish come from the East European Jewish cuisine. They were not part of the culinary culture of the German Jews—not to speak of their Oriental brethren, whose *falafel* and *humus*, in their turn, were not part of the fare of European Jews."

Much the same can be said about such aspects of high culture as music and literature. "What passes for 'Jewish music' in many parts of the United States—and in Israel—is the musical style brought with them by the masses of East European Jewish immigrants. Again, it is not identical with the musical tradition of the Western Jews, while the music of the Oriental Jew is, to the untrained Western ear, indistinguishable from the music of the Arabs." Similarly, there is no such thing as a common "Jewish literature," in which the totality of Jewish life is reflected—and which, in turn, can be certain of the aesthetic appreciation of all Jews. This is no wonder, since—as Petuchowski explains—literature is "so very dependent upon the particular environment whence Jews come."[12]

But if the Jews are not a race, a nation, a religion, or a culture—what, then, are they? Petuchowski would not settle for the thesis that the Jews simply elude all attempts at definition. It is one thing, he argues, to speak in the abstract of a unique phenomenon defying definition. It is another thing again to have to deal with concrete reality.

The Talmud could not avoid laying down some ground rules and setting up some criteria as to who is to be considered a Jew. "According to the formulation of the Talmud, a Jew is either a person born of a Jewish mother or a person of non-Jewish antecedents who has undergone the Jewish rites of conversion. Stripped of its legalistic terminology, what the formulation of the Talmud amounts to is the assertion that Judaism is a family matter. A Jew is a member of the family of Abraham, the first Jew."

Like all other families, this particular family to which all Jews belong reckons its membership in terms of those who were born in it, and in terms of those who come into it from other families.

> Like all families, this particular family also has its "black sheep," its "skeletons in the closets," and those of its members who prefer not to be known as belonging to this family. . . . Throughout its long history, loyalty to the family tradition was never measured in terms of the language which members of this family spoke, or of the culture in which they participated. Not even in matters of religion was absolute uniformity ever a desired goal. . . . There is enough of a recognition, among members of this family, of the greatness of God, and enough of the healthy awareness of human limitations, to permit the frequent application of the incomparable Talmudic wisdom which proclaimed: "Both points of view are words of the Living God."

Another term sometimes used to describe the Jews as a collectivity is "people." In some ways, Petuchowski agrees, "people" is a more satisfactory term than any of those dealt with in his article (that is, "race," "nation," "religion," and "culture"). Certainly no one can say that its very definition renders it inapplicable: "People" is an imprecise term, and it is virtually impossible to prove that it is being used wrongly in defining Jews—or any other group of people.

But this very vagueness is the weakness of the word. To say that the Jews are a people, and leave the word "people" undefined, is begging the question. By doing so, we at best offer half a circular argument. "It may be convenient to refer to the Jewish 'people,' knowing that we are at least not misleading in our choice of words: but we must assume that by avoiding misinformation we have given an explanation."

"I suspect," says Petuchowski, "that the use of the word 'people' originates in the biblical term 'am yisrael—People of Israel. But it seems strange that another biblical term, one that is part of our regular prayer services, has not pointed the way to a far more meaningful phrase: b'nei yisrael—Children of Israel. Throughout the Bible the Jews are conceived of as a family."

One final point. To assert that the Jews constitute a family is not—as Petuchowski is careful to point out—equivalent to making a racial statement. One is born into a family, but this is not the only way of becoming part of a family. One can also marry into a family or be adopted into one. An aunt or uncle by marriage may be no less dear than one related by biological ties. An adopted child is as fully a part of a family and as well loved as the child who is born into the family.

It is no accident that a part of the ceremony of conversion to Judaism is virtually an adoption. The convert receives a Hebrew name, and for a father's name he or she becomes "the son (or daughter) of our father Abraham." The convert becomes a member of the family. Family traditions develop. "A family remembers its home, even when it leaves it. No matter how scattered, a family can share in all those joys and sorrows that befall any one of its members. Thus do Jews forge a common history for themselves."[13]

The Birth of a Pan-Movement

As a collectivity, then, the Jews can best be defined as a family, "the family of Abraham." Throughout the ages, the fortunes of this family have been so intertwined with those of a religious faith that it is impossible to speak of one without the other. Moreover, since Judaism in its earliest days was associated with (in fact, comprised an integral part of) what today would be designated as a nationality, no understanding of the present-day problem of Jewish nationality can be complete without some knowledge of the historical developments which, about two millennia ago, once and for all severed this organic link between the Jewish religion and Jewish—or Hebrew—"nationality."

What happened was that, in the year 586 B.C., when the Babylonian armies defeated the forces of the kingdom of Judah, a process was set in motion that was to result in the complete transformation of Judaism. The destruction of the temple in Jerusalem and the forceful expulsion of many of the inhabitants of Judah to Babylonia placed Judaism, as a religion, face to face with the painful alternative of extinction or drastic revision. Nonetheless, Judaism was to survive, and it is clear that Judaism as we know it today—based as it is upon a period of earlier Hebrew religion—was the creation of an era of the long Babylonian exile.

The transformation of Judaism was complete. In the words of a noted contemporary student of Judaism, "The newly reborn religion revised the older conception of God, now no longer the God of *a* nation, but the God of *all* nations, whose power is universal and who uses every people as an instrument of His Providential purpose."

The revised religion did something more.

It replaced the older Hebrew conception of divine service as sacrificial ritual by a new conception of divine service as study of the Word of God as contained in the Torah. It substituted the idea of "kingdom of priests and a holy nation" for that of a nation divided by a rigid caste system into priests, "Levites" and Israelites. And it provided food for hope in a miraculous return to the homeland and the restoration of political independence under the leadership of the "anointed one" of God, the Messiah.[14]

This new version of Judaism, a blend of religion and "political" messianism, was to sustain the Jews in both East and West through long centuries of hardship, oppression, and victimization. In Western Europe, however, the age-old tradition of oppression and persecution of the Jews was to be broken by the onset of the Enlightenment, which brought the Jew "emancipation." But those few short years of kindness and acceptance were to prove costly in their destructiveness. For at the same time as the Enlightenment and the emancipation were weakening the Jews' attachment to their messianic vision, they brought new, unprecedented demands on the European Jew: The new nation-state, while granting Jews emancipation, began to ask them to define their precise "national" identity.[15]

Among the questions that the new European nation-state asked its Jews was (to quote one of the twelve questions put to the so-called Grand

Sanhedrin of Paris, held in February 1807), "Do those Jews who are born in France and who are treated as French citizens regard France as their native country, and do they feel obliged to defend it, to obey its laws, and to submit to all regulations of the civil code?" In response to such demands, for which the Jews were not quite prepared, came (after a century of groping and soul-searching) an answer that was to prove so fateful and so galvanizing: a secular Jewish nationalist movement modeled remarkably faithfully on the pan-movements of nineteenth-century Central and Eastern Europe.

For if the Jews of France were being asked merely to answer questions— difficult questions, to be sure, but not impossible ones to answer at a certain cost, as the Grand Sanhedrin was to demonstrate—the Jews of Russia, Po- land, and Rumania were to be confronted with problems of a more practical and far deeper nature. There, in the villages and townlets of the Pale of Settlement, young Jewish intellectuals had to take the leap from the old into the new without any transition. "No half-way stations pleased these stormers; the modern life beckoned from without, Israel must step into it, preferably in a Hebrew form, but if necessary in Russian."[16]

At best, the Jew was to be a Jew at home and a *man* abroad, as Judah Loeb Gordon (1831–1892) sang in purest Hebrew verse. Gordon was, from 1872 on, secretary of the Society for the Spreading of Enlightenment among the Jews of Russia, founded in St. Petersburg in 1863 by Baron Joseph Gunzburg and his son Horace.[17]

The intellectual careers and misadventures of this group of impatient enlighteners may be gleaned from the life story of two of its pioneers. Moses Loeb Lilienblum (1843–1910) decided early in the proceedings that "the ways of the Talmud" were nothing but superstition and declared his early Jewish education a veritable "sin against youth." Peretz-Smolenskin (1843–1885) pictured himself as one "astray in the ways of life" and, in the pages of the literary Hebrew periodical *Ha-Shahar* (The dawn), battled against dark orthodoxy. Nonetheless, both Lilienblum and Smolenskin were to "come back"; however, they came back not to Jewish orthodoxy, but to Jewish nationalism.

The tragedy of the disappointed assimilationist was embodied in Smolenskin's fortunes. In Vienna, whither he had transplanted himself in 1861, he gained the perspective that taught him the folly of what he called "the wisdom of Berlin" (the source and center of the Enlightenment). "Over against the Western movement of reform he scorned the casting aside of the messianic hope, which to him was expressive of Israel's character as an 'everlasting people'."

However, on the road between the Pale of Settlement and Vienna something had happened. The messianic hope was no longer one of the miraculous return to the homeland. "It is time to act!" Smolenskin wrote after the Russian pogrom of 1881. "Turkey will give us the land of our inheritance, because in what matter are we inferior to Greece, Serbia, Rumania, Bulgaria and other small nations which yesterday were born on Turkish soil? And if they will object, 'They live on their land,' you can answer 'We will seek what belongs to us not with the sword or spear but with money'."[18]

Secular Jewish nationalism, or political Zionism, thus was a product of the impossible circumstances into which initially assimilationist "emancipated" Jewish intellectuals and *literati* in Central and Eastern Europe were thrown following the refusal of the Gentile environment to receive them. In 1882, a year after the Russian pogroms, Leo Pinsker (1821–1891) published a pamphlet in which he admonished his fellow Jews to look for salvation in "auto-emancipation"—in the creation of a national retreat somewhere on this earth, preferably on the banks of the Jordan, but if necessary on those of the Mississippi.

While Pinsker's pamphlet was still being printed, a group of young Jewish university students formed themselves at Kharkov as the circle of the Bilu (abbreviation of the Hebrew phrase meaning "O House of Jacob come ye and let us go"). Their plan was to establish an agricultural colony in Palestine.

Leo Pinsker's life and opinions furnish another example of the plight of those disillusioned Jewish assimilationists. To an even greater degree than Smolenskin, Pinsker had committed himself to the integration of the Jews into Russian life. After the Crimean War, he was decorated by the Czar for his medical services to the Russian army. This made him an even more ardent advocate of the Russification of the Jews. Moreover, Pinsker was one of the active members, right from its founding, of the Society for Spreading the Enlightenment; even the pogroms of 1871 did not shake his belief that assimilation into Russian culture and society was the most desirable course for the Jews to follow.

After the 1881 pogroms, which were manifestly instigated and encouraged by members of the Russian upper classes and even the government of the Czar, Pinsker's confidence in the advantages of assimilation began to be shaken. He resigned from the society and sought an alternative solution to the Jewish problem.

The result was Pinsker's pamphlet entitled "Auto-Emancipation: An Appeal to his People by a Russian Jew." The deadly influence of the various tribal nationalisms surrounding Pinsker was evident in almost every page of his detailed prognosis. It was because the Jews were not "a living nation," he wrote, but everywhere aliens, that they were despised. Civil and political emancipation was not sufficient for raising the Jews in the esteem of other peoples. The only proper remedy, therefore, was the creation of a Jewish nationality, of a people living on its own soil.

That was the "auto-emancipation" of the Jews—their emancipation as a nation among nations by the acquisition of a home of their own. The Jews, Pinsker wrote, should not persuade themselves that humanity and enlightenment would ever be radical remedies for the malady of their people; the lack of national self-esteem and self-confidence, of political initiative and unity, were the enemies of their national renaissance.

In order not to be obliged to wander from one exile to another, Pinsker thought, the Jews must have an extensive and productive place of refuge, an in-gathering center of their own, which their ablest representatives— men of finance, science and affairs, statesmen and publicists—should combine to create.

Summing up the helpless and humiliating position of the Jews, Pinsker wrote: "We do not count as a nation among the other nations, and we have no voice in the council of the peoples, even in affairs that concern ourselves. Our fatherland is an alien country, our unity dispersion, our solidarity the general hostility to us, our weapon humility, our defence flight, our originality adaptability, our future tomorrow. What a contemptible role for a people that once had its Maccabees!"

Theodore Herzl (1860–1904) was younger than Pinsker and far more convinced that assimilation was the best and only way out for the Jews. In the autumn of 1894, however, something happened that was finally to shake even him. Captain Alfred Dreyfus, an Alsatian Jew attached to the French general staff, was arrested on charges of having furnished staff secrets to the German authorities, condemned by a court martial for high treason, and sentenced to life imprisonment in a fortress.

Herzl was then living in Paris as the correspondent of a Vienna daily, and in this capacity, he attended Dreyfus's first trial. A confirmed assimilationist, Herzl had been "but little concerned with Jewish matters; his knowledge of Judaism was meagre." Witnessing the degradation of the Jewish captain on trial, Herzl decided that France had revoked the principles of her great revolution. Feeling keenly "the blow struck at the whole Jewish people in the person of one Jew," he was an altered man. "Suddenly, as if by inspiration . . . the Jewish question preoccupied his thoughts—and it presented itself to him neither as an economic nor as a religious, but as a political national one."

The Jews, Herzl became convinced, were a nation, and a united one at that. In keeping with the general trend of nationalist thinking in his time and place, he predictably concluded that the Jews must gather and form a state of their own, in the Argentine or in Palestine. Feverishly, he sat down and wrote *Der Judenstaat* (The Jewish state), which he finished in 1894 and published, with revisions, in 1896.

Predictably, Herzl's starting point was anti-Semitism. The Jewish question, he contended, exists wherever Jews live in perceptible numbers. "Where it does not exist, it is carried by the Jews in the course of their migrations." Modern anti-Semitism was the outgrowth of the emancipation of the Jews, Herzl thought, and it was therefore not to be confused with the persecution of the Jews in former times, "though it does still have a religious aspect in some countries."

More central to Herzl's approach, however, was his belief that the solidarity of the Jews was itself one of the by-products of anti-Semitism. This is the way he formulated this aspect of his new stand:

> Perhaps we *could* succeed in vanishing without a trace into the surrounding peoples if they would let us be for just two generations. But they would not let us be. After brief periods of toleration their hostility erupts again and again. When we prosper, it seems to be unbearably irritating, for the world has for many centuries been accustomed to regarding us as the most degraded of the poor. Thus out of ignorance or illwill they have failed to observe that prosperity weakens us as Jews and wipes away our differences. Only pressure drives us back to our own; only hostility stamps us ever again as strangers. . . . We are one people—our enemies have made us one whether we will it or not.

Having thus established his whole national doctrine on an essentially negative, patently deterministic interpretation of Jewish history and Jewish existence, Herzl considered the ideological-theoretical part of his task finished and accomplished.

The common link of the Jewish people, he decided, was neither religion nor language, neither culture nor race, neither a common history nor a common homeland. It was, simply, affliction and collective distress. "Distress binds us together and, thus united, we suddenly discover our strength. Yes, we are strong enough to form a state and a modern state. We possess all the human and material resources necessary for the purpose."

So convinced was Herzl of the Gentile world's inevitable and everlasting hatred of the Jew that he wrote with complete confidence: "Prayers will be offered up for our work in temples and in churches also; for it will bring ease from a burden which has long weighed on all men. . . . The world will be freed by our liberty, enriched by our wealth, magnified by our greatness." The Jewish state, he concluded, was "essential to the world; it will therefore be created."

One more European-style pan-movement was born.

Herzl's Jewish State: Dream and Reality

For all its woolly reasoning and its shaky historical basis, Herzl's blueprint for a Jewish state proved remarkably realistic in its consequences, and events of the fifty years that followed the publication of *Der Judenstaat* can be said to have reasonably vindicated his approach. Yet the basic flaw in his overall argument became apparent even before his dream finally was to come true with the proclamation of the state of Israel in 1948.

On the fiftieth anniversary of the publication of *The Jewish State*, Hannah Arendt wrote an article for an American Jewish periodical in which she set out to evaluate Herzl's work and vision. Herzl, she pointed out, regarded anti-Semitism as a perpetual immutable force which the Jews must learn to use to their own advantage. He pictured the Jewish people everywhere and at all times "surrounded and forced together by a world of enemies." In his oversimplified picture of history and reality, she observed, "any segment of reality that could not be defined by anti-Semitism was not taken into account and any group that could not definitely be classed as anti-Semitic was not taken seriously as a political force."[19]

Regarding the situation of his own time and place as an eternally durable one, Herzl accordingly proposed a solution based upon the premises of his time and place—namely, to constitute the Jews, whom he considered a biological and even a racial group, as a nation like all other nations in their own state. At the beginning, he was interested neither in the history and character of the Jews and of Judaism nor in the land where they were to settle. At first, he did not think of Palestine as the needed homeland, or of a Jewish cultural life expressed in its own language. The solution was simple—to give to the people without a land a land without a people. What kind of people this was or whether such a land existed were not Herzl's primary considerations.

The vagueness, the confusion, and the sheer ignorance of such an approach did not take long to come to the surface. Though Herzl had no definite idea as to the land on which the Jewish state was to be established, his contacts with the Eastern European Zionist movement eventually made him decide on Palestine. But Palestine was not a land without people—and Herzl, under the influence of the liberal ideas that still prevailed when he grew up, duly took this fact into consideration.

In his diaries, Herzl wrote, "My testament for the Jewish people: So build your state that a stranger will feel contented among you." He did not, however, bother to explain just how "a stranger" can feel at home and contented in a state which, by definition, was to identify itself with "the nation," and consequently citizenship with "nationality."

Herzl, however, visited Palestine only once and very briefly—not in order to get in touch with the Jewish inhabitants of the land but to submit a request to the German emperor, who was then visiting Turkey. Herzl, it would seem, wished to avoid all serious thought on what he must have felt was a very probable conflict between the national claims of the Jews over Palestine and the rights of the indigenous population. This was, perhaps, because such a conflict ran counter to his liberal background—or probably because he felt that such a conflict might end in the ruin of the Zionist movement.

In his last book, *Altneuland,* which he left as a testament to the movement he had inspired and founded, Herzl drew a picture of the future Jewish state, depicting it as a new society. In its basic traits, this society reflected the liberal views of the Viennese Jews at the beginning of the twentieth century.

Life in the Jewish state, for instance, was not based on the Jewish traditions, nor was Hebrew spoken there. It was not a new ghetto, living in seclusion from the world and animated by a feeling of hostility to its environment. Herzl thus summed up his vision of his new, open society:

It is founded on the ideas which are a common product of all civilized nations. It would be immoral if we would exclude anyone, whatever his origin, his descent, or his religion, from participating in our achievements. For we stand on the shoulders of other civilized peoples. . . . What we own we owe to the preparatory works of other peoples. Therefore, we have to repay our debt. There is only one way to do it—the highest tolerance. Our motto must therefore be, now and ever: Man, you are my brother!

Envisioning an election campaign in the new state, Herzl went so far as to direct his wrath against the nationalist or chauvinist party, which is depicted as wanting to make the Jews a privileged element in the land. He regarded such a program a betrayal of Zion, for to him Zion was identical with humanitarianism and tolerance. That was as true in politics as it was in religion. "Matters of faith were once and for all excluded from public influence," he wrote. "Whether anyone sought religious devotion in the synagogue, in the church, in the mosque, in the museum, or in a philharmonic concert, did not concern society. That was his private affair."

In *Altneuland*, Herzl described conditions in Palestine twenty years later. He aimed—to quote Israel Cohen, the historian of the Zionist movement— at "achieving a propagandist rather than literary success."[20] When the book appeared, in October 1902, Herzl was bitterly disappointed, however, to find it assailed on the ground that it failed to depict a background of Jewish cultural life, with Hebrew as the national tongue. Curiously, the most-scathing criticism came from the moderate (cultural) nationalist thinker, Ahad Ha-Am. Nonetheless, the sharp controversy that was to ensue did not prevent *Altneuland* from achieving a measure of popularity or from being translated into several languages, while the motto on its title page, "If you wish it, this is no fairy tale," became an oft-quoted maxim in the Zionist world.

That *Altneuland* posed far more questions than it answered was, however, amply shown in Ahad Ha-Am's sharply critical comments on the book. In an extended review of Herzl's romance, he inquired (something no one else among the Zionist leaders of the day had done), "Wherein is the Jewishness of this cosmopolitan society of Herzl's imaginings?" There are theaters in *Altneuland*, to be sure, where plays can be staged in several European languages. Also present are an opera house and an academy modeled on those of France. In Jerusalem, there is a temple of the best German-Jewish type. There are newspapers in several languages, museums, concert halls, and all the other signs of a highly civilized life.

But there is no sign of the Hebrew language except in the synagogue service and in a song of welcome sung by schoolchildren to admiring visitors. There is not a single trace of Hebrew literature or Hebrew culture, of a recognizably Hebraic pattern of life and thought, of anything whatever to differentiate this "Jewish" society from one that might be created, Ahad Ha-Am concludes, by Blacks if they had the means and set about to build themselves a new life modeled on the latest ideas and inventions of Western civilization. In fact, Ahad Ha-Am complained, Herzl's utopia, with its repeated insistence on the absence of any kind of originality in the Zionist haven of refuge, is a glaring example of the assimilationist mentality.[21]

It would be useful and instructive, at this point, to dwell briefly on the difference between the respective approaches of Herzl and Ahad Ha-Am. Arthur Hertzberg, in the introduction to his anthology *The Zionist Idea*, notes that "the key to Ahad Ha-Am, no less than to Herzl, is in his estimate of the world of the gentiles." The vital difference between the two, he asserts, is that at bottom Herzl trusted this world and Ahad Ha-Am did not.

The deeper roots of this difference is explained by Hertzberg at some length:

> This deep distrust [on Ahad Ha-Am's part] was compounded out of several factors. Underlying it all was the attitude of the ghetto within which Ahad Ha-Am had been nurtured till early manhood, which held that the surrounding world was the unchanging and hereditary enemy. His intellectual emancipation, the period of his life when this autodidact was entering "the palace of general culture," coincided with the pogroms of the 1880's, in the aftermath of which his own economic future . . . was undermined by a new ukase of the government forbidding Jews to act as factors of country estates. . . . In a significant way, his experience of Pan-Slavism set the final seal upon his pessimism and coloured the whole of even his theory of Jewish nationalism.[22]

This experience of pan-Slavism (one of the most powerful pan-movements of his time) was to color Ahad Ha-Am's whole outlook, and his so-called cultural, or spiritual, Zionism was little more than a Jewish version of the ideologies of those movements. As he wrote to Judah Magnes in 1910, "In my view our vision is national—that is to say, it is a product of our national spirit." In his essay "The Jewish State and the Jewish Problem" (1897), Ahad Ha-Am tried to clarify the difference between the political Zionism of the emancipated but disappointed assimilationist Jews of Western Europe and his own "cultural" Zionism, based on the age-old love of the Jewish culture of the unemancipated Jewish masses of Eastern Europe. He wrote:

> The eastern form of the spiritual problem is absolutely different from the western. In the West it is the problem of the Jews; in the East, the *problem of Judaism*. The first weighs on the individual; the second, on the nation. The one is felt by Jews who have had a European education; the other, by Jews whose education has been Jewish. The one is a product of antisemitism, and is dependent on antisemitism for its existence; the other is a natural product of a real link with a millennial culture, and it will remain unsolved and unaffected even if the troubled of the Jews all over the world attain comfortable economic positions, are on the best possible terms with their neighbours, and are admitted to the fullest social and political equality.[23]

Ahad Ha-Am and "Spiritual Zionism"

Ahad Ha-Am addresses himself to "the problem of Judaism" in his essay "The Jewish State and the Jewish Problem." This problem is, he opines, that Judaism's older national form is no longer adequate to modern life, but that to abandon that form before a substitute has been produced by the national spirit of the Jews themselves will destroy Jewish life. However, Judaism cannot develop its individuality in its own way as long as it remains in exile. The solution, therefore, is to be found in the return to Palestine and in the natural emergence there of a modern Jewish national culture. The Jews, Ahad Ha-Am believed, were ideally fitted to perform such a spiritual renaissance, since they were naturally endowed with higher ethical values.

In this connection, it is worth referring to another of Ahad Ha-Am's essays, the one on Nietzsche. In that essay, he does not argue against the idea of the Superman; he only denies that the highest human type is necessarily identical with the Aryan "blond beast." The Superman exists in a Jewish version—as the *tzaddik*, the moral hero; indeed, if the Superman is to be "a permanent feature of human life and not just a freak, there must be a suitable environment." And such a people does exist, Ahad Ha-Am maintains: the Jewish people, "whose inherent characteristics make it better fitted than the others for moral development and whose scheme of life is governed by a moral law superior to the common type of morality."

For Ahad Ha-Am, all national identities are fashioned and sustained by a quasi-biological will to live. However, it makes a vast and essential difference whether the dynamism of a nation expresses itself in the quest for power or in the service of the moral ideal. While gentile nationalism is rooted in power, "the secret of our people's persistence is . . . that at a very early period the Prophets taught it to respect only the power of the spirit and not to worship material power."[24]

Hertzberg's comment on this passage is worth quoting:

> What Ahad Ha-Am is thus, in effect, proposing is a dual explanation of nationalism: there is nationalism in general, that of power, which is a genus comprising many species and individuals—i.e. all the nations of the world; counterposed to it there is the nationalism of the spirit, a unique genus of which there is only one species, the Jewish. It necessarily follows that the main axis of history is, indeed, as defined by Nietzsche (and the Pan-Slavs), the hatred of the sword for the book.[25]

Here, obviously, was the root of Ahad Ha-Am's peculiar view of Jewish nationality. It is a mistake, he wrote, to think that Jewish nationality exists

only when there is an actual collective national ethos. No doubt this national ethos came into being in consequence of a life lived in common over
a number of generations. However, "once the spirit of nationality has so
come into being . . . it becomes a phenomenon that concerns the individual
alone, its reality being dependent on nothing but its presence in his psyche,
and on no external or objective actuality."

"If I feel the spirit of Jewish nationality in my heart," Ahad Ha-Am explains, "so that it stamps all my inward life with its seal, then the spirit of
Jewish nationality exists in me; and its existence is not at an end even if all
my Jewish contemporaries should cease to feel it in their hearts." Here, to
quote Elie Kedourie's incisive comment, "are no superfluous appeal to
philology or biology, no laborious attempt to prove that because a group
speaks the same language, or has the same religion, or lives in the same
territory, it therefore is a nation. All this is casually brushed aside, and the
nation, says Ahad Ha-Am, is what individuals feel in their hearts is the
nation."[26]

It will be apparent, however, that the roots of this attitude go far deeper.
Ahad Ha-Am's Zionism is commonly called "cultural" and "spiritual."
Though this has its origin in his call for a "national spiritual center" in
Palestine and in his opposition to certain opportunistic manifestations of
"political" Zionism, no really satisfactory exposition has ever been furnished of just what Ahad Ha-Am's "spiritual Zionism" actually signifies or
in what respects it differs fundamentally from its "political" counterpart.

Ahad Ha-Am himself was constantly preoccupied with such concepts as
"national spirit" and "national creative power"—both of which no doubt
led to talk about his "spiritual Zionism." On two occasions, he was to offer
fairly clear statements of his concept of Judaism and its relation to nationality. In 1910, when consulted by Magnes about his project of founding a
society "to propagate national religion and religious nationalism," Ahad
Ha-Am took exception to this formulation. He fully agreed, he wrote
Magnes, that Judaism was a national religion, but he could not accept "religious nationalism" unless it was merely another way of saying "national
religion." "In my view," he explained, "our religion is national—that is to
say, it is a product of our national spirit—but the converse is not true. If it is
impossible to be a Jew in the religious sense without acknowledging our
nationality, it is possible to be a Jew in the national sense without accepting
many things in which religion requires belief."[27]

In 1913, again, in a letter to Israel Abrahams, Ahad Ha-Am tried to answer the question as to the meaning of Judaism. He wrote:

> The answer to the question what Judaism is depends, of course, on the meaning one attaches to the vague terms "Judaism," "religion" and "culture." In the sense in which I understand these terms, I should say that religion itself is only one particular form of culture and that Judaism is neither the one nor the other, but is the national creative power, which in the past expressed itself in a form of culture which was primarily religious.

While the "national creative power" of the Jews was in the past expressed primarily in the Jewish religion, however, "we cannot foretell . . . in what form it will express itself in the future." Thus, no matter what happens, the "national spirit" and the "national creative power" will always be with the Jewish people—even if religion should cease to be the primary expression of this spirit and that power.[28]

However, while the national creative power and the national spirit of the Jews may have manifested themselves in, or even created, a moral ideal which historically has been associated with Jewry, what is not at all clear is why, on Ahad Ha-Am's own showing, they should continue to be bound to that ideal. As Leon Roth writes:

> The "spirit" may well change. The "national creative power" may well create something else. Its old manifestations may be out of date. The past is the past. It has no permanent validity. It is the subject of historical investigation and of the curiosity of the learned. It is what we think and do now that counts, not what past generations thought or did (or what we think they thought and did), or what we find written in the records of another age.

Ahad Ha-Am's account of the nature of Judaism, Roth argues, may hold good for some few individuals—Moses and Elijah and the like. It does not hold good for Moses' people:

> The "spirit of the people" in the time of Moses worshipped the golden calf: The people consistently accepted the "false" prophets, not those whom we call (why do we?) the true. . . . Ahad Ha-Am talks easily about "absolutes"; and it may be that he is right in thinking that moral commands *are* absolute. But we can extract an absolute from the ever-

changing face of the "national creative power" which is in practice the ever-changing face of national opinion.[29]

It is noteworthy that, his opposition to "political Zionism" notwithstanding, Ahad Ha-Am's thought and his philosophy can, in the end, be comprehended only within the mainstream of the ideology of the pan-movements of his time and place. Leon Roth has reminded us that in his formulation of the theory of Judaism, Ahad Ha-Am attaches himself not to the modern social psychologists who provided him with his method and vocabulary, but to Nachman Krochmal. Krochmal (1785–1840) was one of the creative Jewish minds of nineteenth-century Europe; but he was strongly influenced by the writings of the German romantics and particularly by Hegel.

Krochmal, Roth notes, made much play, in a chapter of his *Guide for the Perplexed of the Time,* with the "spirit" (*geist*) of the different peoples, which he identified with their various "princes" (i.e., their gods). He saw, as the "spirit" of the Jewish people, the Absolute Spirit of God. Krochmal himself, Roth points out, recognized specifically that these phrases are to be taken as pictorial thinking or metaphor, "but like other members of the Hegelian school he tended to move indifferently between immanence and transcendence, with the result that the distinction between human and divine was liable to be overlooked or obliterated."[30]

This same tendency, Roth concludes, was even stronger, owing to his psychological bias, in Ahad Ha-Am, and it was to come to full fruition in many of his followers. "It is a sad perversion of an age-old tradition," Roth writes in referring to this tendency. "It is difficult [for one] to reconcile oneself to the reduction of the God of Judaism to a 'national creative power' or 'national spirit,' or a 'national will to survive'."

In sorrow more than either in anger or jest, Roth then produces the following horrifying parody of the reduction of the God of Judaism in which the Jewish Hegelians were indulging: "In the beginning the National Creative Power created heaven and earth. . . . What doth the National Spirit require of thee but to do justly and to love kindness and to walk humbly with thy National Will to Survive? Replace God by glaring and dismal humbug about *Geist*—that is what "spiritual Zionism" ultimately amounts to."[31]

Leon Simon, Ahad Ha-Am's biographer, draws a curious analogy between his subject and Maimonides. Asserting that "in character and temperament there was more than a superficial resemblance between the two men," Simon goes on to enumerate some of the two men's presumed common qualities: "a burning passion for truth, a lofty morality, a love of order and clarity in thought and its exposition, and a dislike of mysticism."[32]

There is, however, one fundamental and rather decisive difference between these two Jewish thinkers—namely, their diametrically opposite approaches to Judaism and Jewishness. Though he speaks merely of the Jews' "national spirit," "national creative power," and "national will for survival," what Ahad Ha-Am actually does is to set the Jews apart as a unique people with a unique historical and "spiritual" heritage. All of this would be perfectly true, however, were it not for Ahad Ha-Am's firm belief that this uniqueness is in some way hereditary, that the Jewish people, the Jewish "spirit," the Jewish moral ideal to which that spirit gave birth—and ultimately Judaism itself—are all inextricably and everlastingly bound to one another.

This, of course, is as far from Maimonides' concept of Judaism as it could possibly be. For Maimonides, as it has always been for the mainstream of Jewish thought, Judaism is a *voluntary community*. It remained so, too, until the emergence of the pan-movements and their racial theories (also often clothed in highly transcendental jargon about "spirit," "national will," and "national creative power") which grew on the continent of Europe during the nineteenth century.

The contention of Judaism—and of Maimonides—is totally different. Here one can do no better than quote Leon Roth again:

> When Abraham is said to have "made" souls; when the Rabbis of the Talmud forbade the wronging of a stranger "even in words"; when Maimonides addressed the convert as a genuine member of God's household and gave him an even higher place than the "born" Jew because [he said] the convert was like Abraham our father in recognising the truth by his own effort and conviction and not through the mere fact of birth; when even Halevi, although he gave primacy to the born Jew and to the soil of Palestine, yet emphasized the fact that in the last resort Judaism is a matter of choice;—they all repudiate racist doctrine *ab initio*, following the lead of Scripture which opens with the creation of one man who is the one ancestor equally of all the families of earth, and which tells that the man who was "raised on high" to receive God's "everlasting covenant" was the direct descendant of a poor girl from the alien tribe of Moab.[33]

Jewish nationalism, whether it be designated as spiritual, political, or cultural, has one feature that renders it hard to distinguish from the nineteenth-century tribal nationalist doctrine encountered in the European pan-movements of the time. In all its forms, Jewish nationalism is based on a claim of hereditary and exclusive privilege for one branch of the human family as determined by biological descent.

PART 2

Prospects

Death and Life were not
Till man made up the whole,
Made lock, stock and barrel
Out of his bitter soul.

W. B. Yeats

4

In Search of Identity

I don't quite get it. Is this the State of the Jews or the State of Israel?

Shlomo Qatar, member of Israel's national basketball team, pleading
in January 1986 to critics who objected to his demand that Israelis
who are not Jews ought not to be included in the team.

The subject of Israel's identity—national, religious, and cultural—is as old as Israel itself. At issue is whether Israel is, or ought to be, a strictly Jewish state or an *Israeli* state, a European or a Middle Eastern country, a theocracy or a secular-liberal polity and, above all, the precise nature of the status of its non-Jewish citizens. The first two pairs of alternatives are manifestly closely interconnected: In one short fortnight in June 1987, the country found itself plunged into a bewildering assortment of heated debates, all of which, in one way or another, centered on the subject of identity. The events leading to these debates are best given in chronological sequence:

- An Israeli citizen, 'Izzat Nafsu, a Circassian, was released from prison after proving in court that he had been sentenced to twenty years' incarceration on the strength of false evidence extracted from him by past colleagues in the secret security service, where he worked.

- The Druse inhabitants of Beit Jan (likewise full-fledged citizens of Israel, who send their sons to serve in the Israeli defense forces) were claiming back huge plots of land previously confiscated by the state and currently comprising part of a nature-preservation forest.

- The inhabitants of two border Christian villages in the north, 'Ikrit and Bir'am, were again clamoring for the right to return to their homes, from which they had been expelled in 1949.

- A young Palestinian Muslim, a convert to Judaism, a scion of Hebron's ruling family, the Ja'baris, was apprehended in the act of attacking the refugee townlet of Dehaisha, situated not far from the Gush Emunim stronghold, settlement of Kiryat Arba', where the young fanatic convert (now named Jacob Ben-David) lived.

- More recently, in the late 1990s, 'Azmi Bishara, Arab Knesset member from Nazareth, caused a noisy stir in political quarters when he announced he would run for the premiership in the 2000 elections, with some Jewish MKs calling for an amendment to the elections law stipulating that candidacy to the post of prime minister be confined to Jews.

- The influx of immigrants from the republics of the former Soviet Union and Ethiopia was accompanied by a wave of protests from the country's religious establishment, which claimed that as many as 40 percent of these newcomers were not Jews.

These, and many other similar phenomena in recent years, served to blur the very meaning and import of the term "Israeli," and obviously have a bearing both on Israel's self-view and—in the long run—on the Arab-Israeli relationship.

A Tapestry of Cultures

One of the Middle East's most basic problems—and the one with the most relevance to the Arab-Israeli conflict—is that of national identity. This problem continues to beset both Israel and the Arab world, even though it seldom seems to come to the surface. It is now more than a century since the modern concept of nationality first was introduced into the political consciousness of certain groups of Jews in Central and Eastern Europe. At roughly the same time, the rising educated classes among the Arabic-speaking Muslims and Christians in the countries of the Middle East began to be swayed by the same sort of nationalist jargon. Yet few—very few—serious students of the Arab and Jewish national movements would apply to these the terminology of European-style nationalist ideologies without reservations.

The Arabs themselves, though they speak with certainty and a great deal of enthusiasm about themselves as a single "nationality," generally admit that, ultimately, the term "Arab" connotes a mixed population varying widely in ethnic origin, religious affiliation, and cultural background. Many of them now readily acknowledge, too, that what really gives the Arabs their consciousness of belonging to one nation is, in the final analysis, merely their common language and the pride they take in a shared past.

In Judaism, too, the "nation" concept is open to much question. As one confirmed Jewish nationalist and Zionist has written, at no time were the Jews "a nation in the Western sense." He explained:

> The "nation" image which Judaism projected was an outcome of its non-proselytizing nature. . . . The exclusiveness of the Jews and their identification with a specific religious faith and regime of precepts led Western thinkers to classify them as a nation and Zionism as their national movement. Zionist ideologists employed the term "national-ism" as a means of adapting their movement to the *zeitgeist*. And since they could readily explain Zionist aims in such terms, and more important, because they themselves were assimilated into the culture of their surroundings, they in the end came to believe in their formulas.[1]

Relevant or not, accurate or otherwise, these formulas have produced some highly tangible results. Thus, what can be termed the exclusively Arab view of the Middle East (typified, among others, by Muhammad Hasanein Haykal's massive claim that in this region there is room only for "the Arab nation") is fully matched by the equally exclusionary view of Israel which so many Israelis—and the country's present political-cultural establishment first and foremost—take completely for granted. It has al-ready been argued that the whole concept of a Jewish nationality had no basis either in race or in religion, and that therefore there was no substance in speaking of Israel as a Jewish state in either of these two senses.

What then do those who speak of Israel's Jewish identity have in mind? The clue to Israel's Jewish identity, and to the oft-repeated wish to preserve the country's Jewishness, must be sought in the cultural sphere. In Jewry, there developed through the long centuries of exile at least three easily distinguishable cultures: the Judeo-Arabic (Middle Eastern/Sephardic); the Neo-Hebrew/Ashkenazic (Eastern European Pale of Settlement); and the Western (North American/Western European).

Both Zionism and the state of Israel itself were the creations almost ex-clusively of the Neo-Hebrew Ashkenazic culture of Eastern European Jewry. Possessed of a long heritage of exclusiveness and imposed cultural segregation and having little experience of contact with the outside world, the Jews of Eastern Europe gave the Zionist movement many of its lofty qualities; but they also brought with them to Palestine the ingrained fear, suspicion, and contempt for the outsider (often including Jews different from themselves), which centuries of endeavor to preserve their identity and self-esteem under adverse conditions could not have failed to instill in them.

The result, quite naturally, has been a state of Israel conceived and established in an exclusivism which—perfectly appropriate though it had proved to be for a ghetto existence in a hostile environment—was hardly suitable for an enlightened modern nation. Those Israelis who had hoped that the prevalence of this approach was a passing phase were to be disappointed. The fact is that even today, when far-reaching, wholly unexpected demographic changes have rendered the old Eastern European element in Israel a diminishing numerical minority, the dominance of this element in the politico-cultural sphere continues to prevail almost unopposed, shaping the policies, determining the attitudes, and generally setting the cultural tone of the country.

As far as the Arab nationalist argument is concerned, the countries of the area now called the Arab world have in the meantime undergone many important changes. They secured separate independent statuses; Arabic has become the official language in each of them; a League of Arab States was formed; and there has been endless talk about pan-Arab unity. All these, however, have so far failed to add up to anything like a definable "Arab nationality." In fact, the emergence of such a nationality now seems to be farther than ever from materialization, and the Arabs in their various lands are coming to realize this and to reconcile themselves to it.

There is, to be sure, an Egyptian nationality, and also Iraqi, Saudi Arabian, Lebanese, and Syrian nationalities. But from this statement to talk about one single Arab nationality is a very far cry indeed. Similarly, of course, there is an Israeli nationality; and instead of the artificial and baseless opposition between Arab and Jewish "nationalities," the Middle East seems destined to continue to accommodate a rich mosaic of cultures, nationalities, languages, and religious groups: Syrians, Iraqis, Palestinians and Israelis; Arabs, Turks, Persians, Kurds and Armenians; Muslims, Jews, Christians and Druse.

Despite recent tensions and antagonisms, the part that Israel can play in encouraging and stabilizing such a pluralistic Middle East is considerable. Moreover, although the dominant view in Israel so far has tended to envisage the future of the area in exclusivist terms of Arabs and Jews, there have been in the recent past some indications that a different approach may yet develop.

These signs, despite all appearances to the contrary, are discernible on the official as well as unofficial levels. In an article printed more than thirty years ago Abba Eban, then deputy prime minister of Israel, made the astute observation that the key to peace between Israel and the Arabs did not lie in any of "the conventional themes which the diplomats have agitated since

1948," but rather in a new and common understanding of the Middle Eastern structure. "The destiny of this region," he said, "lies in a pluralistic interaction of Asia, Europe, Africa; of Judaism, Christianity and Islam." Besides being worthy of contemplation in itself, this view of the Middle East, in fact, constitutes a radical departure from the old, monolithic opposition of "Arab" and "Jew" as belonging to two different "world entities" or "world nations."[2]

It is essential, however, that this understanding of the Middle Eastern structure be shared by all sides concerned. Israelis are of course right in telling the Arab nationalists that the Middle East never can be comprehended in exclusively Arab or any other ethnic terms—but then, neither could any of the countries of the region, taken separately. If we exclude Saudi Arabia, we find that there is not a single country in the region that, by itself, can be comprehended in exclusively Arab or other ethnic-cultural terms. In a pluralistic Middle East—where Asia, Europe, and Africa, Judaism, Christianity, and Islam interact freely—the Israelis, too, will be called upon to cease viewing their country in exclusively Jewish terms.

Naturally, it will take a good deal of reciprocity on the part of its neighbors to make official Israel proceed in such a novel and rather revolutionary direction. They, too, will be called upon to abandon the view that the Middle East as a whole, or any of its countries taken separately, has room only for Arabs or for the "Arab nation" generally. Such a fresh approach to the problems of the area may well work and at the same time be augmented, on a deeper cultural level, for, as has been indicated, an additional factor has been at work here. That factor is the introduction into Israel's homogeneous, overwhelmingly Eastern European sociocultural fabric of an important Middle Eastern element in the form of the mass influx of Jews from countries of the Middle East and North Africa.

The temperament of these Middle Easterners, their cultural background, and their long experience of living side by side with Arabic-speaking Muslims must, in the end, leave a lasting imprint on Arab-Israeli relations. For one thing, from what has been described as "just a patch of Europe transplanted to the Eastern shore of the Mediterranean," Israel is bound to become increasingly "Oriental"—what has been described as "a normal Middle Eastern country at home with itself and its problems." However, it will perforce develop its own unique culture and way of life, neither Western nor Eastern but a special kind of Mediterranean cocktail.

Naturally, there is nothing automatic or deterministic about these things. The picture often is especially confused where the attitude of the Middle Eastern element itself toward the Arabs is concerned. In general discussions in Israel about the country's future relations with its Arab neighbors, it is sometimes argued that—far from being better-inclined toward the Arabs—Israeli Orientals are actually more "anti-Arab" than their European compatriots. There is an element of truth in this observation, at least on the surface and where the initial emotional reactions of many of these Arabic-speaking Jews are concerned.

Reasons for this, however, are not difficult to determine. During their first years in Israel, immigrants from the countries of the Middle East and North Africa were bound to feel a good deal of resentment, both at being victimized in their lands of birth as Zionists and as a result of the great hardships they had to face in Israel. It was only to be expected that these Arabic-speaking newcomers should go out of their way to dissociate themselves from their origin and their culture, given that they had come to a society whose whole set of attitudes, mores, and sentiments were strongly slanted in the direction of European ways—a society that was openly contemptuous of the East and its culture and in which, moreover, the most readily observable prestige criterion was affinity to Europe. In this endeavor, these immigrants often found no better way than to direct their resentment at their former compatriots and hence at the generality of "Arabs."

This, however, was bound to be a passing phase, and there is now reason to believe that these Arab Jews are gaining enough self-confidence and self-esteem and discovering enough new things about themselves and their surroundings to have a more balanced view of their situation. To be sure, there is still talk about the Israeli Orientals "hating" the Arabs, while their European counterparts can be said to merely "despise" them. It will readily be seen, however, that while hatred is an emotion that can change overnight (often to be replaced by its very opposite), contempt is a far more serious proposition.

Jews beyond Judaism

The thrust of the argument advanced by those who reject the idea of a Middle Eastern Israel is that the appellation "Middle Eastern" is merely a geographical concept, standing in sharp contrast to "Jewish," which is a national, cultural, and religious concept of primary relevance. One cannot, this particular argument goes, be both Jewish and Middle Eastern.

This is patently untenable. To be Middle Eastern (or West European, Far Eastern, Latin American, or Caribbean) involves far more than geography; it denotes certain cultural traits and a well-defined cultural identity. To the extent that some insist that Israel is, or should be, Jewish *rather than* Middle

Eastern, this means that they view Jewish culture as being of a piece, and they view Israel as belonging to this culture and as having a monolithic cultural identity.

Yet the question of what constitutes Jewish culture or Jewish identity—and whether there is, in reality, such a uniform culture and uniform identity—is by no means all that easy to answer. To be sure, the term "Jewish culture" generally is used very liberally by the overwhelming majority of those who write and speak about it. Moreover, these writers and speakers usually see Jewish culture as being equivalent to and interchangeable with "Judaism," "Jewish religion," and "Jewishness." However, as more than one Jewish scholar and historian have pointed out, Jews have acquired, in their many and various environs and through their long history, as many and as various sets of cultural traits. Thus, it has become virtually impossible to speak of "Jewish culture" as if it were in any meaningful way uniform or monolithic.

Since the exile, Jewish culture ceased to be uniform, and a process started whereby there developed several Jewish cultures. At the same time, however, Jewish culture—any Jewish culture, anywhere—cannot be said to exist in vacuo. This is, as Raphael Loewe has pointed out, because without being informed by Judaism and by Jewish ethical values, Jewish culture becomes "but a behaviourism and a skill, comparable to that of a radio-maniac who understands electronics."[3]

When one sets out to define and to delineate a certain Jewish culture, one has to take into consideration at least four kinds of influences that had been at work in the crystallization of that culture: (1) the economic (how Jews lived), (2) the sociological (how the Gentile environment behaved toward them), (3) the ethnological (the extent to which the Gentile environment regarded them as aliens), and (4) the historical (how they got where they did).

The reason why all these factors have to be taken into account is that, wherever Jews chose to live, self-isolation was simply not possible for them. If we consider only one aspect, that of language, we find that invariably and in every instance, Hebrew confronts a vernacular. Indeed, bilingualism has so long a Jewish history as to have become virtually endemic long before the close of antiquity. It is generally taken for granted that modern Hebrew, in Israel, has now changed all this (or at least has made it possible to change all this). As Loewe notes, however, "Contemporary Hebrew has, of its own volition, tended to become a satellite European language . . . rather than an organic continuation of the linguistic dimension of traditional Jewish culture."

In this satellite European language, Loewe adds, "the vocabulary, which is the least important part, is basically Hebrew—or where possible formed on Hebrew patterns—while the syntax, the crucial element, is allowed to become progressively Westernized; and a Jewish flavoring is imparted by the retention from traditional Hebrew of such idioms as do not presuppose too much understanding of the inner workings of the older Jewish writings." Very significantly, moreover, "the idioms of *halakhic* Hebrew—the language of jurisprudence and of rabbinic administration—are among the least frequent of the older expressions retained in popular contemporary Hebrew."[4]

What is true of the Hebrew language is true of Jewish culture as a whole. Loewe argues:

Jewish culture may very well be an indispensable "incarnation" of Judaism. But if its specifically religious dimension is either repudiated or ignored, Jewish culture becomes . . . a technique. It is of course possible for the Hebrew language to be used neutrally, that is to say having been purged, almost sterilized, of theological presuppositions, even if their echoes remain as idiomatic phrases; but if it is thus used, it ceases . . . to have cultural significance in the generally understood sense of "culture." Important it will no doubt continue to be for the psychologist, just as experiments with monkeys at the keyboard are important. But even if a monkey happens to type correctly the whole of, say, Milton's *Ode on his Blindness*, there would be no cultural significance in the event (at any rate for the monkey).[5]

What happened in Israel in the linguistic-cultural sphere has also been happening in the patently far more important field of "Jewish education" or—as some Israelis like to call it—"education for Judaism." To deal with the subject of Jewish education and Jewish learning in contemporary Israel, however, calls for a brief historical recapitulation.

In the year 133 C.E., while "the sword without and the terror within" ravaged Jerusalem, a venerable old teacher quit the walls that harbored misfortune and fled to the enemy. The Roman general Vespasian gave the fugitive a friendly reception and promised to grant one request that he would choose to make of him. The fugitive, who was none other than Rabban Yohanan Ben Zakkai, modestly asked that he be allowed to open a school in a small townlet called Yabneh, where he might teach his pupils. This seemingly harmless request was granted promptly.

There are, to this very day, Jews who would reproach the grand master for having had seen fit to carry on "academic discussions" with the archenemy of his people when the noblest among them were shedding their blood at the altar of liberty. But there are, on the other hand, others who criticize Vespasian for his shocking shortsightedness, for his failure to see that the consummation of Rabban Yohanan's desire would enable Judaism—then visibly so weak and helpless—to outlive Rome, for all its iron strength, for thousands of years.

The last eighteen hundred years of Jewish history offer the best justification for the wisdom and insight that had informed Rabban Yohanan's course of action. As one prominent modern Jewish scholar, Louis Ginsberg, explains: "That the Jewish nation has survived the downfall of its state and the destruction of its national sanctuary is above all due to this great genius, who made of religious study a new form in which the national existence of the Jews found expression, so that by the side of the history of nearly two thousand years of suffering we can point to an equally extensive history of intellectual effort."[6]

The light that Yohanan Ben Zakkai kindled in Yabneh was never to be extinguished. Others took up the work begun there, and when the sun of learning in Palestine had passed its meridian, it made its appearance further to the east. Nehardea, Sura, and Pumbeditha, in Babylonia, kept the flame burning for eight hundred years. And when, toward the beginning of the eleventh century, darkness descended over the Jews of Iraq, bright days dawned in the Iberian Peninsula and subsequently in Germany and Provence, and then in Poland and Lithuania. As Ginsberg has written, "A plant native to Palestine, which flourished by the rivers of Babylon, blossomed out luxuriously in Spain, and bore savoury fruit in icy Poland, must indeed have been tended by the hands of gardeners who combined love and knowledge in the highest degree."[7]

Where does Jewish education stand now, after the tragic destruction of its last European centers? Normally, one would point to Jerusalem, to the Hebrew University, to the Israeli secondary and primary schools. But do these schools and institutions offer a *Jewish* education? In 1964, the newly founded Council for Jewish Education convened in Geneva. The council had been formed at the initiative of the Conference of Jewish Organizations, and its purpose was to find ways of aiding and expanding institutions of Jewish learning in the diaspora. Prior to its first session, the question as to whether the council's permanent seat should be in Jerusalem was discussed at some length.

At these discussions, opposition to Jerusalem had a rather broad basis among the bodies represented, including some Zionist organizations. Although this opposition was explained in all sorts of polite ways (such as that Israel was too busy with other matters and had no time to spare for problems of Jewish education!), it was not difficult to gauge the real cause for the opposition. This was the widespread feeling that Israel did not care enough about the Jewish content of the education it offers its own school children, and that it can thus contribute very little to the task at hand.

Three Major Jewish Identities

Culturally, contemporary Jewry can be said to possess three major identities, the result of long historical and environmental influences that have been at work since the exile. These are: the Eastern European/Ashkenazic, the Middle Eastern/Sephardic, and the Western European/North American. Each of these major Jewish cultures, or identities, may have a number of "subcultures." Thus the neo-Hebrew Zionist subculture is part of the Eastern European/Ashkenazic culture; the Israeli "sabra" subculture may be considered a part of the Middle Eastern/Sephardic culture; and the Soviet Jewish subculture is increasingly part of the West European/North American Jewish culture.

Many of the features that determined Israel's attitude to its immediate surroundings stemmed from the independent, rather exclusivist culture of the Ashkenazi Jews of Eastern Europe and its neo-Hebrew Zionist subculture. The failure of the early Zionist settlers in Palestine—who had hailed almost exclusively from this culture—to establish a meaningful dialogue with the people who inhabited the land before they made their appearance (including the Jews among them) can perhaps be explained best as a by-product of their cultural heritage of exclusiveness and spiritual as well as physical segregation.

The same peculiar cultural heritage also furnishes a possible explanation for the conviction, common among members of the Israeli establishment, that Israel must at all costs remain monolithically "Jewish," a state in which, ultimately, no non-Jew can really be or feel at home. So rooted is this outlook, in fact, that its impact has not been confined to Jewish or Israeli affairs but is also to be discerned in the country's overall concept of other peoples and states.

We have already seen, for example, that in their dealings with the Arabs, the Zionists have managed to mold (if not actually to bring into being) concepts like Arabism and Arab nationalism in their own exclusivist, black-and-white image. According to this ethnocentric view of the world, Arabs everywhere constitute one self-contained "nationality" or "world entity," a separate politico-cultural entity standing, almost by definition, in permanent and inevitable opposition to the Jews, who themselves make up a single, all-inclusive nationality or world entity.

One particular aspect of the three major Jewish cultures enumerated above is worth considering at some length: that is, their respective historical experiences of dealing with non-Jews. In this respect, even a most superficial study of the facts would show that, of the three cultures, the Middle Eastern/Sephardic and the Western European/North American are the only ones whose Jewries have had the experience of leading a full and flourishing Jewish life without being forced to remain socially, culturally, and politically cut off from the mainstream of the environment in which they live.

This point hardly needs elaboration. For Middle Eastern, Sephardic, and North African Jewries, this tradition of living side by side and freely discoursing with their non-Jewish neighbors dates from time immemorial. For the Western European and North American Jews, it is true, the experience has been relatively a recent one; yet it has lasted long enough to leave its stamp on their attitudes toward their immediate surroundings and toward the world at large.

There are signs, too, that the Jews of the former Soviet Union and its Eastern European satellites are also well on the road to establishing a similar tradition of coexistence and interaction with their non-Jewish neighbors—and thus clearly emerging as a subculture of the Western European/North American Jewish culture. That many Soviet Jews have chosen to leave the Soviet Union in no way contradicts this premise, since obviously the desire is shared by many of their non-Jewish compatriots. Indeed, the refusal of a substantial percentage of Soviet Jewish emigrants to go to Israel tends rather to show that their desire to live outside of the former Soviet empire has little if anything to do with the wish to live with fellow Jews and/or away from their Gentile neighbors.

It is also of some interest to note that between 70 and 80 percent of Soviet Jewish emigrants who choose to live in the West rather than in Israel hail from the European parts of the Soviet Union, while an equally large proportion of those who emigrate to Israel come from Soviet Asia, where the impact of Western ideas and attitudes are far less in evidence.

The emerging culture of Israel—what I have called, somewhat arbitrarily perhaps, the Israeli "sabra" subculture of the mainstream Middle Eastern/Sephardic culture—remains rather difficult to place or to define. On one hand, the sabras (native-born Israeli Jews of European extraction) have never had the experience of living in the ghetto; on the other hand, it is by no means certain that, should Israel choose to continue to be the close, exclusionary "Jewish" society that it has been so far, it will not itself develop into a large, institutionalized voluntary ghetto.

While it is difficult, in the realities of the concluding years of the twentieth century, to contemplate such a development, it is clear that the character of Israeli society and culture as a whole may depend on the course of action taken by the Israelis themselves in that direction. Suffice it to say here that, with the growth both of religious fanaticism and exclusivity on one hand and tribal ethnic nationalism on the other—as well as a far more ominous combination of the two—the signs do not seem in the least encouraging.

Be that as it may, the fact remains that it is the Eastern European/ Ashkenazic culture and its Neo-Hebrew Zionist subculture that continue to set the tone and make the decisions. This culture, with its continuous and unbroken experience of ghetto life throughout its known history, has left what appears to be an indelible imprint on practically all aspects of the country's life and affairs, and the trend toward ghettoization and exclusivity sometimes seems to be increasing rather than declining.

True, Zionism itself is generally considered to have been a revolt *against* the ghetto. One reading of its history and its ideology, however, would indicate that, by virtue of being essentially a disillusioned reaction to the world outside the ghetto walls for refusing its founders admittance, Zionism was in fact little more than a call for a return *back to the ghetto,* albeit a ghetto of another kind and of different dimensions. This, of course, accounts for Zionism's lack of appeal to Jews who either were already finding their way in the Gentile world (such as those of Western Europe and the United States) or who had never experienced ghetto existence to begin with (such as the Middle Eastern and Sephardic Jews).

As modern Israel's most vital need is to accept and be accepted by its non-Jewish environment, it is one of the sad ironies of history that its policies and cultural orientation should be determined by the very Jewry that has no experience of living in social or cultural proximity with groups (Jewish as well as non-Jewish) different from itself and whose historical experience renders it the least equipped for the task at hand.

The brief history of the Eastern European Zionist elite in Palestine, as far as matters of cultural contacts and group relations are concerned, amply speaks for itself. Since the first immigrants started to arrive in Palestine from the *shtetls* and ghettos of Eastern Europe over a century ago, this elite has had several encounters with cultural groups different from itself. And, in each and every one of these encounters, it failed dismally to establish a meaningful relationship or dialogue with the group concerned:

- It failed to establish a meaningful relationship with the Jews—Ashkenazim as well as Sephardim—who had lived in Palestine before its arrival.

- It failed to conduct a dialogue with the Arabs, who constituted a majority of the population.

- It did not establish a common language with Jewish immigrants from Germany who sought refuge in Palestine in the early 1930s.

- It dismissed as primitive, "Asiatic," and "Oriental" the masses of Middle Eastern immigrants who poured into Israel shortly after the establishment of the state, and made every effort to deculturate and "absorb" them.

- And, finally and most dismayingly perhaps, it failed to establish a dialogue with its own offspring and creation, the sabras.

Clearly, such an exclusivist and segregationist temperament is not of the kind needed for cultural integration and pluralism, and for intergroup cooperation and coexistence. For Israel to become a Middle Eastern state, or rather *more* of a Middle Eastern state, would entail no loss of whatever measure of genuine Jewishness it may now have. It would largely mean accepting its Middle Eastern inhabitants—Jews and non-Jews—as equals, as people entitled to have their own culture and way of life. It would also require Israel's being accepted by and fitting into its surroundings.

There is, in fact, a fundamental contradiction between the Israelis' genuine belief that they have returned to the Promised Land in order to revive and resume a lost inheritance, and the widespread view that integration into the area and its culture spells assimilation or, worse still, "Levantinization."

Hugh Trevor-Roper, the British historian, has called it an irony of history that the Jews, having first entered Palestine as the tribesmen of the Eastern desert, should now return to it as "the spearhead of the avenging West." "Ironically, too," he writes, "they [now] find facing them the truer heirs of their own lost tradition. For history is only accidentally the continuity of peoples; fundamentally it is the continuity of countries and ideas. In fact they can hardly be surprised if the Arabs of Palestine, still poised upon the historic hills of Judea, looked down upon these sea-born invaders of the coastal plain as the ancient Hebrews looked down, in their day, upon the encroaching settlers from the West—the Philistines."[8]

The Uses of Ambiguity: Israel and Diaspora Jewries

Ambiguity is endemic in Israeli-Zionist ideological discourse. The debate on the issue of who—and what—is a Jew is only one example of this phenomenon, albeit the most vexed. Others concern such crucial subjects, slogans, and objectives as the nature of Israeli nationality, "Jewish cultural values," the status of Israel's non-Jewish citizens, "Jewish survival," "ingathering (and *mixing*) the exiles," and many no-less-problematic conceptual and ideological hurdles.

Arising from these ambiguities (and in turn constituting an inseparable part thereof) has been the rather difficult question as to the precise relationship, as seen through Israeli eyes, between the state of Israel and the Jewish communities of the diaspora. The 1948 Declaration of Independence speaks of "the Jewish people" and of how *Eretz Yisrael* (the land of Israel) was where this people's "spiritual, religious and political identity" was forged. The Law of Return grants automatic Israeli citizenship to any Jew who opts to immigrate into Israel. And on every Israeli Jew's identity card, the bearer's "nationality" is clearly stated to be "Jewish."

This last instance has significant ramifications as far as Israel's attitude to diaspora Jewries and its definition of their "national" status are concerned. For if the nationality (which in Israel is equated with citizenship) of an Israeli Jewish citizen is "Jewish," it logically follows that the nationality of a French, British, Argentinian, Moroccan, or U.S. Jewish citizen is also "Jewish."

This fundamental ambiguity—which does not always seem accidental—has from time to time given rise to certain misgivings among Jewish community leaders outside Israel and especially in those countries, such as the United States, where Jews enjoy full citizenship rights. David Ben-Gurion, then prime minister of Israel, was no doubt fully aware of these misgivings when, at an official luncheon given in honor of Jacob Blaustein, late president of the American Jewish Committee, in Jerusalem on August 23, 1950, he declared:

It is most unfortunate that since our State came into being some confusion and misunderstanding should have arisen as regards the relationship between Israel and the Jewish communities abroad, in particular that of the United States.... To my mind the position is perfectly clear. The Jews of the United States, as a community and as individuals, have only one political attachment and that is to the United States of America. They owe no political allegiance to Israel.

These words were warmly welcomed by Blaustein, who in response, expressed confidence that this statement would "be followed by unmistakable evidence that the responsible leaders of Israel, and the organizations connected with it, fully understand that future relations between the American Jewish community and the State of Israel must be based on mutual respect for one another's feelings and needs." Blaustein then described Ben-Gurion's statement as propounding "a fundamental and historic position which will redound to the best interest not only of Israel but of the Jews of America and of the world."

Yet less than one year later, Ben-Gurion found himself speaking in a somewhat different voice. "When we say 'one Jewish nation,'" he asserted in an article, "we must ignore the fact, favorable or unfavorable as the case may be, that this Jewish nation is scattered over all the countries of the world and that Jews living abroad are citizens of the states in which they live, . . . and that they possess rights or demand rights or we demand rights for them."[9] That Ben-Gurion hastened to add that these Jews "also have duties," and that "we must not disregard the situation of those Jews who are not among us," seems only to be a part of the utter ambiguity with which official Israeli positions on these matters are usually explained.

Since these pronouncements were made, a lot of things happened that tended to make such issues seem obsolete. "To the world outside," William Frankel of the *Jewish Chronicle* of London said at an American Jewish Committee gathering in New York on May 16, 1971, "Jews and Israelis (whatever we may say about it) are practically interchangeable terms." This, said Frankel, "is now beginning to generate a condition of unease among world Jewry—and once again the pressing question revolves around a precise or at least a working definition of the relationship between the State of Israel and the Jewish communities abroad."

The dilemma was put briefly and succinctly by Frankel. He said, "We *are* often referred to by Israelis as being partners in Israel's rebuilding. The area of concern in Jewry today is to what extent we are bound to trail along and give greater or less support to all Israel's policies and postures and, if not, what are the limits of dissent."[10]

One area in which world Jewry must be affected by what Israel does is the way in which it views the status of Jews living outside its boundaries. This, however, remains shrouded in considerable ambiguity and vagueness, and this vagueness sometimes leads to what is tantamount to a veritable conspiracy of silence. A typical example of this was a piece of legislation quietly passed by the Knesset in June of 1971 and officially known as Citizenship Law (Amendment No. 3), 1971. The bill reads in full:

Amendment of Article 2:

1. The following shall be added to Article 2 of the Citizenship Law, 1952 after paragraph (4):

(5) The Minister of the Interior shall be empowered to grant citizenship by virtue of the Law of Return to a person who has applied therefor and who has expressed his desire to settle in Israel, provided that such a person would be entitled to an Immigrants Certificate under Article 2 of the Law of Return, 1950 on his arrival to Israel.

Translated into less-technical terms, the amendment means that the minister of the interior—on the strength of his or her own discretion—can confer Israeli citizenship on virtually any Jew abroad who desires to emigrate to Israel and applies for such citizenship.

Now while there is little doubt that the said legislation was meant to affect only Jews who are prevented by their respective governments from coming to Israel, and that it was meant mainly to help Soviet Jews in such a position, it is equally obvious that it can have widespread repercussions on the status of Jews as citizens of their respective native countries. One question that remained unanswered was whether the amendment referred only to Jewish citizens of the former Soviet Union and other "countries of distress" or was meant to establish a general rule embracing Jews everywhere. Another—in some ways, more intricate—question, which was not clarified, was whether Israeli citizenship under the new amendment may be granted to those who still held their own citizenship or was confined to those who had lost their citizenship while still in their countries of origin.

Neither of these questions received a satisfactory answer. In his address in the Knesset on May 5, 1971, during the debate on the first reading of the amendment, interior minister Yosef Burg assured his listeners that "this is not an anti-Soviet law," thus refuting a previous impression that the new legislation was directed solely at Moscow's continued refusal to grant emigration visas to all Jews who desired to settle in Israel.

However, on another occasion, the interior ministry spokesman explained the position in somewhat different terms:

If a Jewish citizen of, say, Greece, France, Britain or the United States should apply for citizenship on the strength of the new amendment, he will be told that he can obtain Israeli citizenship immediately upon coming to Israel; [since] these countries have not been known to refuse exit or emigration visas to Jewish citizens who apply for it, there is no room for applying the new legislation to them. However, if a Jewish citizen of a country whose authorities bar their Jewish citizens from leaving to settle in Israel should apply, his application will be considered in the light of the new law, and the minister will decide accordingly.

The amendment, however, is couched in general terms, and (whatever its real purpose) it is clearly ultimately applicable to all Jews without reference either to their countries of origin or to the specific policies of those countries vis-à-vis Jewish emigration.

To the second query—namely, whether under the new amendment Israeli citizenship is conferred only on those Jews who for one reason or another had lost their citizenship while still in their countries of origin—the answer seems equally clear: The amendment embraces all Jews, whether they lost their citizenship or still hold it. This has become evident from the fact that, barely a day or two after the bill became law, several immigrants from the Soviet Union brought with them applications made by Jews still living in the Soviet Union and still holding Soviet citizenship.

Be that as it may, the general impression at the time was that the authorities themselves, once they had succeeded in passing the legislation, did not really know what precisely to do with it—at least for the time being. To be sure, it was something that in a vague sort of way was nice and convenient to have around when the time was appropriate—but how and in what specific circumstances such a time would come no one seemed to know; or if they did, they were not in the mood to elaborate.

In conclusion, it may be of interest to note that the only active opposition to the amendment inside the Knesset came from *Rakach* (the new Communist party) and Poalei Agudat Yisrael. Tawfiq Toubi, speaking for the former, pointed out: (1) that the new law constituted interference in the internal affairs of other countries, (2) that conferring citizenship on a person while still in his or her country of origin was a contravention of international law, which prohibits the extension of political sovereignty of a country across the recognized boundaries of that country, and (3) that the new measure was part of the plot being hatched between Zionists and U.S. imperialism to stir up trouble inside the Soviet Union.

Rabbi Abraham Werdiger, speaking for the ultra-Orthodox Poalei Agudat Yisrael, on the other hand, spoke of the possibility of "pseudo-Jews" slipping into Israel with the help of the new law or—what was even worse—Gentiles who sought merely to flee from the Soviet Union. The minister of interior, he warned, could not possibly have a way of checking the credentials of an applicant from Vladivostok, for instance, who claimed that he was a Russian Jew in distress.

To this latter objection, Burg replied that, since the bill was meant to aid individuals rather than masses of people, the danger of an influx of "pseudo-Jews" into Israel was negligible. If the result of the bill, he added, was to help just one single Jew in jeopardy, it was more than justified.

All of this left the larger questions unanswered—especially the one concerning the legislation's possible repercussions on the status of Jews as citizens of their native countries. However, this is not the first, last, or only large question that is likely to remain unanswered within the Israeli ideological context.

The Majority/Minority Syndrome

In the summer of 1968, the American Jewish Congress (AJC) held its annual "American-Israeli Dialogue" in Rehovoth. The subject of the dialogue was "Jewry as a Minority in America and a Majority in Israel." In his opening remarks, the organization's president, Rabbi Arthur Lelyveld, elaborated on the thesis which he said was at the core of the subject: "There is a difference between the experience of a people living as a minority and the experience of that same people living as a majority."[11]

It is arguable, however, that, as applied to contemporary Jewry, this otherwise valid thesis contains three basic assumptions that can be substantiated neither in fact nor in theory. First, to speak of "a people" living as a minority and about "that same people" living as a majority would be to beg the question. The group of people we call the American Jewish community is plainly not "that same people" as the group or groups of people that today constitute the majority of Israel's population. This was true even before the state was established, considering the traits and attitudes the first pioneers brought with them from Eastern and Central Europe to Palestine.

The second basic assumption in Lelyveld's thesis is that the distinction between majority and minority is a purely numerical one. This is definitely not the case—or at least not *always* the case. Sociologically, where ethnic groups and ethnic-group relations are concerned, a more important and therefore more meaningful distinction would be that between dominant and subordinate groups.

The would-be antithetical presentation in the very title of the AJC dialogue is thus rather shaky. This is because one cannot speak in the same breath about Jews being a minority in America and a majority in Israel—

any more than one can speak in the same context of Jews as a minority in Britain and as a minority in, say, the Soviet Union or present-day Egypt. The minute we start speaking in terms of majority/minority in the United States and in Israel, we enter two quite different political and sociocultural realms. American Jews are not a minority in the same sort of context as Israeli Jews are a majority, since (to put it in a slightly different way) U.S. Jews are not a minority in the same sense in which Israel's Muslims are.

Again, while Jews form a clear majority in Israel, there is no corresponding group in the United States that constitutes a majority—either in terms of numbers or of political dominance. There will, of course, be American Jews who would say that the majority in the United States consists simply of all those who are not Jews. It seems certain, however, that none of the participants in that dialogue could have subscribed to such a theory.

The third and last basic assumption implicit in Lelyveld's clarifications is that the Jews who do constitute a majority in Israel are all of a piece. This, of course, is true only in a most limited and extremely superficial sense. It cannot stand any serious scrutiny on the cultural, religious, socioeconomic, or even ethnic planes.

There is no need to engage here in a detailed elaboration of this particular point. Suffice it to say that, insofar as ethnic-group relations always tend to assume an in-group/out-group, majority/minority, or dominant group/subordinate group character, it is impossible to speak in this sense of the Jews of Israel forming a single in-group, a majority, or a dominant group. All that one can say with accuracy is that the dominant group in Israeli society consists of members of the numerical Jewish majority.

In this connection, it may be useful to remember that as far as ethnic divisions are concerned, Israel is a multi-ethnic society rather than a bi-ethnic one consisting of a Jewish majority and an Arab minority, since the Jews themselves embrace many ethnicities and cultures. This may explain the rather complex scale of group hierarchy that prevails in the society—a hierarchy in which each ethnic group tends to occupy a somewhat different social position.

Louis Wirth has noted that, in the United States, "There is little doubt but that the [African American] . . . has become the principal shock absorber of the anti-minority sentiment of the dominant whites." Other ethnic groups within this white majority—Catholics, Jews, Italians, and even Japanese—suffer far fewer disabilities and are more readily able to become full-fledged members of American society. Indeed, these groups often share antiblack sentiment and follow the usual patterns of discrimination and exclusion as does the dominant white group. In pursuit of acceptance, in fact, they may even outdo the latter in their hostility and prejudice toward blacks.[12]

In today's Israel, too, various ethnic groups within the Jewish majority—aware that they are not of the in-group except in the limited and negative sense of not being non-Jews—often go out of their way to demonstrate their hostility to the "real" minority, the out-group that constitutes the principal shock absorber of the antiminority sentiment of the dominant Jewish in-group. I refer, of course, to the Arab citizens of Israel.

Often in my personal contacts with Arabs from East Jerusalem, the occupied territories, and even from pre-1967 Israel, I am struck by the uniformity of their experience in this field: All of them complain that in their dealings with Israeli officials they find that, of these officials, those who hail from Arab-Muslim countries treat them far more harshly and with far less cordiality and consideration than do those who come from Europe. For the sociologist, this will simply offer another illustration of the workings of the pecking order—a glimpse of the group hierarchy system prevalent in Israel. For the Arabs involved in the experience, it remains a mystery.

Here I feel I must append a footnote: This same phenomenon—so easily to be explained on the simplest sociological level—is often used by the in-group as a proof that Arabic-speaking Jews in Israel are "even more hostile" to the Arabs than their European coreligionists. Therefore, it is argued, one can hardly pin any hopes for peace on the alleged cultural affinity between Middle Eastern Jews living in Israel and their non-Jewish neighbors.

From these preliminary observations we can now turn to the more political aspects of the majority/minority syndrome in Israel. As has already been suggested, what marks a people as a minority is essentially the relationship of their group to some other group within the society in which they live. Moreover, many ethnic and "racial" groups are often described as "minorities" simply because they occupy a subordinate position in society—even when they are more numerous than the nominal majority.

Furthermore, minorities are not necessarily always penalized or discriminated against; nor do specific characteristics make a group intrinsically a minority in the social sense. "In pre-war Poland," Louis Wirth writes, "under the Czarist regime the Poles were a distinct ethnic minority. When they gained their independence at the end of the First World War, they lost their minority status but reduced their Jewish fellow Poles to the status of a minority. As immigrants to the United States the Poles again became themselves a minority." Again, "During the brief period of Nazi domination the Sudetan Germans of Czechoslovakia reveled in their position of dominance over the Czechs among whom they had only recently been a minority."[13]

It would seem, however, that though it is not ethnic or racial characteristics that mark a people as a minority, certain minority traits must persist even after a group has changed its status from a minority to a majority. This is what has happened to the Israelis—or rather to those of them who direct the country's destinies, form its attitudes, and set its general cultural tone. Lelyveld rightly pointed out that those Jewish communities in Europe that were not granted the kind of freedom known in the liberal West and were cut off from the outside world "constituted an enclave." As such, they were minority communities that lived as if they were majorities within their own areas.

Being a majority in a ghetto is not quite the same as being a majority in a multi-ethnic society. Nonetheless, this was the case until certain "enlightened" members of those ghetto communities started to lose that psychological security and religious faith which had induced in them the conviction that they, as a group, had a valid role to play and an important task to perform.

Political Zionism was not invented—and the state of Israel was not established—by the psychologically secure, devout Jew of the ghettos and *shtetls* of the Pale of Settlement. They were the work of that disillusioned, confused, and psychologically lost Jew whom the onset of the *Haskalah* (Enlightenment) and Emancipation had thrown off his feet spiritually.

It can thus be said that the Jewish majority in Israel—the country's dominant group—has the mentality of a minority. Paradoxically, this minority stance increases rather than decreases those hazards of majority living evident to the keen observer: self-aggrandizement, chauvinism, triumphalism, xenophobia, intolerance, and loss of sensitivity to the opinion of others.

But this is not really as paradoxical as it may sound. After all, these are not common majority traits or characteristics; they are the traits of a certain kind of insecure, minority-minded majorities constantly afraid of being submerged or subdued numerically, politically, and culturally. In Israel's particular case, the minority stance that seems to characterize Jewish majority mentality and behavior has been the result of two sets of reasons—one historical, one ideological.

The historical reasons are easily discerned. The various groups that make up Israel's Jewish majority—and especially those that constitute a majority in the sociopolitical and cultural rather than numerical sense—

come from backgrounds where they were either persecuted minorities or what can be called ghetto majorities. Neither of these backgrounds seems conducive to the kind of broad-minded, tolerant, and pluralistic approach necessary to maintain a modern, open society in which the perils of majority living can be reduced to a minimum.

The ideological reasons are more complex. To put it succinctly, according to the prevalent ideology, the Jewish majority in Israel (again, in the sense of a dominant ethnic group) has reason to experience the feelings of a minority not once but three times:

1. By dividing the world into Jews and Gentiles, Jewry as a whole is seen as a minority since there are a few more Gentiles in the world than there are Jews.

2. By dividing the Middle East between what David Ben-Gurion once described as two "world entities"—the Arabs and the Jews—the Jews of Israel remain a tiny minority in a sea of Arab "nationals."

3. Finally, by viewing the Jewish situation itself in narrow cultural (or culturist) terms, the dominant Eastern European Zionist establishment in Israel has every reason to acquire a minority mentality vis-à-vis its own internal *Jewish* minority groups.

The foregoing remarks may well impart an impression of inconsistency. At one stage, they seem to imply that the Jews in Israel are very much a majority in the sense that their dominance is too distinctly felt. At another, they suggest that there is no such thing as a clear homogeneous Jewish majority—and that it is a relatively small minority within the numerical Jewish majority that constitutes the dominant group. At yet another point in the discussion, this group is at once criticized as possessing the mentality of a minority *and* as behaving in the worst possible manner in which a dominant ethnic majority could behave.

It would therefore be appropriate to present here in very brief terms a vision—and "vision" here is used advisedly since we are dealing with complex historical processes—of the future of Israel as a state. Inevitably, such a vision must be formulated in terms of what Israeli society ought to be like. This can be summed up in two main trends.

First, the emphasis ought to be shifted from what I called the majority/minority syndrome to a pluralist, multi-ethnic stance. Such a society would be able to accommodate without too much effort the whole mosaic of cultures, religions, and ethnicities, as well as various shades of religiosity among the Jewish part of the population.

Second, the problem of nationality—difficult and extremely vexed as it is—can be solved on the basis of its equation with citizenship. In this way, Israeli citizenship can embrace (as it does now) both Jew and non-Jew living in Israel. But it would include non-Jewish Israelis as Israeli *nationals* rather than as *Arab* or *Druse* ones.

In this way, too, Israeli Jews will cease to be plagued by a feeling of being a minority—and thus, one hopes, will cease to think and behave like a hunted minority, with all the fear, the intolerance and the extremism that go with such a feeling.

5

Israel as an Open Society

I have brown hair and blue eyes—and I don't have a
Jewish nose like the Arabs have.

Momo (Muhammad) in Emile Ajar, *La vie devant soi*

In that classic of bristling social criticism *Knowledge for What?*, renowned American sociologist Robert Lynd speaks with great dismay of a culture "preoccupied with short-term statements of long-term problems"; he proceeds to recommend to social science the task of bringing the lagging culture "not peace but a sword."[1]

For decades now it has been apparent that, in the Middle East, politicians and opinion leaders—Arab as well as Israeli—have been persistent in offering stopgap, short-term solutions for the staggering assortment of long-term and extremely complex problems comprising what is generally known as the Arab-Israeli conflict. Quite inadvertently, however, the actions taken by both sides during the past three decades helped start a potentially reasonably beneficial chain of events.

One of the few good results of the 1967 Six-Day War was that it brought Arabs and Israelis face-to-face with each other in places other than the battlefront. The 1973 Yom Kippur War, too, could claim at least one benefit: It served as an object lesson to both sides in almost equal measure. Egypt, Syria, and the Arabs generally came to the realization that force alone will not do, and the majority of Israelis became convinced that, with all their military might and their power of improvisation, they cannot be completely safe from unpleasant and even perilous surprises.

These events, in short, forced both Arabs and Israelis to start facing the problems confronting them, thus making basic, long-term statements of these problems not only desirable but imperative. It is a measure of the efforts made by both sides in that direction that the Egyptian-Israeli peace treaty, signed in March of 1979; the Oslo Accords with the Palestinians in 1993; and the peace treaty that Israel and Jordan signed in 1994 so far have stood the test of several petty disputes and setbacks, including the full-scale war that Israel waged in Lebanon in 1982, euphemistically dubbed Operation Peace-for-Galilee, and the slow pace at which the Oslo agreements are being implemented.

In this chapter, a number of long-term issues besetting Israel since its birth are given what is hoped to be a long-term look: the cultural face of Israel and the role of the Middle Eastern component of its population; the official Israeli concept of Jewish education; the still-unresolved subject of church and state; aspects of the ongoing controversy between orthodox and secularist; and the issue of nationality and the Law of Return.

Role of the Middle Eastern/Sephardic Element

The presence among Israel's Jews of a Middle Eastern majority opens up new vistas. First, the prevalent image of the Arab as just another version of the European anti-Semite is bound to disappear; it is readily to be observed that the Israeli Oriental tends to treat his Arab neighbor as a full equal rather than a dreaded outsider. Furthermore, now that Israel has established formal relations with Egypt, Jordan, and the Palestinians—and with Israel becoming, for better or for worse, increasingly involved in developments in and around the region—the Israelis themselves are learning considerably from having a closer, more realistic look at their habitat.

The founders of the Zionist movement, who had set out to build a model European state, had scarcely been aware of the existence, let alone the status and significance, of Middle Eastern and Mediterranean Jewries. This probably accounts for the fact that, for five long decades, the Israeli leadership—itself almost exclusively Eastern European by birth, by background, and by culture—should have found it so difficult to reconcile itself to the idea of an increasingly Middle Eastern Israel.

The Arabs themselves, of course, will have their own share of common sense and moderation to contribute. First and foremost, they will have to realize—as Egypt under Sadat's leadership was the first Arab state to have realized (among certain other current Middle Eastern facts of life)—that they cannot possibly have it both ways.

The ultimate irony of Israel's gradual transformation into a Middle Eastern country is that it was brought about by the way the Arabs themselves behaved over the past six or so decades. They would not accept the establishment of a Jewish state in Palestine on the basis of unique Jewish historical claims. They also insisted that the claims of the "natural majority," the Arabs, were paramount. Then, by the work of their own hands (by mistreating their own Jews, among other actions), they have turned Israel into a country in which the natural majority demands an independent state of its own.

The members of this majority—the Middle Eastern Jews and the Palestinian-born Israelis—have never known or lived in any other area but the Middle East, and now live in that part of the Middle East in which the Arabs themselves have decided they should live! This the Arabs will one day have to grasp. For the truth is that these developments have virtually changed the very raison d'être of Israel. From the somewhat dubious basis of the Balfour Declaration and special Zionist claims, the right of Israel to be in the Middle East now rests on the perfectly normal basis that the majority of its inhabitants are bona fide Middle Easterners.

One naturally can never be certain whether such arguments, had they been advanced by Israel, would have carried much weight with its neighbors. The fact remains, however, that the reigning Eastern European elite in Israel has continued doggedly to proceed in such a manner as actually to lend credence to the Arabs' standing complaint that Israel is an intrusion, an alien element in the area, "a cancer in the Arab body."

Not long before the Six-Day War, the late Pinhas Sapir, then an influential Labor party leader and minister of finance, told a correspondent from *Le Monde* that Israel was an integral part of Europe, "culturally, politically and economically," being Middle Eastern "only geographically."[2] Plainly, this sort of proclamation is neither likely nor was it meant to induce the Arabs to accept Israel as a permanent and integral part of the region.

The impact on the Middle Eastern element itself in Israel of the establishment's uncompromisingly Eurocentric attitudes and policies has been neither less pronounced nor less negative. Apart from the fact that self-proclaimed Westernness on Israel's part constitutes an obvious taunt and an insult to this element—since it is tantamount to saying that Middle Easterners and other non-Westerners are not equal human beings—the truth is that the Israeli power structure's real goal all along was to "de-orientalize" this element of the population and acculturate it as swiftly and as thoroughly as possible.

This objective has been pursued with every conceivable means: through legislation, military training, the various communications media and, above all, in the kindergarten and the classroom. In the end, moreover, it was not attained—and remains unattainable. Apart from the fact that a policy of intensive acculturation tends to be the surest way of marginalizing these Middle Easterners and bringing on them the curse of alienation, Israel (should it go on depicting itself as an integral part of "the

West") may ultimately manage to fulfill the Arabs' prophecy that it is destined to remain alien to the region in which it lives.

A few words may be added here concerning Israel's relations with diaspora Jewries. It is often argued that Israel must remain an exclusively Jewish state because 10 million Jews who now live outside its boundaries want it to be so. On the face of it, this may sound fairly convincing. However, the factors that had determined the attitude of non-Israeli Jews to Israel prior to the Six-Day War may be said to have undergone a certain measure of change.

A coherent sociological statement of this change was made shortly after the war by two social scientists writing in an American Jewish periodical. Pointing out that Israel's victory in the Six-Day War "may be the great historical watershed separating the Jew and the Israeli," Irving Horowitz and Maurice Zeitlin spoke of the possibility that this victory "will establish a relationship between Israel and Jews much like that between other nations and their own dispersed national minorities."

Horowitz and Zeitlin went on to say that "Israel's military victory, if it endures, compels a re-evaluation by all sectors of world Jewry of its *freedom from* Israel, just as the defeat of Israel would have compelled re-evaluation of Jewish *responsibility to* Israel." "For the American Jew," they added, "a generalized sentiment in favour of kith and kin will now have to yield to the realization that Israel is a prime military force. . . . In other words, support for a powerful nation [other than one's own] is not the same as philanthropic underwriting of a poor nation."[3]

Such a normalization of relations between Israel and the Jews of the diaspora, though it may not yet be at hand, should be aided and augmented not only by Israel's becoming "a powerful nation" but also if and when it attains the kind of stabilization of relations with its neighbors that it has already attained with Egypt and Jordan. When such normalization with world Jewry comes, it may well lead to a further normalization in Israel's position—this time vis-à-vis itself, its environment, and the world at large.

There are several keys to a way out of the present Arab-Israeli impasse. One of them certainly lies with the Middle Eastern element in Israeli society. These Jews have had a long and firm tradition of dealing and discoursing with Muslim Arabs and often have played active roles in the affairs of the countries in which they resided. An Israel in which this important element gets its share of responsibility and leadership is bound to have a substantially different image of its neighbors as well as of itself, and thus will be better able to attain a meaningful coexistence with them.

It is conceivable, too, that the Arabs—when they have come to know themselves and the area better and acquire a better and more balanced view of their new neighbors—would then begin to see Israel in a different light: as an integral part of a pluralist Middle East, fitting fairly well into the region's mosaic of peoples, cultures, and faiths. There is, after all, sufficient cultural and spiritual common ground between Judaism and Arabic Islam to make such coexistence not only feasible but also desirable and fruitful. Fundamentally, there exists no opposition between the Jewish tradition and the Muslim-Arab tradition.

Despite lingering signs to the contrary, moreover, there are clear indications that Israel's neighbors are gradually shedding their narrow image of the Middle East as an exclusively "Arab" area. They do, however, seem to insist on viewing it as a non-Western area culturally. In this sense, a stubbornly "Western" and ethnically exclusivist Israel will, in all probability, continue to be considered an alien creation and a legacy of Europe's cultural intrusion.

It is probably no exaggeration to say that this question of identity will always be crucial in any appraisal of Israel's future relations with the Arabs and ultimately its position in the Middle East. Charles Malik, in an oft-quoted article, makes a few very pertinent points on this subject. Pointing out that to establish a state is one thing and to ensure its continued existence is another, Malik asserts that "entirely different moral qualities" are required for this latter task."

Malik explains:

In the struggle for establishment, you treat the others as alien forces, to be crushed or pushed back or at least prevented from encroaching upon you; your relation to them is external, summary, destructive, negative; under no circumstances can you allow internal, positive intercourse with them on a basis of equality. But in the struggle for enduring existence you must come to terms with them; you must take their existence positively into account; your idea must be softened and modulated and trimmed to accommodate their idea; you must enter into interacting relationship with them, based on mutual respect and trust. Whether the leadership and the ethos of Israel are adequate to the requirements of existence, of course only the future can disclose.[4]

Jewish Learning versus "Jewish Consciousness"

The nature and status of Jewish studies in Israeli schools today is of some relevance to the problem of identity and, ultimately, to the question of what kind of society Israel is. What kind of Jewish education, or "education for Judaism," is furnished in these schools? Israeli state schools are of two kinds: general (secular) and religious. It is only in the religious schools, which make up less than 30 percent of all state schools, that instruction in religious observance is given, in addition to intensive courses in the Torah and the Talmud.

Responding to calls emanating both from the religious sector and from certain secular quarters that became somewhat worried about the lack of "Jewish consciousness" among Israeli youth, the ministry of education decided, in September 1959, to take steps to foster in that youth a deeper understanding of the spiritual heritage of Judaism.

The decision came in implementation of the government's educational program, which had been approved by the Knesset more than three years previously. This program had stated clearly and at considerable length that the government would "endeavor to contribute to the deepening of Jewish consciousness among Israeli youth in the primary and secondary schools as well as in the institutions of higher learning, to ground them in the past of the Jewish people and in its historic heritage, and to imbue them with the feeling of belonging to world Jewry, springing from an awareness of their common destiny and historical continuity, which united the Jews in all countries and throughout all the generations."

After a long and heated debate, the Knesset appointed two committees whose terms of reference stated that they should recommend ways of implementing the new program. These committees (one headed by the then minister of education, the late Zalman Aranne, the other by his deputy) between them found that, roughly speaking, there was need to introduce "Jewish-Israeli consciousness" both in the general schools and in the religious schools. The idea was that in general state schools the emphasis should be placed on the religious aspects of the subject, while in religious state schools emphasis was to be placed on fostering the national Israeli consciousness of the children. In practice, teachers were instructed to inculcate "Jewish consciousness" in their pupils by: (1) grounding them in the spiritual heritage of the Jewish people, (2) grounding them in the past of the Jewish people, and (3) instilling in them a feeling of belonging to, and of being part of, the Jewish people as a whole.

But how *Jewish* was this "Jewish consciousness"? To appreciate fully the problem that confronted the ministry of education in its endeavors in this respect and to have an idea of the true dimensions of the impasse, we need only quote further from the Knesset debate of 1959. Aranne himself summed up the difficulties faced by his office very briefly and cogently:

From its very beginning, the Hebrew school in Israel had to tackle four baffling problems: How to foster in Israeli youth the feeling of belonging to the Jewish people when the overwhelming majority of this people lives outside the boundaries of the State; how to root the youth in the history of the Jewish people when half of that history occurred outside the boundaries of the State; how to reconcile the Zionist teaching of "rejection of the diaspora" with the authorities' wish to inculcate in Israeli youth an awareness of the unity of the Jewish people everywhere; and how to bring closer to children educated in secular schools a culture permeated by religion.

Clearly, these problems were all but insoluble, and the effort made by the Israeli ministry of education to deal with them was doomed to failure right from the start. In his concluding address at the end of the same Knesset debate, Aranne in fact hit the nail squarely on the head when he declared: "We respect religion, because religious faith in its pure form elevates man. We adopt the Jewish tradition which embodies both the national and the religious elements because it epitomises the glory of former times and ancient glory never wanes. . . . Therefore love and respect for tradition must permeate our national schools—*not in order to educate for religion but in order to uphold the national character of our educational system*" (italics added).

This is a weighty statement. It sums up the whole subject of "Jewish consciousness" in a manner that, for clarity and candor, is difficult to match. Its implications are equally clear. In a book published in the 1960s and from which much of the information given here is taken, the author—Zvi Kurzweil—refers to Aranne's pronouncements on this subject. Aranne, he writes, "makes it abundantly clear that 'Jewish Consciousness' does not imply education towards religion and the observance of religious commandments."

What Aranne was saying, Kurzweil explained, "was *information* about Jewish tradition is to be imparted, i.e., pupils are merely to be instructed about the various facets of Jewish life and customs." "Similarly," he continues, "the reading of the prayer book at school is intended to make children acquainted with Jewish prayers, but does not imply that teachers have to encourage children to pray or attend synagogue services . . . The official programme introducing the study of 'Jewish Consciousness' into Jewish schools was meant to eradicate ignorance of things Jewish—and does not go beyond that."[5]

In other words, what was to be served up to the children was a strictly scientific and historical—that is, secular—concept of Judaism. Clearly, this has very little to do with meaningful Jewish consciousness, and the results can readily be observed. The indifference of Israeli youth to Jewish tradition (which is said to make Israelis abroad feel closer to the Gentiles than to their fellow Jews in the diaspora) has been decried often enough. "Jewish consciousness" as it is being imparted in Israeli schools can do little to rectify this state of affairs. The fact, as Kurzweil points out, is that in the diaspora the difference between Jew and Gentile is mainly religious. In contrast "the Sabra, having no religion, has nothing in common with the Jew of the Diaspora; and the Jewish people, once united, are thus in danger of being divided."[6]

But if the Hebrew language itself can virtually be stripped of all meaningfully Jewish content, and if Jewish consciousness can be reduced to mere fragmentary Jewish knowledge, how far more thoroughly can an individual Jew or even a whole Jewish collectivity become devoid of genuine Jewish solidarity and identity! The insistence on Israel's "Jewishness"—an insistence habitually coupled with an even more emphatic one on the country's "European" or "Western" character—can thus denote little more than sheer culturist bias. What concerns us here, however, is Israel's attitude to its Middle Eastern element—and ultimately to its own physical and cultural environment.

It is in the nature of a truism that people's attitudes to the world around them are determined by their respective collective historical experiences. It is obvious that the prevalent official Israeli perception of Israel as an exclusively Jewish state has its roots largely in the collective historical experience of that part of Jewry that has had the most-decisive and enduring influence on the establishment and growth of Israel and on shaping its present outlook.

In speaking of present-day Israel, however, one must guard against the danger of viewing it culturally as being all of a piece. Israel is still a nation in the making, about which no generalizations can be made with any measure of certitude. Presenting a rich mosaic of ethnic groups, cultures, and habits of thought and approaches, Israelis often speak with many voices and react in widely divergent ways.

This is nowhere more in evidence than it is in Israeli attitudes to the outside, non-Jewish world. For example, what some Israelis may view as their country's integration into the Middle Eastern world, other Israelis may dread as "assimilation" and consequent loss of Jewishness. Rather inevitably, however, the view of the Middle East and of the Arabs prevalent in Israel today is the one determined by the collective historical experiences and general outlook of that group of Israelis from whose ranks the country's present political and cultural establishments are overwhelmingly drawn.

There is no difficulty in discovering which Jewish group this was. Isaiah Berlin has written that it was "almost self-evident" that, if there had existed only the Jews of the Western world and those of the Eastern, Muslim countries, "there would have been no Israel." Neither of these Jewries, he suggested, had any influence on the building and early character of the state of Israel.

Even the German Jewish element has had no such influence. "For all the crucial contribution which the German settlers have had . . . to every walk of life," Berlin asserts, "the heart of the national life is almost untouched by the values dearest to the German Jews. It is they who are expected to adjust to an outlook often alien to theirs." The community, therefore, that is to be considered as the most closely concerned with laying the early foundations of Israel, comprises "the Jews of Eastern Europe, and specifically those of Russia and Russian Poland."[7]

What may one infer from this fact as far as Israel's present attitude to its own habitat is concerned? To the Zionist cause, the Jews of Eastern Europe brought many singular gifts and attributes: dynamism, idealism, a great singleness of purpose, and an uncommon devotion. However, beside these rare qualities, this Jewish community possessed something that neither the Jews of the West nor those of the Middle East and North Africa have ever had. As a result of their own unique historical experience and circumstances, the Jews of Eastern Europe—unlike their coreligionists further to the west and the southwest—had to maintain an independent, self-contained existence of their own and thus had grown to be a kind of state within a state.

"The Jews of Russia and Poland," Berlin has written, "as a result of political and social persecution, had found themselves cooped up in a kind of single extended ghetto, called the Pale of Settlement . . . [where] they remained within their medieval shell and developed a kind of internal structure of their own." Within this fairly independent, virtually isolated structure, this Jewish community developed a powerful and very rich inner life, but in a certain sense, it "remained less touched by modern developments than any community of Jews in Europe."[8]

Again, unlike the Jews who lived in Middle Eastern and North African countries, the Jews of this extended Eastern European ghetto had very little opportunity to mix freely and have day-to-day discourse with the non-Jewish world surrounding them.

Synagogue and State: The Everlasting "Status Quo"

The state/synagogue—or state/rabbinate—problem in Israel is as old as the state itself, and in the course of the years it tends to get progressively more difficult to resolve. In the late 1980s and deep into the 1990s, with the influx of nearly a million immigrants from Russia, the various republics of the former Soviet Union, and Ethiopia and the many questions these waves of immigration raised as to the Jewishness of some of the newcomers and, ultimately, to their rights as immigrants as stipulated in the Law of Return, fierce controversy flared up again concerning the dual question of who is a Jew and who is a bona fide convert to Judaism.

Not only were the rights and privileges to be granted these immigrants affected but also such matters of personal and family status as who is eligible for a proper religious wedding ceremony and whose offspring can legally be registered as Jews. A brief summary of two stages of the controversy spanning a period of almost three decades, and its roots in the so-called "religious status quo," follows.

In 1972, a dispute over the meaning and precise implications of this "status quo"—not the first of its kind and certainly not the last—threatened to rock the country's cabinet coalition. It is useful to point out here that the oft-disputed term "status quo" refers to a somewhat shaky modus vivendi reached more than fifty years ago (on June 19, 1947) between the Orthodox parties and the secular Zionist left group within the Jewish Agency and the national institutions. The compromise formula sought to regulate relations between the religious and secular camps inside the Zionist movement and, eventually, in the ruling institutions of the embryonic state.

Curiously, though, the debate that gave rise to the 1972 crisis was conducted not between the Orthodox and non-Orthodox factions in the government coalition but between different coalition factions within the secularist camp. The ball started rolling when the Independent Liberal party (ILP) decided to authorize one of its Knesset members to table a private member's bill on civil marriage and divorce.

The proposed bill was not meant to introduce civil marriage in Israel for anyone who sought it; it was to provide for civil marriage/divorce facilities solely to those Israeli Jews who are denied all rights to lawful wedlock because *halakhic* rulings disqualify them. In other words, the bill was meant to enable those couples (such as a *cohen* and a divorced woman) whose marriage the rabbinate would never handle, to raise a legally recognized family in Israel.

Now as members of the coalition the Independent Liberals were bound by what is termed "coalition discipline," which in turn was based on the government's platform, whose main guidelines had been approved by the Knesset on December 15, 1969. This lengthy document contained seven fateful Hebrew words under the heading "Religion in the State." Translated literally, these words read: "The government will observe the status quo [prevalent] in the state in matters of religion."

At the time that the Independent Liberals made known their decision to initiate legislation on civil marriage, there was talk in the press concerning the question as to whether the non-Orthodox faction in government and Knesset would grant its partners in the ILP permission to go ahead and submit their proposed bill.

Two crucial issues were involved. First, the Orthodox faction was certain to argue that tabling such a bill by a coalition partner constituted a violation of the status quo, a development that would have made them free to leave the coalition. Second, the non-Orthodox faction had to decide whether the bill did not in fact constitute a violation of the government's platform (and consequently of the coalition agreement) on the Independent Liberals' part and thus a breach of "coalition discipline," making it incumbent on the latter group to leave the coalition.

In any event, a week before the bill was to be tabled, the Labor-Mapam Knesset faction unanimously decided to deny the ILP the right to table the bill. They argued that the coalition platform jointly agreed upon with the National Religious party (NRP) left no room for such legislation since it would constitute a clear violation of the status quo. Alignment spokesmen went on record that in making their decision they were not casting any aspersions on the bill itself, but were merely saying that the measure constituted a breach of coalition discipline as well as a violation of the status quo.

However, to the sensible-sounding argument that a bill on civil marriage tabled by a coalition partner constitutes a violation of the status quo in matters of religion and state, the ILP and its supporters presented a case that cannot be easily dismissed. The bill, they argued, changed nothing in the status quo since civil marriage, for all practical purposes, existed in Israel already (witness the fact that the authorities for some time had recognized marriages made in the civil courts of Cyprus, Mexico, and other foreign countries). Moreover, they added, the bill dealt only with those cases of marriage that the rabbinate never had and never would want to handle itself.

Now while this argument may sound convincing enough, the fact is that the leading document on which the status quo rests—the letter sent to

Agudat Yisrael by the Zionist coalition on June 19, 1947—has a section dealing with marriage, which says that all members of the Zionist Executive "appreciate the gravity of the problem and its great difficulties," and promises that "on the part of all bodies represented by the Executive of the Jewish Agency everything possible will be done to satisfy in this respect the profound needs of adherents of the faith, so as to prevent the division of the House of Israel into two parts."

Translated into practical terms, this passage meant far more than it seemed to be saying. This is because the new arrangement was to introduce a radical change in the sphere of personal law that in turn would have far-reaching implications on much wider spheres. For the fact is that under the British Mandate, the government had dealt with the Jewish community as a sort of club, with individual right of entry and withdrawal. True, the writ of the rabbinate over personal law ran up to the limits of the Jewish community, but these limits were set by the voluntary choice of its individual members.

In the Jewish state, however, such right of entry and withdrawal would be denied to all Jewish citizens, whose position would be defined by objective legal standards. This being so, if the authority of the rabbinate in the sphere of personal law was at all to continue (as the "status quo" clearly indicates it would), the Rabbinical courts were perforce to be entrenched as part of the judicial apparatus of the state itself, and their writ was to run throughout the Jewish community, no matter what its individual members' views happened to be.

All this was to apply in what was to be, by definition, a secular state granting religious freedom. It was an odd bargain and a one-sided one. David Ben-Gurion, who first initiated the "compromise" and then as prime minister enacted it, was fairly frank about his reasons: "I knew that we required the widest possible political backing to carry out the gigantic tasks that I envisaged," he said. "I was prepared to limit my programme to the basic urgencies and offer concessions on what I regarded as subsidiary issues."

Viewed objectively, however, marriage and divorce laws in Israel certainly constitute no subsidiary issue—neither for the Orthodox, nor for the secular, nor yet for the state itself. The reference in the status quo document, as quoted above, to the danger of "the division of the House of Israel into two parts" is by no means fortuitous or rhetorical. Since, for instance, an Orthodox Jew could not marry the child of a Jewish father and a non-Jewish mother and a *cohen* could not marry a divorced woman, the real alternative to the present imposition of *halakhic* law on secular Israelis would ultimately be the development of two mutually exclusive, nonintermarrying Jewish communities within the state. This, in turn, would affect the position of Jews in the diaspora, since such a cleavage between two types of marital regime would be worldwide. This would be especially true of the position in the United States, where the percentage of mixed marriages was estimated to be as high as twenty.

This is a cardinal point whose significance advocates of new legislation on civil marriage in Israel either overlook or belittle, while the dominant secular faction (not to speak of the Orthodox groups) cannot afford to do either. It is possible that advocates of civil marriage, if pressed, would argue that a cleavage such as that which the religious status quo has ostensibly come to prevent already exists in practice. After all, they may well argue, no Orthodox Jew today marries into a non-Orthodox family unless either he or his spouse decides to change his or her way of life drastically. The educational system itself, they may add, with its sharp division between religious and secular schools, is based on this cleavage and helps maintain and even deepen it.

However, they cannot be unaware of the fact that, with Israel being designated a Jewish state and with the *halakhic* definition of a Jew being still the only authoritative one available, a person who does not answer to this definition would not be eligible for membership in the Jewish community—and ultimately would be disqualified as a full-fledged citizen of the Jewish state. Like Ben-Gurion, prime minister Golda Meir declared on more than one occasion that, without their religious tie, the survival of Israel and the Jewish people was uncertain.

Sure enough, Mrs. Meir also acted accordingly in the matter. A day before the ILP was to submit the bill to the Knesset, she told representatives of Mapam that if their Knesset faction should vote in support of the civil marriage bill, she would not hesitate "to draw personal conclusions"—that is, to submit her resignation to the president. She also made it quite clear that the Independent Liberals would pay fully for their breach of the coalition agreement by being ousted from the cabinet, in which they held the minor portfolio of tourism. The following day, hours before the tabling of the bill, the Mapam secretariat decided by a two-thirds majority to support the proposed bill. When this decision was made known, Mrs. Meir's resignation became almost certain.

As usual on these "dramatic" occasions, however, someone came up with a saving formula. The bill was to be tabled as planned, but a way was to be found for it not to be put to the vote. Intensive last-minute consultations were held. Mapam approached the Independent Liberals asking for time to enable their political bureau to discuss the matter further, and experts in Knesset rules and procedures were asked for advice. The result was that the crisis was averted when the MK (member of the Knesset) who tabled the bill himself asked that voting on his bill be deferred until some unspecified future date.

Synagogue and State: Power through the School System

The late Yeshayahu Leibovitz, Hebrew University professor, editor of the *Hebrew Encyclopedia*, and a deeply religious man, said once in a television interview that David Ben-Gurion, Israel's first prime minister, "wanted the state to dominate religion" and attained this objective by turning the chief rabbinate and the religious establishment as a whole into a government department like any other. Leibovitz also used to call the religious political parties (foremost among them the National Religious party) "the kept woman of the Zionist establishment."

If one accepts this definition, one has to admit that the lady in question has been a very expensive one to keep. In fact, maintenance costs rose incessantly since the unhappy match was made some fifty years ago. With its periodic and usually extremely well-timed threats to cause cabinet crises, the NRP managed through the years to exact such a high price for its partnership in cabinet coalitions that an uninformed observer cannot but wonder why—year in, year out—the senior coalition partner continued to put up with what was always seen as something bordering on blackmail.

In virtually all coalition governments formed since 1948, the NRP definitely held more positions of power than its representation in the Knesset warranted. In the 1970s, for example, its representatives occupied three cabinet portfolios—social affairs, interior, and religious affairs—all of them of extreme importance to the party in its persistent attempt to consolidate and reinforce its power. In addition, it had a deputy minister of education, appointed against the will of the minister, the late Yigal Allon. In these four sensitive ministries, the NRP maintained a hold whose strength could hardly be overestimated.

In the late 1980s and throughout the 1990s, the power of the religious parties was substantially augmented by the rise of the ultra-Orthodox Shas, an almost exclusively Sephardic/Oriental party whose spiritual guide is former Sephardi Chief Rabbi Ovadia Yosef. In the 1996 elections, Shas won ten Knesset seats and four ministerial posts. Together with the NRP—with whose increasingly hawkish stands Shas is not often in agreement—they held the power to make or break any coalition government that does not include the Labor Party.

Put briefly, there are two main reasons for the fact that the ruling majority parties have accepted this situation with apparent equanimity. First, the secularized Zionist establishment is eager to maintain at least an appearance of "authentic" Jewishness in a state formally designated as Jewish—even at the price of a certain measure of "religious coercion" in matters of personal status. Second, an open clash with the leading religious parties, especially the NRP, could lead to a split in the World Zionist Organization and would ultimately disrupt its wide-ranging fund-raising activities.

The National Religious party feels, for these two reasons, that the various Israeli governments will do anything to avoid a break-up of the coalition with it. Proceeding on experience they gained in the past five decades, therefore, NRP leaders regularly threaten to withdraw from the coalition unless they attain virtual autonomy for religious education. Realizing that neither of the two major parties would contemplate an open split, the party in 1972 issued an ultimatum, complete with a deadline. "The NRP," its late leader Yitzhak Raphael told the Knesset gravely on June 24, 1971, "does not want a political upheaval at this grave hour; but religious education is very important to us and we will not tolerate seeing it harmed." Similar threats are made by Shas representatives whenever measures are contemplated that the party deems detrimental either to the poorer classes or to the ultra-Orthodox educational Torah institutions, or *yeshivot*.

There is no doubt but that religious education, known as "state religious schools" as distinct from *yeshivot*, is "very important" to the NRP—and in more ways than one. Above all, it is important as an apparatus helping to maintain and enhance the party's political and material hold. But before going into this aspect of the subject let us first have a look at the origin, nature and development of this "religious education."

Education in the prestate Jewish *yishuv* was divided into three leading "trends": the Mizrahi-religious, the Labor-left, and the General-right. This state of affairs was maintained until August 1953, when the State Education Law was enacted by the Knesset.

According to the new law, the trends were to be abolished—though not quite. Instead, state elementary schools were now to be divided into two categories—state schools and state religious schools. The curriculum was to be laid down by the ministry of education, and the bulk of it was to be common to both school categories. Clause 2 of the law formulated the aims of state education, common to all schools: "The object of state education is to base elementary education on the values of Jewish culture and the achievements of science; on love of the homeland and loyalty to the State and the Jewish people; on practice in agriculture and manual work; on *halutzic* [pioneer] training; and on striving for a society built on freedom, equality, tolerance, mutual assistance, and love of mankind."

Already at that early phase, the religious parties saw to it that they would lose nothing by the new arrangement. Under the new law, a special "Council for Religious State Education" was set up to supervise and guarantee the religious character of the curriculum in religious state schools, and of their teachers and inspectors alike.

This arrangement (to which, incidentally, the ultra-orthodox Agudat Yisrael refused to be a party) left the Mizrahi and Hapoel Hamizrahi (later to be merged into the NRP) an unusually wide scope for maneuver. To be sure, with one concession after another and the periodic threats of coalition crises, "religious education" became virtually a state within a state.

There have, of course, been more general adverse results. As Joseph Bentwich points out in his *Education in Israel*, "a result of the separation of 'religious' from plain 'State Schools' has been to emphasize the non-religious character of the latter; and this is a source of continual friction." "Schools in neighboring villages," Bentwich goes on to point out, "even of immigrants of the same communities, often belong to different categories. Complaints appear in the Press, either of party discrimination against this or that school, or of the religious wishes of parents not being complied with."[9]

Be that as it may, a crisis erupted in 1972 over religious education, ostensibly caused by the implementation of a planned reorganization on the part of the government affecting the ministry of education. The NRP claimed that the reorganization introduced "far-reaching and substantial changes in the status of the Religious Education Division as laid down by the existing State Education Law." The result was the appointment of "district inspectors" of schools, who were to be responsible for all state education, including religious schools.

But this was not all. The NRP and its spokesmen now argued that if the district inspector took charge of the state religious networks as well, then the nationwide state religious education division—until then in charge of all religious state schools—would be "emptied of all content." The division, it was argued, would thus be prevented from giving guidance and from supervising such crucial matters as the appointment of teachers and inspectors, laying down curricula, and approving textbooks.

The NRP argued further that its demands were purely pedagogic, not administrative. If the long-standing status quo cannot be preserved and reorganization must be introduced, its leaders argued, then each district must have a senior and separate religious inspector, working independently and being answerable in pedagogic matters only to the religious division at the ministry of education in Jerusalem. Such a solution, had it been accepted, would have amounted to something like a division of the education ministry into two separate ministries—and this no one in the government or the non-Orthodox public seemed willing to tolerate.

Formally and legalistically, the NRP's arguments were weighty. In the course of the years and with the Labor group wanting to avoid an open clash at all costs, several "precedents" were established which now tended to strengthen the position of the religious sector. One NRP Knesset member presented his party's case with considerable force. Basing his argument on a 1956 law regulating the work of school inspectors, Dr. Y. Goldschmidt claimed that while according to that law a district inspector is entitled to hold meetings with inspectors and teachers and examine with them matters of pedagogy, "this clause does not relate to inspectors and teachers belonging to state religious education."

This, Goldschmidt argued, was reinforced and finalized by another clause in the same law, which states that "an inspector or teacher in a State Religious institution shall be answerable in pedagogic matters to the Director of the State Religious Division [at the ministry of education], who in turn will give them instructions in their work and maintain direct and permanent contact with them." In contravention of this clear division of authorities, Goldschmidt asserted, the minister of education, in an order issued on February 14, 1971, invested district inspectors with general authority over all matters of pedagogy, both in state and state religious institutions.

More credence was lent to Goldschmidt's argument when he cited the considered opinion of the government's legal advisor. "The 1956 regulations," the legal advisor wrote, "gave expression to the tendency of the State Education Law to introduce a certain measure of well-defined separation, as far as inspection of schools is concerned, between state schools as such and state religious schools."

In reply to this seemingly impeccable argument, however, education ministry officials cited another clause in the legal advisor's letter. This clause allowed that district inspectors are entitled to convene "pedagogic meetings" with religious-school inspectors as well as with state-school inspectors provided this is done in coordination with the director of the religious education division!

However, the 1956 regulations concerning school inspectors set forth that "authority in pedagogic matters, insofar as they affect the religious character of state religious educational institutions, is vested in the Director of the [religious education] division." The problem here, of course, is who decides what affects "the religious character" of these institutions and what does not? What is the borderline between mere "pedagogy" and pedagogical administration? And, finally, what does "coordination" entail?

It is in the attempt to find answers to such intricate—and ultimately unanswerable—questions that the unending controversy between the NRP and the minister of education resided. With commendable persistence, consistency, and single-mindedness, the religious parties have been exacting concession after concession. One of their demands was that state religious schools should have their own special English-language courses (and therefore English readers and exercise books) so that the books can offer more religious-oriented reading matter. This demand was duly met by the ministry of education.

But this was only one in an endless series of similar demands. Previous demands—all of them duly met—concerned such subjects as books of instruction in the Torah and the Oral Law. They embraced "controversial" subjects like history and civics, and finally were extended to such ostensibly neutral subjects as biology and geography. Biology books used in state schools, for instance, refer to Darwin's theory of evolution—a theory obviously not in keeping with "the religious character" of state religious schools. In geography, especially natural geography, frequent references are made to the "millions of years" that elapsed before certain geological changes could take place, as well as to current land masses that once were covered with water. All of this, too, is considered to be out of keeping with the religious character of state religious education.

The list can be extended almost endlessly—and would in the end embrace almost everything taught at state schools, including the Hebrew literature of the *Haskalah*, modern Hebrew poetry, and so on. It is no wonder, therefore, that one of the NRP's ultimatums concerned the establishment of a special division whose sole task would be to formulate and lay down school curricula for state religious education.

Leaving to Caesar What Is Caesar's

There is obviously a great deal to criticize, deplore, and even condemn in the general behavior and the tactics commonly used by the religious parties in Israel. Their decades-long campaign for an amendment in the Law of

Return on the subject of conversion—and ultimately on the "who is a Jew" question—however, is not one of the grounds on which such criticism and such reservations can reasonably be based.

To be sure, there is a great deal to be said about the true nature of the religious lobby's motives as well as its immediate practical goals. There is also much truth in the complaint voiced by Conservative, Reform, and Reconstructionist rabbis in Israel and in the United States about the attempt on the part of the Orthodox establishment virtually to disenfranchise them. Nevertheless, both on religious and on logical grounds, the Orthodox stand on this particular subject remains valid, and the complaint (justified though it is) is being addressed to the wrong party.

This is so because the real question is not whether *giyur* (conversion to Judaism) should be conducted according to the *Halakha* (Jewish law); it certainly should. Nor is it whether the religious parties are entitled to insist that it should be so conducted; they obviously are. This issue is not, again, whether the Law of Return should be amended to stipulate *halakhic* conversion; it should, as will be explained presently.

The issue, rather, is whether Israel, as a state and as a polity, ought to be formally and officially involved in this controversy. After all, as Shimon Peres, then prime minister, said in the course of a highly recriminatory and noisy debate in the Knesset on January 17, 1985, the issue is "more in the realm of *Torah* than in the realm of government." The government, he added, was not a religious authority, and it cannot, therefore, resolve such problems. On the same occasion, Peres went on to assert that the Law of Return was a Zionist law, not a religious one, and that as such it has no implications with respect to matters of personal status, nor does it weaken the authority of the rabbinical courts.

The only logical conclusion to be drawn from these statements is fairly clear—that the whole subject should be left to the various religious groups and streams to settle between themselves. However, relations between synagogue and state in Israel being what they are, the practical implications of such a conclusion are bound to be so crucial and far-reaching that no Israeli government or leader is likely to risk responsibility for them.

And indeed, Shimon Peres, in his pronouncements on the subject, sounded considerably less sure (and certainly less consistent) than he usually is. In an address he gave at a party gathering on December 4, 1984, he stated definitively: "We have informed the religious parties that there will be no compromise on the 'Who's a Jew' issue, since the subject touches not on any specific religious outlook." In what must be taken as an attempt at explanation, Peres added: "We are a pluralistic people. Anyone who wants to create a hegemony of any one stream is in my view threatening our unity-through-pluralism. In my opinion, the 'Who's a Jew' issue threatens the unity of the Jewish people. I am in favor of showing very great consideration—and I make no secret of this—for the needs and aspirations of religious Jews; but what is involved here is the unity of the people and its survival." Ostensibly speaking for the state of Israel as a whole, Peres explained further: "We do not represent a single stream of Jewish belief, but rather a totality of Jewish belief that all the streams must flow into the same sea without one blocking the course of the other."

While much of this seems to be generally true and the sentiments expressed by Peres are highly laudable, very little of it is relevant to, and the whole is totally inconsequential for, the issue at hand. That Jews are "a pluralistic people" is true only in the sense that among them are observant and nonobservant; *haredim* and Orthodox; Reform, Conservative, Reconstructionist, and (lately) "humanist" Jews, as well as secularists and atheists. All these are part of the Jewish family, or people, and Israel is the home of an assortment of all of them (as well as of many non-Jews). In order, however, to be a member of this collectivity, a person has either to be "born to a Jewish mother" or converted to Judaism.

Now conversion to Judaism is by its very nature *halakhic*, and the demand by the religious parties to insert the phrase "according to the *Halakha*" after "converted to Judaism" is (in the normal course of events) almost superfluous—all the more so since Conservative and even Reform rabbis have insisted repeatedly that they perform *giyur* according to every requirement of the *Halakha*. However, as will be seen presently, we are dealing here with a more complex issue.

In what way does all this affect relations between synagogue and state in Israel? More importantly, does it help us resolve the ever-recurrent problem posed by questions such as "Who is a Jew?" and "Who is a *geir*?" (convert to Judaism)?

Plainly, Orthodox Jewish circles and parties in Israel are fully entitled to insist on a *halakhic* definition of a Jew and to demand that conversion to Judaism be performed strictly according to the precepts of the *Halakha*. However, both in the theological and the political sense, they are totally unjustified in linking the issue of a person's Jewishness to that of his or her nationality or citizenship.

The dilemma confronting religious people and religious institutions in Israel is not as difficult as it seems. As long as matters of personal status, marriage, divorce, and conversion remain—in Israel—the exclusive prerogatives of Orthodox rabbis and Orthodox rabbinical courts, the problem of defining and verifying a person's Jewishness does not arise. This problem arises only when it comes to deciding a person's *nationality* as a Jew; in this respect, the Orthodox in Israel will be well-advised to leave to Caesar what is Caesar's and content themselves with giving God what is God's.

It may well be argued by some that Caesar (in this case, the self-confessed secularist State of Israel), by insisting on defining itself as Jewish, is itself trying to have its cake and eat it, too. This, however true, must nevertheless be viewed by the Orthodox as the state's own affair and dilemma. If they find this state of affairs to be in opposition to the demands of their own consciences, then they must simply and quietly step out of the political party arena altogether.

Marriage, Nationality, and the Law of Return

Recurring cabinet crises over the "who is a Jew" issue continue. In July 1972, in the course of the prolonged debate on the proposed introduction of civil marriage procedures, a private member's bill was submitted to the Knesset by Rabbi Shlomo Lorincz of the ultra-Orthodox Agudat Yisrael. The bill introduced an amendment in the Law of Return making it clear that "conversion to Judaism" means conversion according to *halakhic* norms. The amendment referred to Article 4B of the Law of Return, which reads: "For the purpose of this law, 'a Jew' means a person born to a Jewish mother or converted to Judaism and who is not a member of another religion."

The burden of the proposed amendment was that the law, as it stood, failed to elaborate on the crucial phrase "converted to Judaism," saying nothing about the nature of the procedure required for such conversion. As Agudat Yisrael's official organ pointed out in an editorial, "the existing loopholes in the Law of Return, allowing for the acceptance of improperly-performed conversions as well as of mixed marriages, undermine the foundations of the Marriage and Divorce Law."

From the point of view of the government, there were thus two different but entirely parallel planes on which the twin issues of civil marriage and the proposed amendment to the Law of Return meet: (1) the tactical/political, and (2) the national/ideological. On the purely tactical/political plane, the prime minister's uncompromising stand against the ILP and their proposed bill was easily explicable: If the Independent Liberals and/or Mapam were to be allowed to vote for legislation authorizing civil marriage *and* stay in the cabinet, then the government would find itself quite powerless vis-à-vis the NRP should *it* choose to vote in favor of Rabbi Lorincz's amendment to the Law of Return.

Not only would this mean the virtual collapse of the so-called coalition discipline, but it could have the added danger of turning the conversion issue (and with it the proposed amendment to the Law of Return) into a part of the NRP elections platform in 1973—a development that might well result in the Labor-Mapam alignment being forced again to bow to NRP pressure and "blackmail."

Grave as the consequences of the two proposed bills (neither of which were passed by the Knesset) on the tactical/political plane, their national/ideological implications are even graver. It is instructive to note here that, while a very good case may be made for the Orthodox contention that civil marriage and "improperly-performed conversions" would lead to the division of the Jewish people, an equally good case can be made for a diametrically opposed argument.

In a statement signed at the time by leading Conservative and Reform Jewish organizations in the United States, together with the Israel Movement for Progressive Judaism, and published in the local press as an advertisement, these organizations argued against the proposed revision of the Law of Return on the grounds that "the consequence of the proposed revision would be to divide the Jewish people at the very time when solidarity is so essential to its well being." Pointing out that the overwhelming majority of Jews in the United States are non-Orthodox, and that there "Orthodox, Conservative, Reform, secular, and Zionist organizations work side by side in coordinating umbrella agencies founded on the principle of Jewish unity through mutual respect for ideological diversity," the statement accused the Orthodox rabbinate of being "motivated by concern for preserving their monopolistic control over the *halakha* and of using the *halakha* to reinforce their political power."

Similar statements made in the same circles over the years are couched in precisely the same terms and in the same threatening tone. Finally, after nearly a quarter of a century of controversy, an agreement was reached on October 19, 1996, between Prime Minister Benjamin Netanyahu and the religious parties which allowed the introduction of a bill designed to invalidate Reform and Conservative conversions performed in Israel.

Spokesmen of the Reform movement, however, feared that such a move would also affect conversions performed outside Israel and thus undermine the rights to which certain categories of Jewish immigrants to Israel are entitled. On October 31, the Jewish Agency Executive reaffirmed its opposition to any legislation that would alter the status quo concerning the Law of Return, whereupon Netanyahu in a broadcast via satellite assured the General Assembly of the Council of Jewish Federations gathered in

Seattle that his government would maintain the status quo concerning conversions performed outside Israel.

Four months later, in March 1997, the issue was raised again in full force, with another bill stipulated and with the Chief Rabbinical Council calling on the Knesset to pass a special bill denying recognition of conversions performed by Reform and Conservative rabbis *both in Israel and abroad.*

However, despite efforts on the part of some parties of the opposition, the Jewish Agency, and a number of Jewish organizations abroad, the proposed Conversion Law was duly put to the vote, and the Knesset approved the first reading by 51 to 32 votes. Further attempts were made to resolve the issue, amongst them a compromise proposal submitted by ultra-Orthodox MK Abraham Ravitz stipulating that, instead of the word "Jewish" in the relevant clause of identity cards, the religion of the holder would be listed by just the first letter in case the person in question had undergone a non-Orthodox conversion!

This proposal was made on May 29, 1997. On June 18, under a compromise approved by the prime minister, Conservative and Reform leaders would suspend all petitions to the Supreme Court concerning conversions till mid-September, by which time a compromise solution acceptable to all parties was to be found.

Four days of intensive talks later, an interim agreement was signed with the Reform and Conservative movements stipulating that the proposed Conversion Law would not be submitted to the Knesset for its second and third (final) readings, while the government would ask the courts to defer their rulings on the issue of conversion. A seven-member committee was appointed by the prime minister to formulate a detailed proposal, satisfactory to all parties, for the registration of converts to Judaism, and on June 26 former justice minister Yaacov Ne'man was appointed chairman of the committee.

Since then, despite intensive efforts and repeated claims that a compromise solution had finally been found, no way out of the crisis was found, and the issue of conversion continues to be very much in the air.

The truth is that, though opponents of the "religious status quo" continue to argue that it is observed only by dint of coalition bargaining and horse-trading, a careful examination of the facts reveals that the support given to the existing arrangement by the secular groups—whether left or right—has far deeper roots.

Paradoxical as it may sound, the most compelling arguments advanced in favor of the Marriage and Divorce Bill when it was first debated by the Knesset in August 1953 came not from the religious parties but from secular ones, like Mapai and Herut. In essence, these felt concern, not about religious observance and *halakhic* norms, but about what they termed "national unity" and "national solidarity." Although they were highly critical of many aspects of the law, they felt that the current generation was not ripe for a change. To regulate marital status afresh at that juncture, they felt, would constitute too violent a departure from Jewish tradition and Jewish life, of which the family was one of the mainstays throughout history. In any case, they implied, the danger to national unity was greater than any advantage that might accrue from bringing the law closer to current sentiment and realities.

This took place some forty-five years ago. Since then, a number of things happened and a few cases were brought to the Supreme Court involving the very essence of the problem and making it fairly obvious that some sort of change will have to be introduced. The government's general attitude has been that nothing should be done in violation of the status quo, especially that the far more substantial demand for amending the Law of Return would certainly gain impetus from any such developments.

Indeed, many of those who advocate change realize the far-reaching ramifications that such change is bound to have on other aspects of the synagogue-state controversy, such as the nationality problem and the continued solidarity of Orthodox Jewry throughout the world. An almost classic illustration of the way in which marriage and divorce procedure can affect larger ideological issues is the case of Benjamin Shalit and his Scottish wife, whom he had met and married in Edinburgh, noted briefly in chapter 3, in the section "Genesis of a Nonquestion." Though not a believing Christian, Mrs. Shalit refused on principle to take the common course of converting to Judaism to avoid possible difficulties for her two children.

Subsequently, insisting that his children be registered as Jews and faced with the ministry of interior's refusal to let them be so registered, Shalit took the case to the Supreme Court. In January of 1970, the court decided (by a five-to-four vote) that the plaintiff was entitled to his case—making it clear, however, that the judgment was passed on a point of procedure and not on ideological grounds.

Because of the immense historical significance of the Shalit case and the developments that were to follow, it may be useful to give here the gist of the majority view and the grounds on which it based its verdict. According to the verdict, the determination of Jewish status is an ideological issue of profound importance, involving not only the foundations of a Jewish state but the position of Jews the world over. Yet this issue is not capable of judicial decision, since the term "Jew" has no fixed and immutable meaning and can be given only a limited definition related to the purpose of the relevant legislative act.

In the case under examination, it was explained, the process of registration was carried out for administrative purposes, largely statistical, and the law must be construed in that context. The only issue the Court was entitled to settle was whether the registering officials were not to register as "Jewish" children who were not so under *halakhic* law—or whether the minister was using his powers properly in issuing his directive.

The administrative purposes of registration were not rightly served by introducing the external consideration as to whether the marriage was validly Jewish under religious law (a consideration that had no place in the decision of a secular court). The Court decided, therefore, that it was the duty of the interior ministry's official to enter what the parents told him to unless it was, on its face, plainly untrue.

Thus, what the Supreme Court really did in the Shalit case was to treat the issue as a technical one and not as one of fundamental principle. Yet the case was precisely that; witness the fact that four out of nine judges insisted on penetrating what they considered the technical and legal facade and dealing with the essence of the matter. It would be an evasion, they felt, not to deal with the "awesome and weighty issue pertaining to whether national and religious affiliation can be separated—as the plaintiff was obviously trying to do by his plea that in Israel Jewishness ought to be identified with 'Jewish-Israeli' culture."

But if the majority in the Shalit case tried to evade the fundamental issue of principle confronting them, the Orthodox groups in Israel immediately realized the implications of the majority decision. Chief Rabbi Unterman attacked the decision as "rooting out a cornerstone of Judaism which has preserved the purity of the Jewish family from all incursions of foreign cultures and miscegenation." Minister of religious affairs Zerah Warhaftig declared: "We shall not live by the dictates of the Court." The rabbinate's chief executive adopted the recognized emergency procedure of delaying the reading of the Torah to complain "before the congregation of God" of an injustice that had been perpetrated.

The result was a substantial amendment to the Law of Return reinstating the *halakhic* criterion of Jewish "nationalism" for the purpose of registration, so that the "religion" (which in Israel is equated with "nationality") of children of mixed marriages would not be decided for them by their parents. For the religious, however, the amendment was far from being an unmixed blessing, since it also granted automatic citizenship rights to the non-Jewish spouses and adult descendants of those eligible for immigration under the Law of Return. These rights extended to the third generation and continued even after the death of the man or woman whose Jewish status was the basis of these rights.

Moreover, the amendment left open one point of cardinal importance by again failing to specify the manner of conversion of a non-Jew to Judaism. This is the issue on which the NRP and Agudat Yisrael have since been so determined to fight.

Military Service for Women

One of the concessions made to Agudat Yisrael in the letter related to the religious "status quo" was the exemption of "religious women" from military service. Although secular circles opposed this concession and agitated for its repeal, the arrangement was upheld for exigencies of coalition government. Prior to the formation of the government that took office in October 1951, a promise was extracted from Mapai of a moratorium of at least one year on the recruitment of religious girls.

This promise was honored to the letter—and when, a year later, notice was served that the concession was to be withdrawn, both Agudat Yisrael and Poalei Agudat Yisrael left the coalition, which was finally dissolved in September 1952. The government that succeeded it, however, obtained a majority in the Knesset during the following year for the conscription of eighteen-year-old religious girls for national service of a civilian nature.

The result was a tremendous outcry. Demonstrations were staged not only outside the Knesset and in the streets but also outside the premises of Israeli embassies in New York and London. The Council of Sages—an ultra-Orthodox consultative body of the Agudah parties—placed the matter within the category of decrees to be defied only at risk of death, and even Chief Rabbi Herzog publicly opposed the measure (an act, by the way, that exposed him to complaints that, as a state official, he had no right to condemn a decision approved by a parliamentary majority).

Although the main argument advanced by the Orthodox against the conscription of girls derived from reports of immorality in military camps, opposition to the measure had far deeper roots extending to the *halakhic* code of sexual conduct. The assumption of male lust and of the frailty of the female's will pervades all traditional discussions of the subject. Therefore, the only permitted outlet for the sexual instinct is lawful marriage, which was divinely ordained for the twin purposes of reproduction and subjection of the evil inclination.

Chastity is thus demanded of male and female alike. Accordingly, the *halakhic* code contains detailed regulations aimed not only at avoiding sexual stimulus outside marriage but also at inducing restraints within its bounds. Since according to very strict rules of modesty even the hair and the voice of a woman are considered to be as alluring as her body, numerous preventive measures have been prescribed, among which is a more or less complete segregation of the female outside the immediate family. Any state decree, therefore, that is liable to take a girl out of the confines of her family is considered to be the thin edge of the wedge.

It must be pointed out here, however, that this is no longer the code that all Orthodox Jewish groups follow strictly. Orthodox circles that can be said to be "borderline cases" (that is, somewhere between the openly secular groups and the ultra-Orthodox ones like the Netorai Carta and the Agudah) have gradually relaxed some of these rules. This can be seen, in addition to the many aspects of outward appearance and conduct, in such phenomena as coeducation in Mizrahi religious schools and in the joint activities in its youth movement, the *B'nai Aqiba*. In these religious groups, while segregation at prayer remains unquestioned, men and women sit together and take the rostrums at public meetings; the *hora*, a round dance, is not discouraged (although ballroom dancing is); and married women tend to cover their heads only when they go out of doors.

As summarized here, the Orthodox position on the subject of military service for women was never seriously challenged by any of the coalition governments since the establishment of the state. The exemption boards or committees set up by the ministry of defense were there only to see to it that nonreligious girls could not easily take advantage of the so-called status quo agreement of 1947.

What gave rise to the fierce controversy was the Agudah's goal of securing exemption not only for "religious women" but also for girls who, though not observant themselves, come from observant families. Moreover, some saw the new law as making possible the evasion of army service by girls who neither are observant themselves nor hail from Orthodox homes. For although certain revisions were introduced into the amendment as it was originally formulated in the coalition agreement, it remains true that the "reasons of conscience or religious conviction," which used to constitute grounds for exemption, have been substituted after the amendment by "reasons of religious conviction or the religious way of life of her [the girl's] family."

The amendment no doubt marked a further serious erosion of the position of the non-Orthodox sector of the community and a parallel advantage for the Orthodox sector. What was taken as a significant sign of the times, too, was that the National Religious party (despite some faint sounds made by some of its luminaries) chose to keep fairly silent on the subject, taking the new gain in its stride.

It all goes to show how increasingly costly it is becoming for Israel's nonreligious parties to persuade the country's politicized religious groups to keep helping them patch up a stable coalition government.

PART 3

Middle Eastern Themes

The average Westerner was wont to regard Japan as barbarous while she indulged in the gentle arts of peace; he calls her civilized since she began to commit wholesale slaughter on Manchurian battlefields.

Okakura Kakuzo, *The Book of Tea*

Arab Nationalism and Pan-Arabism

In the Middle East there is no place for both Arab nationalism and Zionist nationalism. . . . To be more specific: In the Middle East there is room
only for the Arab nation.

Muhammad Hasanein Haykal, *Al-Ahram*, February 21, 1969

The difficulties that the Arabs have been experiencing with their "national
question" are not less galling than those that Israeli Jews are having with
their own. Like Jewish Israelis and the way they relate to their religion,
Muslim Arabs, too, are somewhat unsure where Islam stands in relation to
Arabism and the pan-Arab nationalist ideology. Like the so-called enlightened Jews (*maskilim*) of Central and Eastern Europe in the second half of the
nineteenth century, conscious educated Arabs in the last few decades of
that century and of the early twentieth, too, borrowed the narrow ethnic-
racial concept of nationality from the pan-movements of those days and
those parts.

The Arabs, indeed, have had more than their fair share of trouble in this
field. How, for instance, were their nationalist ideologues to reconcile their
genuine pan-Arab zeal with the distressing reality of their nation's division
into so many different and separate "national entities"? Attempts to resolve
this question in any really convincing way have all been half-hearted—as
were attempts to show that, far from being an ethnic-racial ideology and a
pan-movement, Arab nationalism was primarily a political movement bent
on liberating the Arabs and "reuniting" them in a single independent domain.

Added to these difficulties are the claims made in recent years by leaders
of the Palestinian national movement. The arguments and the rhetoric of
these leaders often seem to be in direct opposition to the claims and preten-
sions of the pan-Arabs, whose stance in turn seems to negate the Palestinians' specific claims and demands.

In this chapter, an attempt is made to grapple with these and other issues connected with the rise, growth, and visible decline of pan-Arabism and the ethnic-nationalist ideology that lies at its core.

Arabs and Muslims

In any serious consideration of the subject of Arab nationalism, two issues have to be tackled: the relation between Arabism and Islam, and that between Arab nationalism and pan-Arabism. To clarify the first point, an attempt must be made at some kind of definition of the term "Arab." "To the question 'Who are the Arabs?,'" wrote the noted British orientalist Sir Hamilton Gibb in 1940, "there is—whatever ethnographers may say—only one answer which approaches historic truth: All those are Arabs for whom the central fact of history is the mission of Muhammad and the memory of the Arab empire, and who in addition cherish the Arabic tongue as their common possession."[1] This definition is patently both inadequate in itself and unacceptable to the generality of Arab nationalists. By identifying Arabism so completely with Islam, Gibb leaves out those non-Muslims who have always formed an integral part of the Arabic-speaking world, and who, in some cases, were an equally inseparable part of the Arab nationalist movement in modern times.

Gibb's definition may, to be sure, be regarded by many Western observers as the closest to reality. Yet it is a highly significant and often overlooked fact that the Arabs themselves have always insisted on a broader frame of reference, thus suggesting a nonexclusive, open aspect of their society and culture. A 1913 Arab congress in Paris, for instance, thus defined "Arab": "Whoever lives in our country, speaks our language, is brought up in our culture, and takes pride in our glory is one of us." An even broader and more inclusive definition was advanced almost half a century later by Yusuf Haykal, who in his book *Nahwa al-Wihda al-'Arabiyya* (Toward pan-Arab unity) asserted that an Arab was "anyone whose national language is Arabic and who thinks and expresses his thoughts through its medium, regardless of the racial origins of his parents."[2]

There are, of course, many other definitions. Bernard Lewis, who quotes the 1913 Paris congress formulation and furnishes a brief summary of the various usages of the term "Arab" in different periods, writes in conclusion: "While all these usages have survived in certain contexts to the present day, a new one born of the impact of the West has in the past fifty years become increasingly important. It is that which regards the Arabic-speaking peoples as a nation or a group of nations in the European sense, united by a common territory, language and culture and a common aspiration to political independence."[3]

Be that as it may, it is noteworthy that in attempting to define the Arabs, it is almost always the non-Arabs who usually offer the more restricted, ethnocentric, and religious-bound definitions. The Arabs themselves have proposed broader, more-inclusive definitions denoting, theoretically at least, a more open, pluralistic kind of society.

The attempt to link Arabism, and ultimately Arab nationalism, with Islam is an old one. Nabih Amin Faris, an Arab nationalist thinker of note, once remarked that "the birthday of the Prophet [Muhammad] is the birthday of Arabism."[4] Such a view of the relation between Islam and Arabism is held, with varying degrees of vagueness, by many modern proponents of the Arab nationalist doctrine. Others, however, have disputed it energetically. For these, the main object of Muhammad's mission was—in the words of 'Abd al-Rahman 'Azzam, the first secretary-general of the Arab League—"the creation of an Islamic nation and not of an Arab nation."

'Azzam makes a very clear distinction between Islam and Arabism, arguing that the coming into being of an Arab nation "was never planned or intended by the Arab Prophet or his followers." Those peoples whom Islam Arabized were only a by-product of Arab influence, and this "by-product nation, curiously enough, was never seriously conscious of its ethnic or cultural existence until it was aroused to the new doctrine of nationalism by its European conquerors." It was only after this arousal that it became "convenient for the Arabs, and in certain cases even necessary, to use [the doctrine of nationalism] as an instrument of defence against these conquerors."

'Azzam, indeed, gives the impression that, for him, the fact that "the last great prophet" was an Arab was a mere accident. Muhammad belonged to a great Arab tribe, to be sure; yet "nothing was more distasteful to him than to glorify his tribe or race, because in Islam there was no room for discrimination whatever, on account of either colour, language or race." According to the prophet's creed, his followers should live in the service of the one "God of the universe." "You are one nation and I am your God to worship," says the Koran—and therefore "what the Prophet and his followers planned was not an Arab nation, but one Muslim nation living under one God and one law." It was this Islamic nation that endured for thirteen centuries after the rise of Islam. 'Azzam adds:

> From the seventh to the twentieth century, Arabs, Turks, Iranians, Afghans, Indians, Indonesians, Berbers, Chinese, Europeans and Africans had one citizenship. They were all considered Muslim citizens,

irrespective of their origin or the form of local government under which they lived. They had one loyalty and one permanent devotion to the Muslim nation since, in spite of the breakup of the Caliphate into several states, Muslims continued to live under the *Shari'a* (Islamic law) from which all citizens derived equal rights and duties applicable wherever they happened to be.

However, while Arabism has had a largely accidental relation to Islam, as a religion, it has nothing to do with race, either. All nations are a mixture of races and cultures, and the Arabs are no exception, 'Azzam asserts. He explains:

In order to help clarify this, I proposed to a select few of Arab thinkers, meeting in Baghdad some twenty-five years ago, at the time when Nazi racialist theories were attracting increasing attention, a certain definition of Arabism, as opposed to racialism. This definition ran as follows: "Those who live in Arab lands, speak the Arabic language, live an Arab way of life and feel proud of being Arab, are Arabs." This definition was later accepted by the Conference that laid the Pact of the League of Arab States in 1945.

Having thus disposed of the problem of definition, 'Azzam turns to the subject of modern Arab nationalism, which he describes as a concept of recent origin. Before the turn of the present century, he writes, the Arabs were not conscious of the modern ideas of nationalism. "These Western ideas flourished in Europe and never had any appeal to the rich, human and universal culture of Islam," he asserts.[5]

But while for 'Azzam the fact that Muhammad belonged to a great Arab tribe was a sheer accident of history—while, in a sense, he actually attempted to Islamize Arabism—there are Arab nationalist thinkers whose intent has been to Arabize Islam. For 'Abdel Rahman al-Bazzaz, an Iraqi law professor who in the 1960s became his country's prime minister, "the fact that the Prophet Muhammad was an Arab was not a matter of chance; a genius, he belonged to a nation of great abilities and qualities." In a booklet printed in Baghdad in 1952 with the title *Islam and Arab Nationalism*, al-Bazzaz presents what amounts to a straight antithesis of 'Azzam's theories.

Accusing the *shu'ubiyya* (non-Arab Muslims who reject the identification of Islam with Arabism) of denying the Arabs all qualities, al-Bazzaz attributes to them the desire to separate Muhammad from the Arab nation to which he rightly belonged. These *shu'ubis*, he writes, "confined their interest, their consideration and their appreciation to the Prophet in a forced manner and separated him from others before him, from his contemporaries and his compatriots, converting him into a universal being snatched from his land and sky, freed from his history and people." These *shu'ubis*, al-Bazzaz complains, pictured Muhammad as "a prosperous plant growing in an empty desert, no one having helped him, and himself not indebted to anyone's help."

Remarking on the degree of progress and maturity that the Arabic language and its literature had attained before Islam, al-Bazzaz concludes that the Arabs were the backbone of Islam:

> They were the first to be addressed in the verses of Revelation; they were the *Muhajirin* and the *Ansar;* their swords conquered countries and lands, and on the whole they are, as Omar has described them in a saying of his: "Do not attack the Arabs and humiliate them for they are the essence of Islam." If we may take an instance from contemporary history, we can say that the position of the Arabs in Islam is like that of the Russians in the Communist order, with the obvious difference between the spiritual appeal of Islam and the material principles of Communism.[6]

On the face of it, all these arguments and counterarguments concerning Islam's relation to Arabism may seem of little help in an attempt to define the Arabs. As a matter of fact, the meaning of the term "Arab" has changed and developed over the course of time. The great Arab historian and social philosopher Ibn Khaldun used the term to describe the nomads, the Beduin of the desert.

The term "Arab" in its current connotations is, thus, quite new; we have only to remember that until just before World War I Arabic was not even the official language in any of the countries now designated as Arab. The inhabitants of these countries, moreover, rarely thought of themselves as "Arabs." As Goitein has rightly noted, until fifty or sixty years ago, if one of these inhabitants was asked about his or her identity, the reply would have been, "I hail from this or that tribe, from such-and-such a town or city, I am a member of this or that faith or confession," and so on. It hardly ever would have occurred to that person to describe himself or herself as an Arab.[7]

The Growth of Arab Volkisch Nationalism

For more than four hundred years, most of the area now called the Arab world was ruled by Ottoman sultans, who were primarily religious rulers reigning over a community of Muslim believers under the authority of Islamic law. In such a system of government, the nation-state as we know it in its modern European form had no place whatsoever; the amalgam of races, ethnic groups, cultures, and faiths living under Ottoman rule enjoyed a large measure of communal autonomy and self-government. The Middle East was indeed what many nowadays say they would like to see it become: a meeting-place of cultures, religions, and races, a pluralist multifaith society in which Muslim, Jew, and Christian could coexist in peace and a certain measure of amity.

In contrast, the aspect that the contemporary Middle East has presented to the world has been one not of pluralism but of ethnocentrism and narrow *volkisch* nationalism—not of a society that includes different nationalities without oppressing them but of one which tries to neutralize them. Since the mid-1930s, the region has been the scene of a veritable gallery of horrors perpetrated against ethnic and cultural minorities by the petty national sovereignties which were to succeed the Ottoman Empire. The massacres which were staged, in succession, among the Armenians in Turkey in the 1910s and the Assyrians in northern Iraq in the 1930s—as well as the expulsions and the variety of discriminatory measures taken against Turkey's Greek minority, the Copts of Egypt, the Kurds of Iraq, the Jews in Arab lands, and (more recently) Iraq's Shi'i Muslims—all follow what by now has become a well-established pattern.

The Armenian and Assyrian episodes are now virtually forgotten. The position of the Copts of Egypt, the oldest of the country's inhabitants, has largely been obscured by the steady increase of conversions among them. The problem of the overwhelming majority of the Jews of the Middle East and North Africa was solved through mass emigration to Israel and elsewhere. An examination of the checkered history of any of these groups and communities under the new nation-states of the Middle East would give an ample idea of the way in which the rise of ethnic nationalism in that region rendered life for them intolerable. The story of the Kurds, in particular, offers a laboratory case and furnishes an excellent example of the workings of a historical process that has made the Middle East what it is today.

The problem of the Kurds of Iraq was first brought to the attention of the world following the collapse of the Ottoman Empire. At that time, the Iraqis and their European allies tried to convince themselves and the world that the Kurds, who constituted some 20 percent of Iraq's total population, were variously a communal, ethnic, cultural, or racial minority fairly content to be included within the compass of an "Iraqi nation." This, on the face of it, was largely true. Yet, with the steady growth of Iraq's *Arab* consciousness, the accompanying weakening of a coherent *Iraqi* nationality, and the insistent talk about an overall pan-Arab union in which Iraq was to play a leading role, Kurdish nationalism tended to grow. In this sense, the rise of a Kurdish national movement was a direct result of the growth of the Arab national consciousness among the Iraqis (in the self-same way as the growth of a distinctive Turkish national sentiment in the late nineteenth century had served as a spur to the national awakening of Arabs who lived within the Ottoman's domain).

It all had taken a clear and recurrent pattern. The advent of European ideas in the nineteenth century had led to the partial breakdown of an intricate system of government in which a multitude of ethnoreligious minorities could be tolerated and reasonably well treated. The climax of this process, however, was to be reached only in 1908, when the Young Turks revolution enabled the Ottoman reformers to obtain unlimited power in the empire. It was then that the idea of the supremacy of the Turkish people triumphed over the Islamic pluralism of the sultans. It was then, too, that the idea was entertained that the peoples of the empire (Arabs and other non-Turks included) must be Turkized—if necessary, by force.

At that point, the Arab nationalist movement, which had been merged with the general movement for Ottoman reforms, now began to separate itself. Faced with the prospect of forced assimilation into the dominant ethnic group and culture, the Arabs started agitating for autonomy, if not for full independence. Almost simultaneously, the Kurds also began to organize as a separate national group. Not unexpectedly, these reactions, in their turn, had the effect of pushing Turkish nationalism to further extremes, and the idea of a multinational, pluralistic empire was now discarded completely in favor of a purely Turkish nation-state.

At first glance, World War I and the subsequent dismemberment of the Ottoman Empire may seem to have provided a solution to the problem of national minorities in the Middle East. What it in fact did was to resolve the problem of the "big fish." The Turks were confined to Turkey, where they proceeded to create their own separate national sovereignty; the Arabs, though still deprived of the one united Arab state which they claimed they had been promised by the British, were eventually to get local national entities of their own.

Nevertheless, the tensions that had led to the breakup of the Ottoman Empire did not disappear after the empire finally disintegrated. The struggle, which had been one for influence among factions within a single commonwealth, now became one for land and power among groups controlling different independent states or living within their boundaries. The reason for this was simple enough: Within the empire, these groups had been so intermingled that it was impossible to say where each national minority began and where it ended.

Be that as it may, the disappearance of the Ottoman Empire resulted in a state of affairs that, nationally speaking, did not differ substantially from that obtaining in Central and Eastern Europe a few decades earlier. These regions—unlike, say, England, France, or Spain—possessed no tradition of well-defined and anciently established nation-states. Instead, there were peoples and nations that, in the words of Bernard Lewis, were lost in polyglot dynastic empires, divided into small principalities, or subject to alien rule. "There were Germans, but no Germany; Poles, but no Poland; Italians, but no Italy; Hungarians, but only a shadow of Hungary." To such people, patriotism as such had little appeal. Their profoundest loyalties were given not to state or country but to the nation or people. This loyalty was expressed not in love of country but in nationalism of the linguistic, "racial," and cultural variety rather than one of territory and citizenship.

It was this brand of ethnic, as opposed to territorial, nationalism that the states of the Middle East were to adopt. This plainly was not conducive to a political existence in which ethnic, linguistic, and religious groups could live peacefully together. To pick on a concept of nationality that was so alien to their religious tradition was unfortunate for these peoples. It was also deeply ironic. For while the present-day nationalisms of the states of the Middle East are based primarily on such concepts as race, culture, language, and religion, these factors have all been of a rather secondary importance in the Islamic world.

However, though nationalism is undoubtedly at the root of the present unhappiness of minority groups in the Middle East and elsewhere, there does not seem to be anything inevitable about it. We all speak rather loosely of "nationality," mostly confusing it with racial descent, language, ethnicity, culture, and (in the worst of cases) religion. It is wise to remember, though, that the term has often been used in more than one sense, depending on the locality and the political culture of the user. In England, the United States, and France, where nationality has been a function of citizenship and territory rather than of ethnicity or race, the word *nationalité* indicates the country or state of which one is a citizen. In German, however, there is a special word for nationality as used in this sense. It is *Staatsangehorigkeit*, meaning "state-belonging"; the term *Nationalitat*, on the other hand, is used in an ethnic rather than legal-territorial-political sense. The Russians, too, have two different words for "citizenship" and "nationality": *Grazhdanstvo* and *Natsionalnost*, respectively.[8]

The difference between these two usages—the British, American, and French usage, on the hand, and the Central and Eastern European, on the other—is one of substance. The latter usage has its origin in the German concept of nationality as being linguistic and racial rather than political or territorial. It was this German concept that was to triumph in the successor states of the Ottoman Empire. Nowadays, one speaks habitually of "the Arab world" and of "the Arab nation." The Arab world, it is fairly unanimously agreed, consists of those lands where the majority of the population is Arab or Arabic-speaking. Accordingly, this world is said to extend from the Atlantic Ocean in the west to Iran's borders in the east, and from the Taurus mountains and the southern shores of the Mediterranean in the north to the Indian Ocean and the steppes of central Africa in the south. It includes Morocco, Algeria, Tunisia, and Libya (the countries of what is called the Arab West [al-maghrib al-'arabi]); and Egypt, the Sudan, Lebanon, Syria, Jordan, Palestine, Iraq, and the Arabian Peninsula (which comprise the Arab East [al-mashriq al-'arabi]).

However, while "the Arab world" is fairly clearly defined geographically, the nature of "the Arab nation" (and indeed of the identity of the Arabs) poses two problems in any serious treatment of the subject of Arab nationalism. The first is whether the Arabs are Arabs by virtue of race, history, language, religion, a common culture, a shared mental make-up, or common social structures. The second is whether the Arabs, no matter how they are to be defined, can be said to constitute one nation or, more specifically, one "nationality."[9] So far, no one has succeeded in giving a really satisfactory answer to either of these two questions—least of all, perhaps, the Arabs themselves.

In The Arab Awakening, George Antonius maintains that the cultural evolution that the Arabs set in motion after their great conquests was the outcome of two processes—Islamization and Arabization. The former was a purely religious process, whereby the new faith of Islam transformed the spiritual life of millions of new adherents. The latter process, Arabization, was essentially sociocultural in character and had two aspects: linguistic and racial. Though Arabization was the older of these two processes, after the rise of Islam, Islamization and Arabization worked together; yet they never became identical and never acted within the same frontiers. "Broadly speaking," Antonius writes, "every country which became permanently Arabized became also permanently Islamized. But the converse is not true. There are countries, such as Persia and Afghanistan, where notwithstanding a thorough and lasting Islamization, the progress of Arabization remained . . . negligible."

Thus, in the course of time, the world of Islam reached out to India, China, and the westernmost recesses of Africa, whereas the Arab world remained confined to those countries in which the process of Arabization progressed far enough as to have achieved lasting results: the enthronement of Arabic as the national language, the introduction of Arab manners and ways of thought, and the implantation of an appreciable Arab stock in the racial soil.

After this brief historical survey, Antonius reaches the conclusion that the word "Arab" has come to mean "a citizen of that extensive Arab world—not any inhabitant of it, but that great majority whose racial descent, even when it was not of pure Arab lineage, has become submerged in the tide of Arabization; whose manners and traditions had been shaped in an Arab mould; and, most decisive of all, whose mother tongue is Arabic." To make his meaning clear, Antonius adds that the term "Arab" "applies to Christians as well as to Muslims, and to the offshoots of each of those creeds, the criterion being not Islamization but the degree of Arabization."[10]

In a sense, the definition offered by Nabih Amin Faris and Muhammad Tawfiq Husein sums up Antonius's theory. "The present-day Arabs," they have written, "are all those who inhabit the Arab world, speak the Arabic language, take pride in Arab history, cherish the general Arab feeling, and share in the characteristics of Arab mentality, irrespective of their religious affiliations and their racial descent."[11]

As will readily be seen, this definition is a fairly liberal formulation, coming as it does from two confirmed Arab nationalists. Is Arab nationalism, then, different from other ethnic nationalism? Does it belong in a class all its own? Muhammad Abu Shilbaya, a Palestinian journalist and author, proposes a rather novel approach to the subject. Referring to such concepts as "the Arab homeland," he asserted on more than one occasion that the adjective "Arab" in such phrases must be understood not racially but territorially—"exactly as, when we speak of the American Union, we refer to the American *land*, not to the American *race*."

Though this formulation would seem rather novel if taken in the context of the general run of Arab nationalist thinking, the idea itself is not new. A perceptive American student of Arab society has indeed likened this society to the modern American system. "In many ways," he writes, "like American citizenship, Arab society resembles a club in which membership may be obtained by cooperating in certain good works, in this case by actively sharing in common linguistic, cultural and emotional attributes. Throughout their history Arabs on the whole have formed a flexible community, stretching out to receive and assimilate, in part under the inclusive mantel of Islam."

"Even today," this observer continues, "this passive proselytization and assimilation continue, standing in sharp contrast to the exclusiveness of the nationalisms of Europe, Japan, India *et al.* This non-exclusiveness goes even a bit further. Arab society, again like its American counterpart, tends to impress a general conformity on its organized constituent parts while respecting individualism and minority patterns on a less general level."[12]

Conflicting Definitions—Conflicting Perceptions

Of all the definitions offered of the term "Arab," the one that would approximate historical and contemporary reality most seems to be that which places emphasis not on nationality or ethnicity but on language, culture, and environment. "We may say," W. B. Fisher writes, "that from the point of view of the anthropologist it is impossible to speak with any accuracy either of an Arab or a Semitic people. Both terms connote a mixed population varying widely in physical character and in racial origin, and are best used purely as cultural and linguistic terms respectively."[13] Given, then, that we accept as valid some such definition of the Arabs, there remains the question as to whether the Arabs, so defined, can be said to constitute a "nationality."

Some Arab nationalist thinkers date the emergence of a distinctive Arab nationality, and indeed of the Arab nationalist movement itself, back to pre-Islamic days. The more moderate view, shared by most Arab nationalists today, accepts the proposition that, like all nationalist movements, Arab nationalism is a relatively recent phenomenon dating back not earlier than the second half of the nineteenth century. The ideas and basic postulates of this movement were formulated gradually and not at one go, in a historical process that one historian of Arab nationalism has divided into five distinct phases.

The impact of European expansion marked the first phase, and with it came an Islamic-Arab reaction motivated by an Islamic rather than an Arab nationalist impulse. The second phase (which again had nothing specifically Arab about it) reflected the reformist tendencies in the Arab parts of the Ottoman Empire and the demands for decentralization. With the third phase, which represented the Arabs' response to the challenge of ethnic Turkish nationalism, a specifically Arab movement started to emerge. This was followed by a fourth phase, which came with the increasing contacts between Arab intellectuals and the European idea of nationalism, which manifestly contributed greatly to the articulation of a distinct Arab national ideology. The fifth and final phase in this particular account came with the Arab Revolt of 1916, which was interpreted by the nationalists as signifying the emergence of Arab nationalism as a living force and a popular rather than an elitist movement.[14]

Hazem Nuseibeh's book *The Ideas of Arab Nationalism*, from which the above account is summarized, appeared in 1956. The ideology of Arab nationalism has since undergone certain significant changes. However, regardless of whether this historical account stands the test of subsequent developments, it was inevitable that Arab nationalist thinkers soon would become aware of a certain incongruity.

There is, to be sure, an Arab nation; this nation is entitled to the rights of nationhood; Arab nationalism had been neatly defined, its postulates well and finally formulated. Yet something was missing—namely, a great Arab homeland, strong, prosperous, advanced, but above all united. Instead, the Arab world was fragmented into more than a dozen independent, mandated, or downright occupied geographical entities. The inhabitants of each of these possessed special characteristics of their own: They spoke widely different dialects of Arabic, had their own armies, their own ruling dynasties, their own vital interests and foreign policies.

How are the Arab nationalists to reconcile their concept of one Arab nation with the distressing reality of its division into so many different national entities? Sati' al-Husri, one of the leading theoreticians of pan-Arabism, had the following explanation to offer. Writing in 1951, he asserted:

> The apparent differences among the populations of the Arab states are accidental and superficial, and do not justify the assumption that they are members of different nationalities simply because they are citizens of different states, all of which have come into being as a result of the maneouvres and horse-trading tactics of the powers. . . . There are several Arab peoples, but all of them belong to one nation, the Arab nation. . . . Any member of these Arab peoples is an Arab.[15]

Al-Husri, whose influence on the ideology of pan-Arabism cannot be exaggerated, has developed what Albert Hourani terms "a 'pure' theory of nationalism with all its assumptions clearly understood and accepted, all its problems faced, a theory derived not only . . . from English and French thought, but from its roots in German philosophy; he has read Fichte, as no other Arab nationalist seems to have done."[16]

For al-Husri, a nation is not any group that wills to be a nation; it is something that exists in reality and has an objective basis. Language and a common history (in that order of importance) are the components of this basis. The Arab nation consists of all those who speak Arabic as their mother tongue, he taught. He repeatedly denied that race or blood relationship was a component of Arab nationalism, and he rejected the French view of "will" or "choice." An Arab, for him, "is an Arab whether he wishes to be one or not, . . . whether he admits it or not, . . . whether he be ignorant of it, or careless, or stubborn, or traitorous."[17]

Nor would al-Husri accept that Islam was an integral part of Arabism, although he admits that religion—especially a "national religion"—helps to create the kind of solidarity that reinforces national sentiment. It must be noted, however, that al-Husri's insistence on the primacy of the language factor tends to contradict his claim concerning the nonracial character of Arab nationalism. In nationalist parlance, "race" and "ethnicity" are hardly distinguishable from each other. Further, it is well-known that in nationalist doctrine, language, race, culture, and sometimes even religion constitute different facets of the same primordial entity—the nation. It is, in other words, impossible to accept the kind of language mystique advocated by a Fichte or al-Husri without embracing the fundamental ethnoracial implications of such a mystique.

Indeed, as Kedourie sums it up so deftly:

The theory [of nationalism] admits of no great precision, and it is misplaced ingenuity to try and classify nationalisms according to the particular aspect which they choose to emphasize. What is beyond doubt is that the doctrine divides humanity into separate and distinct nations, claims that such nations must constitute sovereign states, and asserts that the members of a nation reach freedom and fulfilment by cultivating the peculiar identity of their own nation and by sinking their own persons in the greater whole of the nation.[18]

However, while this is strictly true of all nationalist movements, and especially of pan-movements, the fact remains that a number of Arab—and even pan-Arab—nationalist thinkers have persistently refused to admit any racial or ethnic connotations to their doctrine. Gibb once made a distinction between what he called moderate Arab nationalism and pan-Arabism. This was plainly an unfounded distinction; but it is interesting to see how one advocate of both Arab nationalism and pan-Arabism has reacted to Gibb's classification. Asserting that the distinction was not a valid one, Cecil Hourani maintains that the very nature of any Arab nationalism is such that it cannot help embracing within its scope the whole Arab world. Cecil Hourani argues:

> There is no good reason why an Arab nationalist should be interested in the freedom and unification of part of the Arab world and not of the whole, or draw the frontiers of the Arab world at Libya.... There may be differences among Arab nationalists about the order of importance of certain Arab questions, but there is no disagreement about fundamental aims, which cannot stop short of the entire Arab world from the Atlantic to the Persian Gulf, and which embrace all levels of Arab society—the social, economic and intellectual no less than the political.

But in saying that Arab nationalism . . . is Pan-Arabism, it should not be understood that there is any comparison with or resemblance to such movements as Pan-Germanism or Pan-Slavism. There is a radical difference between Arab and European political ideology. In Europe nationalism has been built on two concepts: that of the state inherited from the tradition of Roman law and society, and that of a homogeneous racial group. Arab nationalism is based on neither. On the one hand, Arab society was not based on the Greco-Roman political tradition, and has never had a concept of a strong sovereign state. On the other, Arab society has never been exclusively racial, but has consisted of racially and religiously heterogeneous groups bound together by a common Arabic culture and world of thought. It is thus rather dangerous to compare conditions in Arab countries with conditions in Western societies.[19]

These words were written in the mid-1940s. In the early 1960s, three Egyptian university lecturers, writing jointly on the subject of Arab society and Arab nationalism, went much further in emphasizing the nonracial, nonethnic, and nonreligious character of Arab nationalism. In what was to be a textbook for Egyptian university students in a special course which can only be described as "national indoctrination," these three authors wrote (at a time when pan-Arabism was part of the official ideology of the day): "We consider Arabism to be a political ideology—just like democracy, communism, socialism, the movements for unity in Europe and America, and other ideologies and missions which various nations adopt and for which they fight." According to them, there are three pillars of Arabism as an ideology: (1) liberation of the Arab world from foreign domination, (2) unification of the Arab world within its natural boundaries, and (3) neutralism in the conflict between the two opposing world blocs.

These three pillars are interconnected in a very real sense, the authors assert. "Liberation," they explain, "cannot be realized without unification, and will be attained only through disengagement from the two opposing camps." But before going into these political considerations, the authors make a point of enumerating the fundamentals of Arab nationalism as they collate them from the writings of leading Arab nationalist thinkers. There are four such fundamentals, they assert, and they list them as follows:

- There is one Arab nation living in the territory extending from the Arab (Persian) Gulf to the Atlantic, and it possesses all the requisites of a nation.

- These requisites are: the unity of language, of history and land, of culture and spiritual heritage, and of aspirations and sufferings.

- Neither religion nor race is one of the foundations of the existence of the Arab nation.

- Fragmentation and imperialism—Western, Communist and Zionist—are the chief enemies of Arab nationalism.

The authors then state that they will now "define and delineate the meaning of Arabism," a task which, they make a point of explaining, the Charter of the League of Arab States fails to perform. Yet before embarking on such a definition, the Egyptian academics devote some space to their proposition that neither religion nor race plays a role in Arabism:

Arabism is not founded on Islam because not all the Arabs are Muslims, nor are all Muslims Arab. There are Arabs who are Jews, Catholic or Orthodox Christians, Druse, Baha'is and others. The opposite picture is true too: The Turks, the Afghans, the Pakistanis, the Iranians, the Indonesians and others are nearly all of them Muslims, but they are not Arabs. Moreover, non-Muslim Arabs comprise ten per cent of all the Arab peoples, while Muslim Arabs represent no more than about a seventh of the Muslim peoples.

Nor is Arabism founded on race. "Had it been founded on racial traits, and were it confined to the pure Arab race, it would have been confined to the Arab Peninsula, because the Arabs who had set forth from their peninsula since the beginning of the Muslim conquests mixed with other peoples, and their blood became mixed to such an extent that it became extremely difficult to tell an Arab from an Arabized person." In the Arab world today, the authors assert, live tens of races, distinguishable by the colors of their hair, their complexions, their facial features, and other marks singled out by the sciences of race and ethnography as distinguishing racial traits.

"Though we possess no accurate data on the various races of which the Arab world is composed," the three Egyptian scholars conclude, "it is evident that the pure Arab race totals no more than ten million, the rest descending from a variety of races—Copts, Syrians, Berbers, Nubis, Aramaics, Phoenicians and others who were assimilated into the Arab nationality, thus constituting one nation whose oneness and ties are expressed in the simple statement, 'we are all Arabs'."[20]

Pan-Movement by any Other Name

The claim, made by some Egyptian intellectuals in the 1960s, that the Arab nationalist movement is essentially a political creed—like democracy, communism, socialism—does not stand scrutiny. Merely by stating that there is one Arab "nation" living in a clearly defined geographical area, these intellectuals implicitly accept the thesis that no meaningful distinction can reasonably be drawn between Arab nationalism and pan-Arabism.

A controversy that occurred in those days may be illustrative. In 1964, in the course of a state visit to Egypt, the late Soviet leader Nikita Khrushchev made some remarks about the pan-Arab unity movement which were taken to imply criticism of the Egyptians' preoccupation with the fortunes of that movement, to the detriment of socialist objectives and the cause of labor internationalism.

Egyptian reactions to these criticisms were as instructive as they were sharp and spontaneous. In a brief address delivered in the presence of his distinguished guest on May 20, 1964, Abdel Nasser himself politely rebuked the Soviet leader when he asserted that the pan-Arab unity movement was neither racial nor new. To start with, he said, "the Arab peoples lived as one nation, within a single state, for the longest duration in history [sic], thus developing organic relations between themselves that have made of their existence one indivisible whole."

Nasser characterized the divisions seen at that time as "a recent phenomenon whose history does not date back to more than a few decades." These divisions were imposed by the forces of imperialism "in contradiction to nature and to history and in spite of the will of the people."

Throughout the long centuries, Nasser went on to instruct his guest, this Arab being has been one entity, and has attained for itself two main foundations: "a common conscience springing from the common history which this nation has lived through, and a common mentality springing from a common language." And he summed up: "One material entity [the state]; one conscience; and one mentality—these are the foundations and principles of Arab unity."[21]

Another comment, no less instructive, came from Ihsan Abdel Quddous, a leading spokesman of the Nasserist regime and then editor of Cairo's leading weekly, *Rose el-Yusuf*:

> The difference between the structure of the Soviet Union and that of the Arab Homeland is this. The Soviet Union: several nationalities each of which forms its own republic, all of these republics then forming one entity, i.e. the Soviet State. The Arab Homeland: One nationality spread over several artificial states; the whole of this Arab Homeland, when it has attained its unity, will become similar to one Soviet republic as far as national affiliation is concerned.[22]

Masquerading in any other name, then, Abdel Quddous, Nasser, and the intellectuals who argued that Arabism was no more than a "political creed" are all advocates of a full-fledged pan-creed. Indeed, during the 1950s and 1960s, pan-Arabism was associated chiefly with Abdel Nasser, whose first serious practical step in the direction of Arab unity was the proclamation in 1958 of the United Arab Republic following an ill-fated merger with Syria. Since the dissolution of that merger in September 1961, however, the pan-Arab movement has made no headway whatever.

Despite the pan-Arabs' oft-repeated claim that "fragmentation" of the Arab world was artificial, imposed from above, and was the result of imperialist machinations coupled with plots by "Arab reaction," the Arab peoples in their various lands failed to show any enthusiasm for an all-Arab union.

The revolution of July 14, 1958, in Iraq—hailed as marking the end of the imperialist, reactionary regime of the Hashemites and thought to be a gigantic step toward Arab unity—would soon prove even more hostile to Nasser's pan-Arab designs and plans than the hated regime it had unseated.

In Jordan, similarly, King Hussein's rule was to prove far more durable and stable than the pan-Arabs in Cairo had estimated. Even in Yemen (where an openly pro-Cairo revolt in 1962 led to Egypt's armed intervention there), the venture failed even before Nasser, following the defeat of his army in the Six-Day War and his decision to appease the Saudi regime, was to order the complete evacuation of his troops from there.

The main obstacle to Arab unity, then, was neither the Western imperialist presence nor the machinations of "Arab reaction." The reasons are far more basic and must be sought in the economic, social, cultural, and psychological spheres rather than in the political one. For the fact is that, despite a common lingua franca, a shared history, and a more or less uniform cultural and religious tradition, considerable differences still persist between the various peoples who make up the Arab "nation."

These differences affect such significant cultural-psychological factors as the spoken language (which differs widely in the various Arabic-speaking lands), temperament, local customs, and general environment. The situation, in fact, is remarkably analogous to the one that confronted the pan-Slavs of a century and more ago in Eastern Europe.

Pan-Slavism, like pan-Arabism, aspired to a union of the Slav peoples which was based largely on the language factor. Both were movements in which—in the words of Hans Kohn, describing pan-Slavism—"nationalist elements mingled with supranational and often imperialist trends."

To those who are familiar with certain pronouncements made during the 1950s and 1960s by some of the opponents of pan-Arab unity, the following passage, quoted from the work of Karel Havlicek, a great Czech intellectual who died more than a century ago, will no doubt have a familiar ring:

> I learned to know Poland and I did not like it (Havlicek wrote). With a feeling of hostility and pride I left the Sarmatian country, and in the worst cold I arrived in Moscow, being warmed mostly by the Slav feeling in my heart. The freezing temperature in Russia and other Russian aspects extinguished the last sparks of Pan-Slav love in me. So I returned to Prague as a simple Czech, even with some secret sour feeling against the name Slav which a sufficient knowledge of Russia and Poland had made suspect to me. Above all, I expressed my firm conviction that the Slavs, that means the Russians, the Poles, the Czechs, the Illyrians etc., are not one nation. The name Slav should forever remain a purely geographical and scientific name. Nationality is determined not only by language, but also by customs, religion, form of government, state of education, sympathies, etc.

Much like the Arab critics of Egyptian pan-Arab claims and designs in the 1950s and 1960s, Havlicek found the pan-Slavism of the Russians and the Poles mainly a desire on the part of these two strong Slav nation-states to utilize the other Slavs for their own needs and purposes. "I admit," Havlicek once wrote flatly, "that I prefer the Magyars, who are open enemies of the Czechs and Illyrians, to the Russians who approach us with the

Judas embrace—to put us into their pockets. We are Czechs, and we wish to remain Czechs forever, and we do not wish to become either Germans or Magyars or Russians; and therefore we shall be cool to the Russians, if we do not wish to be hostile to them."[23]

"The Palestinian Revolution" versus Pan-Arabism

If the pan-Arab movement, with all the massive theoretical armory its exponents had marshaled, failed to make any real headway prior to the Six-Day War of 1967, the defeat of the armies of Egypt, Syria, and Jordan in that war made its appeal even more negligible. This was not only, or even mainly, because these Arab regimes failed dismally in their military performances.

The heaviest blow to the pan-Arab doctrine came, ironically enough, from the Palestinians. Politically disillusioned by twenty years of Arab inability to do anything to retrieve Palestine for them, socially rejected by their Arab brethren and Muslim coreligionists, the Palestinians were bound to be the Havliceks of the contemporary Arab world.

The lot of the Palestinians during the twenty years between the adoption of the Palestine partition plan by the United Nations in 1947 and the Six-Day War of June 1967 had indeed been thoroughly unhappy. Whether they lived in refugee camps in Jordan, the Gaza Strip, Lebanon, or Syria; in the cities and towns of various Arab countries; as laborers, teachers, or technicians in the sheikhdoms and emirates of the Persian Gulf; or in their villages and towns in Israel, the Palestinians felt slighted, humiliated, bandied about, and discriminated against.

To cap it all, the defeat of the Arab armies in the Six-Day War brought in its wake what amounted to a second Palestinian dispersion. This would prove to be the last straw. The last remaining spark of pan-Arab zeal and love in the hearts of the Palestinians was extinguished.

Thus was born what was to be known as "the Palestinian revolution." Slogans such as "Palestine for the Palestinians," "an end to custodianship," "time to take matters into our own hands," "no settlement without the Palestinians' consent," and others in the same vein began to be voiced by Palestinian activists.

At first, when Palestinian guerrilla attacks and acts of violence constituted virtually the only Arab war effort and were thus generally hailed as having saved Arab honor, these slogans were tolerated. But as time passed, the Palestinian revolution—though with scant achievements on the battlefield—was beginning actually to be presented as an alternative to the

Nasserist revolution, which certain radical Arab circles suddenly found wanting in both its social and its Arab content.

This would soon provoke a sharp reaction from the assaulted camp. And from these arguments and counterarguments much can be learned about the current state of the doctrine of pan-Arabism.

The steady growth in influence and popularity of the Palestinian organizations after 1967 was not only a standing rebuke to Abdel Nasser and other Arab rulers for their failure to "solve" the Palestine problem; it also seemed to constitute a partial refutation of the late Egyptian leader's hard-core Arab nationalist orientation. Indeed, by the beginning of 1970, a number of Egyptian writers and spokesmen of the regime found themselves involved in a growing "dialogue" with the Palestinians and with advocates of the Palestinian revolution.

One of these, Jalal al-Sayyid, sharply and openly criticized the proliferation of slogans among the Palestinian guerrilla organizations and accused them of resorting to "ideological auctioneering." Al-Sayyid argued that these slogans, far from promoting the cause of the Palestinian revolution, were only spreading confusion and leading to inconsequential debates and controversies about issues that were "as remote from reality as they could possibly be."

As examples, the writer cited the case of those guerrilla organizations that "compete in proclaiming their Leftism"; he deplored the fact that one organization had announced its adherence to Marxism-Leninism and was making a lot of noise about such phenomena as the class struggle, revolutionary cadres, and the Arab petite bourgeoisie; and he pointed out sorrowfully that the Palestinian revolution was now split into left and right.

All this al-Sayyid considered quite irrelevant. The present state of the Palestinian revolution, he wrote, was one of a struggle for national liberation, a task which calls for the mobilization of all national elements. "The issue today," he asserted, "is not one between Left and Right; it is a national issue first and foremost."

The most serious charge, however, which the orthodox Arab revolutionaries (which is what the Nasserists had become by then) leveled against the Palestinian radicals was their declared support of "particularism," which meant the continuation of the present deplorable state of fragmentation in the Arab world. This "particularist trend," it was said, was evident from the Palestinians' advocating a "Palestine for the Palestinians" rather than joining forces with the pan-Arab nationalists, who believe that a united Arab world is the appropriate answer not only to Zionist and imperialist aggression but also to the Arabs' plight in the social and economic spheres.[24]

There is no denying that the emergence of a distinctive Palestinian personality or identity constituted a setback to the pan-Arab cause. This is because what the Palestinians and their ideological allies in the Arab world were actually saying was that it is political ideology and class affiliation, rather than "national" belonging, that really matter. To ask (as Nasser and the pan-Arabs generally did) that one cease drawing distinctions between rich and poor, right wing and left wing, and make "Arabism" the sole criterion for admittance into the fold, appeared to these critics to spell total ideological bankruptcy.

It was this ideological challenge, posed somewhat unexpectedly by the Palestinian movement, that upset the pan-Arabs most—and the response was quick in coming. One of the most detailed and best-reasoned ideological replies came from the pen of Dr. 'Ismat Seif el-Dawla, a well-known Egyptian political scientist and author of several books on Arab nationalism and Arab socialism. An ardent socialist and pan-Arab, Seif el-Dawla tried to demonstrate that there was no contradiction or collision between these two major "isms," nor could there be one.

As he put it: "It is now universally agreed that there exists a social entity with distinguishing characteristics called 'the nation'. Today we want to discover this truth from a new starting point—that of Socialism. We want to start off as Socialists and then to see whether that would lead us on the road of becoming nationalists." The reason why he decided to take such a "detour," he explains, "is that the crisis of the Arabs' future as we now see it is that the Arab Socialist forces are divided into nationalists and non-nationalists, whereas the unity of all Socialist forces throughout the Arab homeland is a national imperative, and Palestinian resistance as we know it stands no chance of success unless it becomes a socialist-nationalist resistance."

The road along which Seif el-Dawla leads his reader from Socialism to nationalism is simple enough. Socialists, he writes, are concerned with creating a better life. But a better life for whom? "For the society to which we belong," he answers and promptly proceeds to show that the society to which one belongs is "the nation." It is not the state, as it would seem at first glance. To be sure, a state has a territory, a people, a government, a capacity to progress and prosper. Yet all this does not mean that it is the state that ought to be considered the society to which one belongs.

"We have to search for the objective reality of this society in order to see whether the State is in keeping with that reality," Seif el-Dawla explains. "If the State is at variance with that objective reality, then the artificial State must be done away with and replaced by the State that conforms to the reality of the society to which we belong."

This, of course, is only a convoluted, almost Germanic, way of saying that it is the "nation" that makes the state and not the other way around. It is a superb specimen of the kind of jargon used by the theoreticians of Eastern and Central European pan-movements of the past century.

Be that as it may, having thus argued his way into a perfect union between socialism and ethnic nationalism, Seif el-Dawla now finds no difficulty whatever in formulating his final conclusions. "The Arab nation," he asserts, "is therefore the society to which we belong, and nationalism is the progressive link that ties us all together.... Nationalism is the guarantee for the victory of Socialism."

Having thus expounded his ideological frame of reference, Seif el-Dawla then turns to the Palestinian resistance movement and its relation to the pan-Arab movement. All that has been said so far in support of the proposition that the liberation of Palestine is the responsibility of the people of Palestine, he writes, is that the adoption by the Arab states of the Palestine cause to the exclusion of its own protagonists—the Palestinians—throughout the 1950s and 1960s had led to the loss of the land. The Palestinians also argue that for twenty years they have been scattered, lost, without a homeland, and without an identity of their own, and that they are now fighting to liberate Palestine in order to acquire a country and an identity card.

All this is true, Seif el-Dawla concedes. "But is it not obvious," he asks, "that Arab particularism was itself to blame for the Palestinians' lack of a country and of an identity card? After all, it was this particularism that viewed the Palestinians as foreigners and strangers and stood in the way of the united Arab state in which they would have found both a country and an identity."[25]

The evil, then, lies in Arab particularism—that same trend that the Palestinian movement was said to be promoting by its call for "Palestine for the Palestinians." And the remedy, the only realistic solution, lies in the creation of one, big, united Arab state, which presumably would materialize only under the banner of Nasser's Arab socialism. According to Seif el-Dawla, indeed, a separate Palestinian entity—just like a separate Syrian, Egyptian, Jordanian, or Iraqi entity—is a myth, to be tolerated only because the Palestinians were now in the throes of a life or death struggle against Zionism.

As Muta' Safadi, another pan-Arab thinker writing on the same subject, put it, the Palestinian revolution must be viewed within the framework of a new, all-Arab mass revolution. This approach, he added, would serve the Arab cause far better than "the mere invention of a name for the Palestinians, a people that has always been a geographical entity possessing no distinctive characteristics and no independent existence—a people that is totally inseparable from its Arabism."[26]

Like Seif el-Dawla's assertions, Safadi's argument is strongly reminiscent of the terminology of the tribal nationalisms and pan-movements of nineteenth-century Europe. What this seems to show is that, despite the many voices occasionally heard in the Arab world criticizing "racial nationalism" and calling for a tolerant, liberal, and pluralistic version of nationalism, it is these European concepts that have triumphed in the Arab world.

As to the Palestinian revolution, it is difficult to predict with any measure of confidence whether it will have a lasting negative impact on pan-Arabism, or whether the repeated failure of all experiments in Arab unity so far will deter the pan-Arabs from continuing in their chosen path.

Whatever name they choose to give it, then, the fact remains that the nationalist ideology which the successor states of the Ottoman Empire in the Middle East have chosen to adopt belongs overwhelmingly to the ethnic-tribal variety. This has made the continuous existence of the amalgam of races, cultures, religions, and languages that one usually identifies with the Middle East all but impossible.

One can only agree with Bernard Lewis's verdict. "The introduction of the secular heresy of nationalism, of collective self-worship," he once wrote, "is the best-founded and least-mentioned of the many grievances of the Middle East against the West. It is a melancholy task to chronicle the successive phases of contact, infection, inflammation and crisis."[27]

East, West, and Other Vanities

The Russian is a delightful person till he tucks in his shirt. As an Oriental he is charming. It is only when he insists on being treated as the most easterly of western peoples instead of the most westerly of easterns that he becomes a racial anomaly extremely difficult to handle.

Rudyard Kipling

"We live in a villa in the middle of a jungle," lamented Ehud Barak, then Israel's foreign minister, in February of 1996. He was speaking to a gathering of American Jewish notables in New York, trying to explain to them Israel's woeful quandary of being situated in the heart of the Arab-Muslim world. Barak's complaint came only a few days after he jeered, again somewhere in the United States, that for him it was not such a big deal to see his prime minister Shimon Peres's vision of an overall peace settlement fulfilled, since he wasn't eager to see twenty or so "*jallabiyya*-clad" Arab rulers sign peace treaties with Israel.

Such pronouncements—made by a somewhat bashful, recently retired Israeli officer with the rank of major-general, speaking to a gathering of dutiful Jewish leaders abroad—came as no surprise (although in the capacity of foreign minister, Barak should have been a bit more careful).

However, sentiments not dissimilar to those expressed by Barak—who in the meantime won the chairmanship of the Labor party and became its candidate for the premiership in the 2000 elections—are aired freely in public and in various ways even taught to small schoolchildren. They are, indeed, part and parcel of the self-image of the average Israeli and of Israel as an integral part of "the West" accidentally and unhappily situated in "the East."

In this concluding chapter, it is argued that to try to "place" Israel or its culture as between East and West is a pretty futile endeavor. Israel is too much a tapestry of cultures, colors, and ethnicities to be defined in either/ or terms of any traits, be they cultural, ethnic, or religious.

Culture and Person

In his autobiographical work, *When Memory Comes*, Saul Friedlander relates how he felt in Germany in late 1962, where he was to meet the former Grand Admiral Doenitz in connection with a book Friedlander was writing. "I would not call it anxiety or panic, but a strange feeling of desolation," he writes. "This Autobahn was shutting me up in Germany forever: on every hand were Germans, nothing but Germans. I felt caught in a blind trap. In the ponderous cars going past me, the faces seemed to be suddenly bloated with rancid, reddish grease; on the shoulders of the roads the signs—in German—represented so many cold injunctions, issued by an all-powerful, destructive, police-state bureaucracy."[1]

Since then, Friedlander has returned to Germany often. He relates:

> More than once, the same sensation has come over me, though less intense and more complex. On the one hand—danger, a trap, desolation—but at the same time a feeling of familiarity, pleasant familiarity: the language, the streets, the songs, the waters of the Rhine that I had seen only once . . . the hillsides covered with grapevines, the old castles and the baroque churches—everything was thoroughly familiar to me. And so, at the archives in Bonn, Koblenz, or Freiburg, I would read my records: . . . but when night came, how many times have I hesitated between the attractions of a *Weinstube* as familiar as everything else and the imperative need to pack my suitcases immediately, flee instantly, go back across the border at all costs.[2]

This strong, piercing ambivalence toward Europe in general and Germany in particular is natural and quite understandable. It is typical of the sentiments of many Israeli intellectuals with roots in the culture and civilization of the West. Friedlander, however, manages to be subtle and circumspect about his feelings. Yoram Bronowski, the prolific Israeli literary critic, editor, and translator, belongs to the same generation as Friedlander, though he hails from what can be described as the periphery of Western Europe.

Paradoxically (though not in the least surprisingly), however, Bronowski's attitude to "the West" is far less ambiguous and seems to have not the slightest trace of ambivalence. In a series of two articles written during a visit to Europe, he practically raves about what he calls "this inexhaustible wonder-place" and testifies that a short visit there made him spend "long days of intensive reflection concerning the sources of this miracle, its marvelous steadfastness through all the hardships of time—and above all and most importantly from my, or our, point of view: the relationship between us and the (mutual?) unending bond between us."[3]

The title Bronowski chose for his articles, "Barbarians in the Garden," is typical, and was meant to be evocative. In Israel, he laments, "Europe has ceased to exist as a living presence, and the anti-European complexes which are typical of Israeli culture since its beginnings are again dominant." These "complexes," he adds, have taken different and variegated forms during the past one hundred years, since the beginning of Zionist settlement. What he finds paradoxical, however, is that "while 'the East' constantly looks up to 'Europe,' these European Jews—who are generally loyal sons of Western culture—had aspired to this very East!"

However, Bronowski seems to find some consolation in the fact that, after all is said and done, "the aspiration toward the East is distinctly *European* in character—so that even in this aspiration genuine Europeans like [Eliezer] Ben-Yehuda were loyal heirs to their culture." The trouble, however, was that "many of those who came after them failed to see the subtlety of this orientation—and thus a fashion, indeed, rather more than just a fashion, was created of a straightforward and open repudiation of Europe."

At the root of the East-West opposition, at least as far as Israeli society is concerned, is a certain approach to the subject of culture. The term "culture" had a hectic and rather checkered history. Humpty Dumpty tells Alice in the course of a heated argument in Lewis Carroll's *Through the Looking Glass*, "When I use a word, it means just what I choose it to mean, neither more or less." In reply to her protestations about the way he seemed to overwork words, he explained with no apparent hesitation: "When I make a word do a lot of work like that I always pay it extra. . . . Ah you should see 'em come round me of a Saturday night—for to get their wages, you know."

When one considers the way certain words are used in daily life in Israel, one cannot help being reminded of Humpty Dumpty's remarkable literary habits and predilections. The word "culture" is a case in point. A statistical survey concerning the frequency with which this unlucky word is used in Israeli public and private pronouncements undoubtedly would yield highly interesting results.

Yet the word "culture," besides being relentlessly overworked, must be one of the most frequently misused in the language. To cite a few examples: "culture" is used freely and variously to denote a sound *education*, a higher degree of *civilization*, good *manners*, and so on. Equally often, the term is appended to specific concepts and notions loaded with value judgments, such as culture *lag*, *higher* and *lower* cultures, cultural *standard*, and *lack* of culture.

In fairness it must be pointed out that the meaning of the word "culture" was never, until relatively recently, unanimously agreed upon even by the professionals. But for the last nearly half-century, a fairly generally accepted definition of the term has existed. According to this definition, culture, generally speaking, is the sum total of all the ways of life that have been evolved by human beings in society. A *particular culture,* according to the same interpretation, is the total shared way of life of a people or a group of peoples; it comprises their modes of thinking, acting, and feeling, as expressed, for instance, in religion, law, language, art, and custom, as well as in material products such as houses, clothes, and tools.

Anthropologist George Kneller, of the University of California, sums it up in these words:

> Our culture is the way we eat and sleep, the way we wash and dress and go to work. It is the actions we perform at home and on the job. It is the language we speak and the values and beliefs we hold. It is the goods and services we buy and the way we buy them. It is the way we meet friends and strangers, the way we control our children and the way they respond. It is the transportation we use and the entertainment we enjoy.[4]

It is essential to remember, moreover, that a culture in this sense is more than just the sum total of its various parts. It is, in addition, the way in which those parts are organized to form a whole. To quote Kneller again: "Just as several buildings can be made of the same materials yet differ in structure and function, so various cultures may share some similar elements yet each may organize them uniquely. Thus, to understand a culture we must grasp not only its parts but also the structure that holds them."[5]

A final important point to keep in mind in discussing "culture" is that the degree of unity achieved by any culture determines the degree of its integration. Every culture contains a multitude of different patterns of behavior, and it is "integrated" to the extent that these patterns of behavior are interrelated. The more integrated a culture, the more these patterns reinforce one another; the less integrated the culture, the more they function independently.

In an integrated culture, resistance to change is far greater—and in cases where the change is enforced, the culture may simply collapse. The case of a certain North Australian tribe is often quoted. The men of this tribe used stone implements to kill animals and cut firewood. The ax was their treasured possession and the symbol of their masculinity. Well-meaning missionaries, however, got it into their heads to introduce steel choppers and give them to both men and women of the tribe. This act of kindness resulted in the ruin of the tribe: The pattern of gender and age relationships was irrevocably upset, destroying the reasons that led children and adolescents to obey their male elders. By making it possible for women, too, to kill animals and to cut firewood, the men lost their self-respect.

As already indicated, it took decades for this final formulation of the concept of culture to take root in modern European languages. A. L. Kroeber and Clyde Kluckhohn rightly express surprise at the fact that, though the word "culture" was defined in its modern anthropological context as far back as 1871 (in which Tylor's pioneering work *Primitive Culture* was published), the first English dictionary ever to recognize this meaning of the term was *Webster's New International Dictionary*, published in 1929.[6]

Be that as it may, the history of the word "culture" presents several highly interesting questions: Why did the concept of "culture" (*Kultur*) evolve and play such an important part in the German intellectual setting? Why has the same concept had such difficulty breaking through public consciousness in countries like England and France? And why has it lately become so popular in the United States?

One explanation for these three phenomena may be found in the proposition (implied but never fully formulated by Kroeber and Kluckhohn) that the less homogeneous a nation's particular culture, the more inclined that nation tends to be to accept the sociological definition of the term "culture." In the nineteenth century, for instance, German culture was less internally homogeneous—at least less centralized in a dominant capital city—than French or English culture in the same period. To be sure, colonial powers France and England were aware of other ways of life; yet—perhaps precisely because of their imperialistic status—they were characteristically indifferent to the significance of cultural differences and tended to resist them. Similarly, the heterogeneous cultural backgrounds of Americans have helped to create a climate of opinion in the United States singularly congenial to the anthropological approach to culture.

But there is another, perhaps more relevant, explanation for the prevalence in nineteenth-century Germany (and later in Russia) of the idea of culture as a complex of qualities, achievements, and behavior patterns which are unique, nontransferable, and local or national in origin and significance. As Alfred G. Meyer, the noted philosopher, points out: "The stress [on the part of German thinkers of the period] on such unique culture patterns, as against the economic, political, scientific or philosophical achievements of Western civilization, can be regarded as an attempt to compensate for a deep-seated feeling of inferiority on the part of German intellectuals once they had come into contact with the advanced nations."

Similarly, Russian cultural nationalism can be traced easily to such a feeling of inferiority. "Quite fittingly, Russian cultural nationalism developed in the measure as Russian contacts with the West intensified. These *kultur* theories were a typical ideological expression (though by no means the only one) of the rise of backward societies against the encroachment of the West on their traditional culture. *They consist in asserting the reality of something which is just about to be destroyed.*"[7]

But this is only one of many cases in which the concept of culture can serve to illuminate historical and intellectual problems. In the social sciences, it is proving increasingly useful—even paramount. In fact, it is now generally regarded as the foundation stone of the social sciences and is being put to use with great advantage in such problematic spheres as education, social work, and psychotherapy. In the words of Kroeber and Kluckhohn, "Few intellectuals will challenge the statement that the idea of culture, in the technical anthropological sense, is one of the key notions of contemporary American thought. In explanatory importance and in generality of application it is comparable to such categories as gravity in physics, disease in medicine, evolution in biology."[8]

It is, indeed, very difficult to dispute this contention. Words, in themselves—as opposed to "deeds"—may not signify much; but one cannot help feeling that in this particular case of "culture," there is much, very much, in a name. A little less confusion and muddled thinking in this sphere can do a great deal of good in countries like the United States and, probably even more, Israel, where the lack of a homogeneous cultural background tends to lead to much unnecessary trouble and headache.

Levantinism Redefined

Nowhere are these difficulties and confusions more apparent than they are in the use that Israelis and others habitually make of the terms "Levantine" and "Levantinism." In the spring of 1961, for instance, commenting on the Israeli scene shortly after the outbreak of the notorious Lavon affair, *The Manchester Guardian*, a widely respected British daily, accused Israel's then prime minister, David Ben-Gurion, of plunging the country into "Levantinism." Yet the late Israeli leader himself, addressing a mass election rally in Jerusalem not long afterward, declared solemnly that his paramount aim was to prevent "the Levantinization of Israel!"

What then is this fearful monster of whose danger everybody seems so acutely aware? The fact is that, like "culture," "Levantinism" is a notoriously elusive concept, and it is scarcely possible to find three serious persons who agree on a single, clear definition of the term. One often hears people exclaim "Levantine!" when encountering someone who comes from certain parts of the world behaving with what seems to them excessive politeness or "exaggerated" consideration and charity. The same people would no doubt have called this self-same man "Levantine" had he behaved in a manner that seemed to them too direct or aggressive. One hears people for whom questions of truth and falsehood, right and wrong, are strictly relative matters describe as "Levantine" any person hailing from the Orient who they catch telling the most innocuous of lies. Again, a non-European who dresses too correctly usually does so simply because he is a "Levantine," whereas another who chooses to dress rather carelessly does it for the self-same reason.

But before making any attempt to answer the question as to who, precisely, a Levantine is, we must dispose of one minor difficulty. Geographically, a Levantine is one who is born and bred in the Levant, a term which my dictionary defines as "the countries of the East, specifically the eastern part of the Mediterranean, with its islands and the countries adjoining." On that score, of course, many, many of us are Levantines—and Israel is and has always been a Levantine country.

But besides being a geographical concept, Levantinism is also—and more meaningfully—a cultural one. It is here that the real confusion starts. According to our definition, culturally speaking, one can come from the Levant and yet be the opposite of a "Levantine"; one can hail from Europe (and not only from Eastern Europe) and be the epitome of Levantinism. Again, you may believe you are checking the danger of Levantinism yet shout your way into thorough Levantinization. Finally, and perhaps most distressingly, you can be a Levantine and happily oblivious to it—and, at the same time, never stop warning others of the supposed perils of Levantinism.

Now the best definition one can find of Levantinism in this latter sense is that to be a Levantine is to live in two worlds or more at once without firmly belonging to any. It is to be able to go through the external forms that indicate the possession of a certain culture without actually possessing it. According to this definition, "Levantinism" denotes a condition in which one no longer has a standard of values of one's own—a state of mind which reveals itself in lostness, pretentiousness, cynicism, and despair. Or, to quote Arthur Koestler's dictum, "Two half truths do not make a truth, and two half-cultures do not make a culture."

Whatever may be said about this definition of Levantinism, one must recognize that it has the distinct advantage of being supported by the latest findings of anthropology, defined as "the science of culture." We have seen how a person's culture tends to pervade every aspect of his or her activities and behavior—how culture shapes us intellectually, emotionally and even physically. To quote an eminent American anthropologist, culture "conditions such physical traits as gestures, facial expressions and ways of walking, sitting, eating and sleeping. . . . [It] prescribes what emotions may be expressed and by whom, where and how. . . . All people laugh and cry, but different cultures find different modes of expression for the subtler shades of anger, grief, joy, shame and other feelings."[9]

If we accept a definition of Levantinism based on these findings and stipulations, it becomes obvious that no group, community, or nation can claim a monopoly on it. This is as true of Israel as it is of any other country. Israel, in fact, must be literally seething with "Levantines." For it is by no means self-evident that an Israeli hailing from Egypt, the Levant, Iraq, or North Africa should find it more difficult to meet the challenge of Westernization than one who comes from an Eastern European country and tries to discard his or her particular cultural identity and background.

It is quite easy, in fact, to notice how—driven by the same powerful urge to adopt a way of life they were taught to consider "superior"—these two types of Israeli usually hasten to disown and even denigrate their own "inferior" cultures. Both go through the same sort of experience: feeling lost between two worlds, neither of which is quite their own; pretending not to belong where they actually do belong; becoming cynical, as they both lose their own respective sets of values and standards; and, finally, despairing of ever really possessing the new ways of life or restoring their old ones.

For to a very great extent, individuals are the prisoners of the culture of their particular group and on which they are brought up. The methods used in rearing and training a child make his or her personality structure correspond to that culture's major values and institutions. This applies even to such seemingly insignificant things as the way in which a baby is nursed, dressed, fed, or put to sleep—all of which tend to condition a person to behaving according to the values of his or her group and culture. According to this view, too, it is the early years that form the pattern of the mature personality; hence similar childhoods will produce similar adult personalities. Finally, since culture determines what parents teach their children and in what ways, we may expect a given culture to produce a distinct personality type.

This does not, however, mean that a culture always and invariably shapes its members in a certain unchangeable way. A rapidly changing culture, for instance, needs and creates a mobile and dynamic personality, even though it may also produce a number of persons who are too disorganized to be able to keep pace with the tempo of change and who finally break down under the accumulating pressures.

There are, of course, always a few who seem to be endowed with such strength of character that they can withstand these pressures successfully. One often hears, for example, of people who proclaim, with a good deal of self-satisfaction, that, thank goodness, they still see themselves as "Europeans." (In the present state of affairs, few Israelis would dream of boasting of being true "Asians" or "Africans"!) This, of course, is all very well as long as it lasts. But by the very nature of things, it can hardly last very long.

Here it may be useful to quote a passage from Arnold Toynbee's *A Study of History.* The passage occurs in the section dealing with the "Phanariots, Oazanlis and Levantines," and reads in part:

> In the earlier centuries of their dominance the Osmanlis, knowing the people of Western Christendom—the Franks, as they called them— only through their Levantine representatives, assumed that Western Europe was wholly inhabited by such "lesser breeds without the law." A wider experience led them to revise their opinions, and the Omanlis came to draw a sharp distinction between the "fresh-water Franks" and their "salt-water" namesakes. The "fresh-water Franks" were those who had been born and bred in Turkey and had responded by developing the Levantine character. The "salt-water Franks" were those who had been born and bred at home in Frankland and had come out to Turkey as adults with their characters already formed. The Turks were puzzled to find that the great psychological gulf which divided them from the "fresh-water Franks" who had always lived in their midst did not intervene when they had to deal with the Franks from beyond the seas.[10]

It is not difficult to see why this was so. The reason why the Turk and the "salt-water Frank" could easily understand one another, while finding the native-born Franks (who were geographically their neighbors and compatriots) psychologically alien to them, was that there existed "a broad similarity between their respective social backgrounds." Both, Toynbee explains, had grown up in environments in which they were the masters of their own houses. Again, both the Turks and the European-born Franks found difficulty in understanding the "fresh-water Franks" or taking them seriously, because these latter had a social background that was equally foreign to both groups. The fresh-water Frank "was not a son of the house but a child of the ghetto; and this penalised existence had developed in him ethics from which the Frank brought up in Frankland and the Turk brought up in Turkey had both remained free."[11]

One need hardly point out that, in the sense of the term that we have adopted, neither the European-born Frank nor the native Turk could be considered a "Levantine."

Israel—"Between East and West"?

In Israel, the subject of East and West, and the alleged opposition between them, became relevant—and rather fashionable—as far back as in the early 1950s, in the context of the so-called absorption of the mass of Oriental and Middle Eastern immigrants arriving in Israel, a state generally described as "Western." Over the years, some Israelis came to view the subject also in the wider context of Israel's place in the Middle East and the roots of the Arab-Israeli conflict. Here I will allow myself to cite a personal experience I had which is of some relevance to the subject. Sometime in November 1979, I received a call from Yehoshua Knaz to take part in a symposium on the subject "Israel between East and West: The Available and the Desirable." The text of the symposium was to be printed in one of the first issues of a new literary periodical coedited by Knaz and Yoram Bronowski. The participants were Saul Friedlander, Bronowski, and me.

I overcame my natural disinclination to take part in such discussions and duly arrived at the appointed place in North Tel Aviv on one rainy day in December. Bronowski, as moderator, opened with a few remarks, the gist of which was that there were in Israel two schools of thought on the subject at hand. The first school maintained that the question of Israel and its place between East and West was "the central concern of Israeli culture," while the second claimed the whole subject was artificially imposed on Israel and was not really relevant.

He himself, he declared, belonged to the former school, adding that, in his opinion, discussion of this subject could serve as a fitting framework for the clarification of many problems that would not, at first glance, seem very relevant. He then proposed that each of the three participants open with a few words about what, for him, was East and what was West. The question as to where Israel belongs culturally, he added, would be clarified in the course of the symposium. But it was essential that we first try to explain what the terms "East" and "West" meant for each of us.

Friedlander opened by saying that he saw the question as one of "subjective feeling" rather than "abstract definitions." He went on to say that while the West for him was a cultural concept, a cultural dimension, a cultural background which goes in "concentric circles"—with their center somewhere in Central Europe, expanding concentrically into a wider circle embracing French culture, and finally including the still-wider circle that takes in British and American culture—the East "poses a problem for me." He simply didn't know it, he said. "For me, it is something exotic in the best sense of the term—but also somewhat repulsive in a negative sense." Nevertheless, he was in a position to say, in an attempt at explication, that "what I know here [in Israel] is not the East; it's some mixture—and on this we will of course dwell."

At this point, Bronowski volunteered: "In other words, your attitude to the East is an example of the classical Western attitude, i.e., repulsion at one extreme, attraction at the other." Friedlander denied he spoke of "attraction"; his problem, he said, was *What was the East?* Is it perhaps some Western image of the East?

Taking my turn, I explained at some length that the terms "East" and "West," or rather the opposition habitually made between them, can be made on a number of different planes. There is, first, the geographical level, on which no one has doubts about the legitimacy of the distinction. There is also the political/diplomatic one, between the Eastern Bloc and the Western Bloc. A third sphere of distinction can be said to be the technological one—the West being technologically far more advanced than the East.

All these three "oppositions," I maintained, can be accepted with some measure of accuracy. However, I added, I had a problem with the *cultural* opposition as between East and West. To start with, I could not accept the habitual identification here between geography and culture—namely, the implicit assertion that all the lands situated in the geographical sphere called "the East" belong to something called "Eastern culture," and vice versa.

I was aware, I said, that there is a distinctive Middle Eastern culture: there is also a culture that one can identify as "Mediterranean." Where do these two cultures—and especially the latter—really belong? Take Greece, for instance, or Spain, or Italy: Can one say with conviction that their cultures are part of Western culture while the cultures, say, of Lebanon, Egypt, and Tunisia are Eastern? And what about East and Southeast Asia? And, for that matter, Latin America?

The opposition—the dichotomy rather—often drawn between East and West, and the subsequent division of the world culturally between these two vague concepts, is thus arbitrary and cannot be taken seriously, I said. I concluded my opening remarks by saying that even if such opposition does exist, and even if it is valid when applied to certain parts of the world, as far as Israel is concerned, the distinction is neither valid nor relevant.

At this point, a word of explanation is in order. For two or three weeks before I went to the symposium, I gave the subject a good deal of thought, and, considering the matter from all its Israeli aspects (which, after all, was what the symposium was all about), I decided that it would be more than useless to enter into a discussion of what orientation Israeli culture ought to take—Western or Eastern.

Moreover, knowing approximately what direction the symposium would take—considering the views of the other participants—I decided I was not going to be drawn into a futile dissertation on the supposed merits and demerits of this or that Eastern or Western culture trait. I also genuinely believed—and continue to believe—that any sort of interference, on the part of the state or any other party, to "help" in choosing the "desirable" way, as between East and West, would ultimately and inevitably smack of regimentation and cultural coercion. And I am strongly opposed to these two forces, no matter which section of the population would, in the end, prove to be the likely victim.

Predictably, my clear-cut dismissal of the whole alleged East-West dichotomy (and especially my firm denial of its relevance to the Israeli cultural scene) was something of a shock to my two interlocutors.

Bronowski was the more insistent of the two. Why, he wondered, didn't I see the distinction? And anyway, where in the world did I belong? Could it possibly be that I had no "problems" deciding whether I belonged to the East or to the West? He himself, Bronowski said, like Friedlander, had his own "autobiographical definition" of the West. He, too, was born and grew up "in this framework of Western culture." Friedlander, it is true, was born in Prague and moved to Paris; but although this was not exactly what happened to him (Bronowski), the account nevertheless "covers the same ground."

Needless to say, Bronowski added, he had his problems with the East. One of the important distinctions between the East and the West, however, was that the latter "took the trouble of defining itself throughout the centuries, each time anew—and there in fact its greatness resides." These repeated attempts at self-definition in the end produced a fairly clear cultural identity.

In the course of this part of his contribution, Bronowski admitted that for him, too, things were not too clear where a definition of "the East" was concerned. While the East, he explained, was for him "a very clear and distinct world," he was aware "that it was in fact a Western world." Somewhere in ancient Greece, the East somehow "integrated" with the West, and Greece accordingly became richer and greater. "It is here," he concluded, "that my East starts, an East that is part of my West."

Friedlander could not understand, either, how it was possible for me "not to feel the difference." And in an attempt "to compel" me to speak of this, he volunteered to tell us how *he* saw the difference. He chose music, and after telling us how he felt about Western music and his reactions to Eastern music, he again turned to me and declared that he was at a loss to see why was I "trying to underestimate the difference." Why did I insist that I did not see "the dividing line," when in reality every single one of us was living these differences, was fully aware of them, and often talked and expressed opinions about them?

In reply, I pleaded that the subject with which we were dealing was not abstract or theoretical. In the first place, the symposium dealt primarily with Israel. Second, we were talking about the years 1979–1980—and for me, the subject of East and West in the cultural sphere is simply no longer relevant to the Israel of our day. Take music, for instance: How can one speak of Western versus Eastern music in Israel when the last word in Western music since the early 1960s has been such indistinguishable mixtures as those presented by the Beatles, the Rolling Stones, Abba, Pink Floyd, and dozens of others whose works cannot by any stretch of the imagination be said to have an affinity with the music Friedlander was talking about?

Inevitably, things came to a head in due course. In reply to my statement that I do not, or at least do not wish to, identify certain human beings with the West and certain others with the East, I was confronted with the assertion that these people nevertheless live within certain cultural contexts and there was no way of ignoring that fact. Certainly, I agreed, but insofar as we were talking about Israeli culture—about what was available and what was desirable for Israel culturally—I was all for letting people be what they are, live in the way they choose. The desire to make a choice for Israel (what was "desirable," etc.) and to act accordingly was for me something dangerously bordering on cultural Zhdanovism.

At this point, Friedlander spoke about the desirability of having and deciding upon "a blueprint," an ideal type, according to which we may want to see Israeli society and Israeli culture develop. When I responded that I had already implied I was against making any such decision, Bronowski asked whether, then, I was in favor of allowing things just "to flow, to develop." I said yes, provided we accept people and their various cultural traits as they are. "But to accept also implies identification of the traits!" countered Bronowski. To which I replied, in brief: "No, we don't even have to identify the traits! What for? What's the use of engaging in such ungainly questions as to what the components of Western culture are and what those of Eastern culture might be—and probably even trying to make some alleged synthesis between the two sets?"

Bronowski thought these were "heretical opinions which are very hard to hear," because, he said, "the aspiration of every individual and every people is to identify and to find a framework for individual or national identity." It was, he explained, "some sort of inner urge, a cultural force." To this, my answer was simple enough: It would, I said, perhaps have been more appropriate for us first to try to define "Israel" before defining "East" and "West." Bronowski spoke of individuals and nations aspiring to identify and so on, I pointed out. How many cultural groups did Israeli society consist of? How can one possibly speak of Israel in this particular context as if it were all of a piece?

I have no intention of giving here a full summary of the proceedings of that symposium (which, for reasons best known to the editors, never saw the light of day). The general impression, however, that I got from it was that here were three Israelis sincerely and earnestly trying to make some sort of sense of the cultural scene in Israel more than thirty years after its establishment—and also the direction that cultural developments were taking. All three, I must admit, were, to a lesser or larger degree, fairly steeped in the West's literary, artistic, and even material culture. The reason why we could not agree among ourselves was simple and quite understandable—and I hasten to add that it seems to me to have nothing whatsoever to do with our respective cultural-geographical origins, widely different as these might have been.

What now strikes me as significant, in fact, is not that we failed to agree; that often happens in such discussions. It is that we could not establish a solid and convincing ground for a meaningful controversy—which, after all, must have been the whole point of the symposium and certainly made the monthly's editors choose the participants in the way they did. Choosing me to represent "the other side" seems to me to have been a mistake of judgment. Both Bronowski and Friedlander can be said to be enamored of Western culture—for what it is—only in the way *outsiders* to that culture can be.

I am not saying that Bronowski, Friedlander, and other advocates of a Western-oriented Israel are strangers to the West and its cultural trappings. None of us is. But in pondering the phenomenon, I cannot help being reminded—for one—of those Indian writers and intellectuals who today are said to be the only real die-hard fighters for the purity of the English language. Another (more extreme and admittedly rather far-out) example is the fellow in Koestler's *Darkness at Noon* who, while jailed in a Soviet prison, was in the habit of drawing maps of the USSR, the land of socialism, where he so desperately yearned to be!

What that symposium needed, in fact, was someone who had it in him to stand up to the Western cultural chauvinism of my two interlocutors—an Eastern counterpart and opposite number. That, in all honesty, I could not do—or be.

The Myth of "Orientalization"

For some time now, and especially since the late 1970s, a dominant theme in political-intellectual discourse in Israel has been the so-called Orientalization of Israel and its institutions by the growing impact of the "Oriental vote." The dangers to Israel and its future inherent in such a process is generally depicted as being little short of mortal by what seems to be an alarmed and panic-stricken, overwhelmingly European and Western-oriented politico-cultural elite. These fears and premonitions are expressed openly, sometimes even by visitors from abroad duly briefed by their hosts about the perilous demographic changes in Israel and their possible repercussions.

In this running debate, a good deal of sociological jargon has been used. Erik Cohen, a Hebrew University sociologist, has written about this subject with considerable feeling. In a paper entitled "Ethnicity and Legitimation in Present-Day Israel," Cohen takes clear stands and makes a number of useful and appropriate generalizations; some of them are fairly well supported by the evidence while others are controversial and arbitrary.

Cohen writes, for instance, that Oriental youths "refused to accept the premise that, in order to become Israelis, they ought to become Westernized." This is a fair enough assessment provided one agrees that what these youths had been asked to do was indeed to become Westernized and not just to adapt to the overwhelmingly Eastern European political culture of the Ashkenazi-dominated state and Histadrut machines. What is unacceptable, however, is Cohen's subsequent remark that these Oriental youths' refusal to accept Westernization as a precondition for becoming full-fledged Israelis amounted to their "rejection of the universalist component of the Zionist ideology."[12]

The assumption on which this curious statement is based is far from being as self-evident as Cohen makes it out to be. Put briefly, this assumption is that political Zionism "strove to integrate two, in principle conflicting, value premises: the collective particularism of Jewish aspirations to an independent national state and the universalism of modern Western civilization." According to this aspiration, "the Jewish state was to be an enlightened one, in which the secular values of freedom, justice and equality for all citizens without difference of race, nationality or religion would be fully realized; though a national state, it was to be fully a democratic one, in which universalistic principles would govern the relations between all citizens." For Zionist idealists, in fact, the new state was to be "a light unto the nations."

In more recent years, however, the emphasis has shifted, Cohen notes. Rather than insisting on both features of Zionism, the particularistic and the universalistic, "the particularistic component of the Zionist ideology" began to take the upper hand; this shift, in turn, "created a more comfortable background against which the Oriental Jews could reassert their ethnicity and their changing attitude to the nature of the State of Israel." According to Cohen, the shift—though it already had begun "under the pre-1973 Alignment [Labor] government"—intensified dramatically following the ascendance of the Likud in the 1977 elections, a development usually attributed to the so-called ethnic vote.[13]

There is, of course, a great deal of confusion here in the very usage of terms like "particularism" and "universalism," and especially in the way Cohen seeks to apply them in dealing with Israel's ethnic problem. In what way, for instance, can the refusal of Oriental youths to accept Westernization as a necessary passport to civic equality and political power-sharing be construed reasonably as a rejection of the alleged universalistic component of Zionism? Why should the contrary not be the case? After all, what the Orientals refused to accept was that they ought to become *different*, to be something they had not been. This is usually a perfectly natural, even healthy, and almost inevitable reaction; rather than amounting to a rejection of universalism, it might well have been considered a laudable affirmation of universalism!

No less problematic is Cohen's assertion that the Orientals—of whatever age group—have rejected Westernization altogether or refused to adopt its ways and its mores. Indeed, insofar as the term "Westernization" has any relevance in the present context, it can be argued safely that these Oriental

Jews, though refusing to accept Westernization as a precondition for being granted full civil and human rights, in fact heartily welcomed Western technology and Western premises—especially that part of Western political culture that stressed the merits of representative government and taught the democratic way of life.

For it was precisely this measure of Westernization that enabled the Orientals to turn the table, so to speak, on what they perceived as a bossy, patronizing, ethnocentric, and politically monolithic Ashkenazi Labor party hierarchy. To put it a little differently, in a strange turn of fortune rarely paralleled in the depth of its irony, the Orientals—who as Cohen asserts were asked to be Westernized "in order to become Israelis"—did precisely that: In 1977, they duly exercised their elementary right as Israelis, in the best Western democratic traditions, in an effort to unseat a regime that they decided was neither to their liking nor in their or the state's best interest.

Another of Cohen's points, which in fact constitutes the core of his whole thesis, is also worth examining briefly. Asserting that "the present crisis of Zionism made it easier for Israel's Oriental Jews to reassert their ethnic identity while claiming acceptance for themselves and their traditions by the wider Jewish society," Cohen goes on to say that "a successful realization of [the Orientals'] aims may significantly change the nature of Israeli society." In the main—and most crucially—such an eventuality will, according to Cohen, "further exacerbate," even "hopelessly extend," the antagonism between Israel and its neighbors, and between Jews and Arabs within Israel.[14]

To argue that the Oriental Jews in Israel had to wait for a crisis to erupt in Zionism in order finally to gain acceptance in the Jewish state and "by the wider Jewish society" is of course to malign Zionism and to make nonsense of both its universalistic and its particularistic components (such as they are). The claim that an Israel in which the Oriental Jews get their share of power and decision-making would be averse to an accommodation with the Palestinians and the "future assurance of the civil rights of Israeli Arabs," as Cohen phrases it, is a wild generalization which has not a shred of evidence to support it. To be sure, the argument has consistently been liberally aired by frustrated Labor party functionaries and self-serving fellow-traveling intellectuals. But from scholars and academics one is entitled to expect more caution and minimally authenticated evidence. Simply voting for the right-oriented Likud provides no such evidence about Oriental Jewish attitudes and grievances.

There is, however, more to this than meets the eye, and Cohen's thesis is only part of a larger argument involving Israel's future as a whole. Israelis, in fact, seem destined to argue and reargue points about problems that one would think had long been settled or forgotten. One such point (as formulated earlier in this chapter) concerns the future cultural face of Israel; it is often formulated in a question like this: Should Israel adopt Western culture and its ways (i.e., be "Western"), or should it adopt Eastern culture and *its* ways (i.e., "Orientalize")?

In the 1970s and 1980s, the controversy tended to become both an outcry and a lamentation. The rise to power in 1977 of the Herut-Liberal Likud bloc was made possible, many believe, solely by the "Oriental vote," resulting in the increasingly religious-nationalist thrust of Israel's policies and stands, the alleged emergence of "street corner politics," and the outspokenness and "lack of sophistication" that characterized Israeli utterances and tactics under the Likud. All these phenomena, in one way or another, were viewed as the inevitable result of a shift away from the values and mores of Western culture and Western civilization under the impact of a variously labeled Eastern, Arab, Oriental, Middle Eastern, or Levantine sociopolitical culture.

Those who propound this version of events are generally designated as "Westerners"—Israeli men and women who for a variety of reasons seriously aspire to enforce a kind of neatly drawn blueprint for Israeli's future cultural face made to fit their own well-defined, if hopelessly outdated, image of the West and its culture. They seem to think of Israeli culture in black-and-white terms and often formulate their outlook as "Israel: East or West?"—as if somebody somewhere, somehow, could actually sit down, draw up, and finally manage to put into effect a cultural plan for the future of any country or society, let alone one, like Israel, that is culturally, temperamentally, and traditionally so heterogeneous and pluralistic. For the advocates of this stand, in fact, the world is divided culturally between "East" and "West"; if you fail to be either one or the other, you do so at your peril—which in this particular case is the danger of "Levantinization," a dismal state said to signify a cultural vacuum and "lostness."

The truth, of course, is far more complex. For the fact is that even if such clear-cut distinctions exist and are applicable to certain parts of the world, they are neither valid nor relevant when applied to the Israeli situation. It is curious, to say the least, that those in Israel who advocate a Western-oriented culture (and especially those who call for some sort of "planning" toward that end) are usually outsiders to that very culture—people who hail, for the most part, from countries of Eastern and Central Europe and for whom the West and its culture are more an ideal than an experienced reality. Moreover, and far more importantly, it seems obvious that any attempt to plan and create an "infrastructure" of Israeli culture based on an East-West dichotomy is bound to lead to something close to cultural coercion.

Culture, it has been said, is the person. Put a little differently, this means that by accepting the person we also accept the culture, while if we reject the culture we likewise reject the person bearing that culture. To be sure, to speak of "persons" is to refer to people with special cultural traits. However, these traits are not classifiable into "Eastern" and "Western."

It is a fact, for example, that in Jewry, Easterners as well as Westerners are vastly different precisely within these two broad designations. Among those said to be of Eastern origin are Moroccans, Iraqis, Yemenites, Levantines, and the Falashas of Ethiopia. Among Jews considered Westerners are Eastern Europeans, Germans, Frenchmen, Italians, "Anglo-Saxons" from several parts of the English-speaking world, South Africans, and Latin Americans. There are also the Georgians, the Kurds, the Bukharans, and other groups from Soviet Asia and the Indian subcontinent. These decidedly do not lend themselves to simple cultural categorization as Easterners or Westerners.

Advocates of Western-oriented cultural planning for Israel, plainly not averse to a system of cultural coercion, bewail the danger of "Orientalization," "Arabization," "Levantinization," and other terms they use to vent their dismay whenever members of the non-Ashkenazi majority voice some of their resentments and grievances. Their anxiety increased visibly since the 1977 Knesset elections, which for them indicated a polarization in Israel of two distinctive political cultures. On one hand, we are told, there is an Oriental community on the upsurge, thanks to its numbers and high birthrate. On the other, there are the Western and European settlers who had been dominant in the Zionist movement and the building of the state, but whose numbers are dwindling because Western immigration is declining and emigration is on the increase.

As a result, it is said, Israel is in danger of becoming just another small, divided Middle Eastern state—one that is often viewed by critics as Jewish in its religious domination by rigid orthodoxy, but in the volatile temper of the majority of its population not much different from its Arab neighbours. Diaspora Jews, too, especially those who consider themselves liberal, have also accepted the validity of what can best be termed the myth of Orientalization. This is the fear that Israel will become just another Middle Eastern state, and "the dumping ground for blue-collar survivors of the North African malaise and ultra-Orthodox fanatics," as an American Reform rabbi once put it.

If Israel is really in danger of Levantinization, this is largely the result of the absence of a cultural live-and-let-live policy. The situation, indeed, has its roots in a wrongheaded concept of immigrant "absorption," which decreed that newcomers from the lands of Islam should be assimilated into and then made to share in a cultural-political milieu totally foreign to them. Those who could not or would not thus shed their old cultural identity for a new and alien one were left behind, marginalized.

This state of affairs, combined with an educational system that presupposed and required active participation by the parents, resulted in the exclusion and alienation not only of the immigrants themselves (conveniently condemned as "the desert generation" anyway) but of their children as well. The last thing Israel needs now is any kind of cultural "planning," be it Western- or Eastern-oriented. Israeli culture is neither Western nor Eastern, and there is no way of forcing its development in either direction without causing great harm to the country's future as well as immeasurable hardship for one or the other of its various cultural and ethnic groups.

Another aspect of this subject is worthy of some consideration here. There is a fairly widespread belief in Israel—especially among the Western-oriented, overwhelmingly Ashkenazi elite—that the Oriental element has become the main impediment to peace with the Arabs. This belief has its roots in the fact that, since the 1977 elections, the Orientals have massively supported the Likud group. The theory is that, since the Likud is a right-wing, ultranationalist, and generally religion-oriented coalition advocating a hard-line policy toward the Arab world, the Oriental Jews (from whose ranks the Likud gets about 70 percent of its votes) are "anti-Arab" and opposed to a peace settlement based on a territorial compromise.

Oriental Jews are also said to "hate" the Arabs because during centuries of life under Arab rule they were subjected to persecution, deprivation, and oppression of the worst kind. In addition, Oriental Jews are often blamed for the growing trend toward authoritarianism and religious fanaticism. Finally, we are told, with the help of a combination of "primitive" Likud politics and a fanatical brand of religious nationalism, these Orientals by their voting habits are now dragging the country away from its Western, democratic, and humanist tradition and into the abyss of "Orientalization."

The only verifiable part of this novel argument is that, in the 1977 elections, a majority of Israel's Orientals decided to change their voting habits, making it possible for a Likud coalition government to rule the country for eight consecutive years and, since the 1984 elections, blocking the way before the Labor Alignment to rule the country uncontested.

This change, however, has been an essentially negative gesture, in the sense that the Orientals in 1977 gave a vote of no confidence in a political establishment and in a cultural elite which they chose to identify and equate with the "Ashkenazis." They voted for Menahem Begin and his party not because they liked their foreign or domestic platforms, not because they could spot the difference (for what it is) between these platforms and the ones offered by the Labor Alignment. They voted the way they did because they thought they had had enough of an exclusively Ashkenazi ruling elite which, they believed, looked down on them and on their culture, prevented them from attaining positions of power and influence, and generally refused to grant them anything like their piece of the national pie.

The argument that the Oriental Jews in Israel are an impediment to peace with the Arabs is, in reality, without foundation. As a matter of fact, the opposite may be said to be true. The fact that a Likud coalition government has nothing to fear from its Oriental constituency on the question of what are called "territorial concessions" (as was demonstrated during the negotiation of the peace treaty with Egypt) proves at least one major point: that the Orientals as a group are not ideologically oriented either to the doctrine of greater Israel or to the Zionist mystique of land. In none of the major ultranationalist groups, in fact—Gush Emunim, the Tehiyya movement, or Kach (the fringe group led by Meir Kahane)—are Orientals prominent or significant numerically. In fact, the contrary is true.

It is indeed something of a paradox, but had Menahem Begin's party's constituency not been overwhelmingly Oriental, he would have been unable to make the kind of concessions he made to Egypt—concessions that the Labor Alignment still holds were excessive, unnecessary, and made in unseemly haste.

It is, in fact, precisely Labor's electoral constituency, estimated at 70 percent Ashkenazi, that would have prevented such a turn of events. Indeed, when the time comes to make more concessions to the Palestinians or to the Syrians, a right-oriented government would be far less hampered to make them than one led by Labor, irrespective of what the latter's foreign-policy platform might say. In this sense, the Oriental vote may yet prove to be no impediment to peace with the Arabs, but rather a significant contribution to that peace.

The Futility of "Cultural Planning"

In the course of his long eulogy-lament, cited earlier in this chapter, Yoram Bronowski quotes from a poem by the Polish poet Czeslaw Milosz and states, almost in passing, that he often thinks Israel's position culturally is analogous to that of Poland—namely, that of "a frontier post between East and West." One cannot but wonder how Bronowski arrived at this analogy. The truth, of course, is that while Poland may indeed be regarded as a frontier post between East and West—and while Israel, too, is situated on the borderline between East and West—the analogy becomes totally false when we realize that in these two instances we are speaking about two entirely different "Easts." The East on whose borderline with the West Poland happens to stand is largely a political-diplomatic concept, a function of the then-ongoing struggle between the two superpowers, and only marginally cultural in character. The East on whose borderline with the West Israel is situated, on the other hand, is taken to be an entirely cultural concept—or rather should be, or was!

To be more specific, the subject of East and West is highly complex, and opinions vary widely—all the way from Kipling's famous dictum that East is East and West is West and never the twain shall meet, to Mahatma Gandhi's outspoken denial of the very concept of a Western versus Eastern civilization. To be sure, thinkers both of the East and the West often have made some sharp distinctions between their respective civilizations and ways of life—and almost always to the detriment of the West. Here are a few examples:

- Sir George Birdwood refers sadly to "the secular, joyless, inane and self-destructive modern civilization of the West"—and contrasts this with the attitude of the Eastern philosopher who, he says, amid the stream of fast-moving traffic, driven by the urge to go somewhere, anywhere, would advise each hectic driver to stay where he is and meditate.[15]

- F. S. C. Northrop, author of *The Meeting of East and West*, believes that the East has its own kind of knowledge based on experience or "the immediately apprehended aesthetic component of the nature of things."[16]

- The Earl of Portsmouth proclaims that "We have much to learn from the East—from high farming to high philosophy."[17]

- And, speaking of philosophy, René Guenon (a Westerner) quotes a Hindu comment on the philosophical works of Europe to the effect that "the ideas in them would only do credit, at the most, to a child of eight."[18]

- Cranmer-Byng, an Eastern thinker, observes that "The everyday men of the West walk faster and talk louder and seek refuge in speed and sound from the self whose narrowing limit they would escape and the non-self whose eternity appalls them."[19]

These are but a few samples. However, to a man like Mahatma Gandhi, the very concept of Western and Eastern civilizations seemed wrong. According to him:

1. There is no impassable barrier between East and West.

2. There is no such a thing as Western or European civilization, but there is a modern civilization which is purely material.

3. The people of Europe, before they were touched by modern civilization, had much in common with the people of the East (at least with the people of India). Even today, Europeans who are not touched by modern civilization are far better able to mix with Indians than the offspring of that civilization.

4. It is not the British people who are ruling India, but it is modern civilization through its railways, telegraph, telephone, and almost every invention which has been claimed as a triumph of civilization."[20]

The truth is that, despite all the loose talk we are accustomed to hear about East and West, no definitive idea exists as to what the terms mean or signify. With reference to "Orient" and "Occident" (terms that are usually used to mean "East" and "West," respectively), Professor Clark Wissler says: "It is not always clear what is meant by those who use these terms, but in most cases merely Asia and Western Europe are meant.[21]

Finally the late Professor Hans Kohn includes in the East Turkey, Persia, Egypt, India, and China. According to him, the Occident is either Europe only or both Europe and America. Russia "represented to a large extent the Orient for the Occident and the Occident for the Orient," and it "has been the meeting place of the East and the West by her history and by her nature."[22]

All these are examples of the thinking of non–Middle Easterners on the subject. We shall now cite what a great Egyptian thinker has to say about his own country's place among the civilizations of the world. Taha Hussein, in a book published in the late 1930s entitled *The Future of Culture in Egypt*, explains that from ancient times, there have been two civilizations on this globe, that of Europe and that of the East. Is the Egyptian mind Eastern or Western in terms of its concept formation or imagination, perception, understanding, and judgment?

In attempting to answer this question, Taha Hussein claimed that there was but one test: Is it easier for the Egyptian mind to understand a Chinese or a Japanese, or a Frenchman or Englishman? The answer, he said, was obvious. There is no evidence of intellectual, political, or economic ties between Egypt and the East (i.e., the Far East) in antiquity. Close ties existed solely with the Near East—Palestine, Syria, Iraq. On the other hand, there is no need to dwell on the well-known connections between Egypt and the Aegean, and Egypt and the Greeks, from the beginnings of their civilization down to Alexander.

All this shows, Taha Hussein concludes, that the Egyptian mind had no significant ties with that of the Far East and that its real ties were all with the Near East. If the Egyptian mind was affected by any outside influence, therefore, this influence was Mediterranean. Mediterranean civilizations interacted, with Egypt holding the precedence of age; but never did her mind enter into contact with India, China, or Japan. However, he added, although all this is fairly well known to everybody, the Egyptians will consider themselves Easterners, closer in mind to the Indians, the Japanese, the Chinese, than to the Greek, the Italian, the Frenchman![23]

Taha Hussein spoke with disapproval of his country's inclusion in what is commonly known as the East. To come closer to our own time and situation, I will cite here two diametrically opposed attitudes to the subject expressed by two prominent Israeli Jews, who according to all accepted notions, are "Orientals" or "Easterners." Some years ago, I used to write a weekly column for the *Jerusalem Post*. One day, while hurrying to finish some piece of work, I got a telephone call from the late Yitzhak Shammoush, then lecturer in Arabic literature at the Hebrew University and a native of Syria. The conversation went roughly as follows:

"Rejwan? Are you the same Rejwan who writes in the *Jerusalem Post*?"

"Yes, I'm the one."

"I read your articles, and I'd like to know where you got your education."

"In local schools in Baghdad, where I came from."

"Are you sure you didn't study at any foreign school or university?"

"I'm quite sure. But why are you asking?"

"Well, er, you see . . . it's just unbelievable. You don't write like an Oriental."

"And how, pray, is an Oriental supposed to write?" I asked somewhat rudely.

To which he replied, "Well, look, you surely know what I mean."

And so on. The truth of the matter was that I did not—and still do not—know what he meant!

My second example is not personal. Sometime in the early 1980s, I had the opportunity of hearing Professor André Chouraqui speak on the subject of Oriental Jews in Israel. One of the points he made was that he, coming as he did from Algeria (which is considered the West—*maghrib*), does not consider himself at all an Oriental, despite the fact that the name Chouraqui seems to originate in the Arabic word *sharq*, or *mashriq*, meaning "east."

It would thus appear that, even from the purely geographical point of view, the terms "East" and "West," "Orient" and "Occident," have no definite or commonly accepted meaning.

While I myself have no clear-cut ideas to offer about this highly complex subject, I do tend to subscribe to the view expressed by Gilbert Murray many years ago in a conversation with Gandhi:

All generalizations about whole nations or groups of nations are superficial and inaccurate, even when made by scientific students without personal bias. And most of these actually current [generalizations] are made by prejudiced and utterly unscientific partisans. People talk loosely of the difference in character between "Nordic" and "Latin" nations, or, in a still looser phrase, "East and West," violently denouncing the one and praising the other. Even when there is no actual prejudice at work, the comparisons, though sometimes suggestive, are never exact. For one thing, neither side of the comparison is uniform: Every German is different from every other German, every Italian from every other Italian. Nor can you make any single statement that will be true of all Indians or of all Englishmen. I am always puzzled by the people who ask me "Do I like Indians," or it may be Americans, or Frenchmen—and can only answer, as I would about my own countrymen, that I like some and do not like others.

Being the great scholar that he was, however, Murray went on to say that the differences are there and are felt, though they cannot be analyzed. "The differences are there: they are real and perhaps to a certain extent they are national and racial, though not as much as people imagine."[24]

To sum up this part of our discussion on a lighter note, here is the text of a heated debate on the subject as presented in a cartoon by the well-known American cartoonist/satirist Jules Feiffer. The debate is conducted between a mild-mannered, bespectacled, lean man and an athletic-looking fellow with a highly aggressive appearance.

- My god is an Eastern god (says the former).

- My god is a Western god.

- My Eastern god is hip, cool, contemplative.

- My Western god is aggressive, macho, a go-getter.

- My Eastern god helps you to be at peace with inevitable failure.

- My Western god clobbers you with guilt if you don't make it.

- My Eastern god offsets material anxieties with cosmic numbness.

- My Western god is easy on redemption even if you cut a few corners.

- My Eastern god grossed 40 million tax free last year.

- !!!(Awestruck)

- !!!(Pleased with himself)

- Are you sure your Eastern god isn't my Western God in drag?

As I tried to show at some length in the preceding paragraphs, this is not a simple question of East versus West. There is no sense, there never has been any sense, in an exercise whereby we first try to define the two terms, then work up some sort of fateful confrontation between them, proceed to make a choice between "East" and "West" (the "better" one, needless to say)— and finally set about drawing up a blueprint, a model, an ideal type, for Israel's culture, its direction and its development. Any attempt to determine a cultural "infrastructure" based on the alleged dichotomy between East and West is bound to lead to something dangerously akin to cultural coercion of the worst kind.

In the course of the symposium on the subject of Israel and its place as between East and West, cited above, I stressed this point more than once. Pressed by the two other participants, however, to state how exactly I proposed to let things take their course and to arrive at the kind of pluralistic society in which there would be no coercion, no dictation from on high, I replied quite simply that, as far as I was concerned, the crucial point was to accept human beings as they were rather than trying to change them into something that they are not and never were. I said, too, that I was a believer in the theory advanced by the sociological school known as "culture and personality," which says, in effect, that culture is the person, and that by accepting the person we also accept the culture, and vice versa.

Needless to say, when one speaks of "persons," one speaks of them as people with special traits of their own. These cultural traits, however, are not classifiable into "Eastern" and "Western"—at least as far as our approach to these persons and their well-being is concerned. Easterners as well as Westerners (at any rate, in the way they are perceived in Israel) are of vastly different colors and hues. There are Moroccans, Iraqis, Yemenites; there are Eastern Europeans and *Jekes* (German Jews); and there are Russians, Ukrainians, Georgians, Kurds, South Americans, and "Anglo-Saxons." These are decidedly not given to a simple and simplistic classification into Easterners and Westerners.

In response to these remarks, one of the participants exclaimed—with apparent sorrow: "Then we are practically back at square one!" The other added: "Yes, as a matter of fact we have merely delineated the circle—a circle which I find vicious and rather tragic." The dialogue continued:

> *Rejwan:* I don't recall how many times you have used the word "tragic" in the course of this discussion. I myself don't see any tragedy here whatever.

> *Bronowski:* Insofar as we cannot break out of a vicious circle, this seems to me to be a tragedy—a tragedy of inertia and the inability to build an infrastructure or a common denominator.

> *Rejwan:* What is it we couldn't find? Is it not simply that we failed to decide which orientation Israeli culture should follow, Eastern or Western?

> *Bronowski:* Precisely! Since we failed to agree on frameworks which are so basic and elementary, we have in fact failed to arrive at any basis; we have merely amplified the controversy.

> *Friedlander:* In other words: Only if we were to start from the assumption that there are two, relatively coherent frameworks, would we have been able to draw up some sort of desirable model.

The truth is that I never managed to understand why failure to determine "frameworks" and draw "blueprints" and decide on "models" should in any way be considered a source of such disappointment and frustration. To put it bluntly, I fail completely to see why—as far as cultural matters are concerned—there ever ought to be such frameworks and such models and such infrastructures.

Blueprints and infrastructures may well be absolutely essential when we are dealing with other fields of human endeavor, such as security, health, economics, and physical development. As far as culture and "cultural growth" are concerned, however, the attempt to decide on what is desirable and on the ways to reach it inevitably leads to conditions that are ultimately objectionable and harmful.

Indeed, in the final analysis, such endeavors can lead only to division and polarization rather than to integration and harmony.

Afterword: A Bold Look Ahead

*Academic and aristocratic people live in such an uncommon
atmosphere that common sense can rarely reach them.*

Samuel Butler

This book makes no pretense of complete objectivity—of treating all aspects of its subject matter: history, sociology, and the various cultural and theological matters discussed—as one would be expected to treat some branch of the natural sciences. Nor do I make any claim to being a disinterested observer or to standing apart from my material in the same way in which a chemist or a physicist would. Such a "positivist" approach, I believe, cannot lead to an understanding of either the past or the present. In the words of Lionel Kochan, summing up Lord Acton's thoughts on the subject:

> If [positivism] did not teach sympathy, then it could not understand or experience the past. It could not understand the Zeitgeist. It could not grasp what made one epoch different from any other. It could not see a man in his totality. Above all, it could not penetrate beneath the surface of an epoch and uncover the process of development and change. It was restricted to seeing in history an unchanging pattern of scientific laws.[1]

Here I would like to cite a personal experience. Toward the end of 1971, I was asked to address the American Historical Association's annual convention on the subject of Arab-Jewish relations. The title I chose for my lecture was "Arab-Jewish Relations through the Ages: A Problem for the Historian." In the opening paragraph of my paper, I remarked that, in addition to the problem referred to in the title and which confronts all contemporary historians writing on the subject, there was the dilemma facing a contemporary student of these relations who—like myself—also happens to be emotionally deeply involved in the current stormy events in the Middle East.

I returned to this dilemma in the concluding paragraphs of my lecture. "His," I said, referring to this specific contemporary student, "is obviously a very difficult position. Hailing from an overwhelmingly Muslim-Arab environment, he is liable to be accused of romanticizing and idealizing his encounter with Muslim society. Like the rejected post-emancipation Jew in nineteenth-century Europe," I added, "he might even be open to the charge that, rejected by the predominantly Western-oriented society of Israel as an Asiatic and an Oriental, it is only natural that he should look to other Asiatics and Orientals for comfort—in this case to Muslim Arabs."

It was the British historian E. H. Carr who first advanced the theory that all history is relative to the historians who write it, and all historians are relative to their historical and social backgrounds. "Before you study the historian," he advised, "study his historical and social background."[2]

Are we, then, to despair of finding plain historical truths? Where do the facts of history lie, and how does one set about looking for them? I am, of course, too ill-equipped academically to answer these questions. I will only venture an opinion as to where the trouble really lies.

To my mind, the main trouble (and I am not speaking only about the subject at hand, bedeviled as it is by current conflicts and bitternesses) must be sought in the general predilection of human beings, historians included, to judge historical periods and widely different human cultures by the standards of their own times and their own culture. To give only one example: It is often argued that, while Islam might have been tolerant in practice to non-Muslims living in its domain, it has consistently opposed the "national aspirations" of its minorities.

Yet Islam is not a nationally oriented religion, and nationalism is a relatively very recent European invention. If Muslim-Arab countries oppose the ethnic-national aspirations of Jews, Armenians, Kurds, and Assyrians living in their domains, they do so partly because Islam opposes all ethnic-national aspirations, including those of its Arabic-speaking followers—and also, of course, because no sovereign state ever has stood idly by while a section of its citizenry made active separatist claims. One of the reflections that a historian is likely to make about present-day pan-Arab nationalists is how fundamentally wrong they are in denying others what they claim to be their legitimate right—namely, the right to have a pan-movement of their own based on secular, ethnic, and pagan premises.

This, however, does not justify leveling retrospective charges against Islam on grounds of its treatment of religious minorities. For one thing, Islam cannot be and has never seriously been identified with pan-Arabism.

For another, there are obvious and dangerous pitfalls in trying to apply our present standards to the history of intergroup relations in a period and within a culture completely different from our own.

By way of conclusion, I believe it would be fairly true to say that, judged by the concepts and the standards prevalent at the time, relations between Jews and Muslim Arabs in the past were tolerably peaceful, humane, and amicable—and that peaceful and fruitful coexistence between the two groups was made possible partly by the affinity between the two religions (an affinity that no one seems to deny today). However, neither Jews nor Muslim Arabs seem any longer to be able to live by the old faith. Through innumerable pressures and influences, both Jews and Muslim Arabs have adopted new faiths and now worship new gods.

It is also clearly evident that whatever form Arab-Israeli coexistence takes in the future, it will be based on an understanding between Arab secularist and Jewish secularist rather than on the old link between devout Muslim and devout Jew. This being the case, one would be justified in asking both sides to have the historical sense and the responsibility to keep Islam and Judaism out of their present quarrels and squabbles.

NOTES

Chapter 1: A Problem and Its Roots

1. Charles Freundlich, *Peretz Smolenskin: His Life and Thought* (New York, 1965), 263–64.

2. Moshe Dayan, "A Soldier Reflects on Peace Hopes," in *A Middle East Reader*, ed. Irene L. Gendzier (New York, 1969), 413.

3. Stephen S. Rosenfeld, "Israelis Face a Shattered Illusion," *Washington Post*, March 22, 1970.

4. I. F. Stone, "The Future of Israel," *Ramparts* (San Francisco), July 1967.

5. Theodor Herzl, *Old-New Land* [Altneuland], trans. Paula Arnold (Haifa, 1960), 94–95.

6. Hans Kohn, "Zion and the Jewish National Idea," *Menorah Journal* (New York) 46, nos. 1–2 (Autumn–Winter 1958), reprinted in *Zionism Reconsidered*, ed. Michael Selzer (London, 1970), 190.

7. Hannah Arendt, "Zionism Reconsidered," in *The Jew as Pariah* (New York, 1978), 131.

8. Cited by Kohn, "Zion and the Jewish National Idea," 194.

9. Ahad Ha-Am, cited in Kohn, "Zion and the Jewish National Idea," 195–96.

10. Chaim Weizmann's dicta on the Arab question are quoted in Meyer Weisgal, *Chaim Weizmann: Statesman and Scientist* (New York, 1944), 55, 58.

11. Robert Weltsch's reflections are taken from an article in *Jewish Social Studies* (New York), July 1951, in Kohn, "Zion and the Jewish National Idea," 191.

12. Kohn, "Zion and the Jewish National Idea," 192–93.

13. Cited by Kohn, ibid., 204–5.

14. Quoted in Paul R. Mendes-Flohr, *A Land of Two Peoples: Martin Buber on Jews and Arabs* (New York, 1983), 88.

15. Judah Magnes, "Solution through Force?," reprinted in *Middle East Reader*, ed. Gendzier, 334.

16. Hannah Arendt, "The Jewish State: Fifty Years After, Where Have Herzl's Politics Led?" in *The Jew as Pariah*, 174–75.

17. Arthur Ruppin, *Pirkeh Hayyai* [Chapters from my life] (Tel Aviv, 1968), 3: 149, 258.

18. Cited in Kohn, "Zion and the Jewish National Idea," 206–8.

19. Weisgal, *Chaim Weizmann*, 58.

20. Quoted in Elie Kedourie, "Sir Herbert Samuel and the Government of Palestine," *The Chatham House Version and Other Middle Eastern Studies* (London, 1970), 78.

21. Joel Carmichael, "The Anatomy of a Fossil: Mandatory Palestine," *Midstream* (New York), March 1966, 72.

22. David Ben-Gurion, *Pegishot 'im Manhigim 'Arabim* [Meetings with Arab leaders] (Tel Aviv, 1967), 48.

Chapter 2: Nationalism Tribal and Territorial

1. Lord Acton, "Nationality," in *Essays in Freedom and Power* (New York, 1955), 141–70.

2. Hans Kohn, *Prophets and Peoples* (New York, 1946), 16–17.

3. Ibid., 100, 105.

4. Lewis Namier, *Facing East* (London, 1947), 38–39.

5. Lewis Namier, *Avenues of History* (London, 1952), 22–23.

6. Hans Kohn, *The Idea of Nationalism*, quoted in Namier, *Avenues*, 23–24.

7. Hannah Arendt, *The Burden of Our Time* (London, 1951), 226.

8. Ibid., 239–40.

9. Kohn, *Prophets and Peoples*, 115–16.

10. Arendt, *Burden of Our Time*, 227.

11. Ibid., 227–28.

12. Elie Kedourie, *Nationalism* (London, 1960), 58.

13. Herder's thoughts are quoted by Kedourie, *Nationalism*, 57, 58–59.

14. Ibid., 59.

15. Arendt, *Burden of Our Time*, 230–31.

16. Ibid., 234.

17. Quoted in Boyd C. Shafer, *Nationalism Myth and Reality* (New York, 1955), 147.

18. Kedourie, *Nationalism*, 74.

19. Ibid.

20. Bauer is quoted in Kedourie, *Nationalism*, 116.

21. Arendt, *Burden of Our Time*, 231–32.

22. Ibid., 239.

23. Ibid., 234.

24. Kedourie, *Nationalism*, 75.

25. Arendt, *Burden of Our Time*, 234.

26. Ibid., 234–35.

27. Ibid., 235.

28. Kedourie, *Nationalism*, 75–76.

29. Karl R. Popper, *The Open Society and Its Enemies* (London, 1962), 2: 50–51.

30. Ibid., 2: 51.

Chapter 3: The Jewish Nationality Issue

1. C. G. Montefiore, "Nation or Religious Community," *The Jewish Quarterly Review* (London) 12: 177–94.

2. E. S. Artom, *Hayyei Yisrael He-Hadashim* [Israel's new life] (Tel Aviv, 1966), 28.

3. J. L. Talmon, *The Unique and the Universal* (London, 1963), 283.

4. On Brother Daniel's trial and the Supreme Court's decision, see Marc Galanter, "A Dissent on Brother Daniel," *Commentary* (New York), July 1963, 10–17; "When Is a Jew Not a Jew?," in *Jewish Heritage Reader* (New York, 1965), 5–10.

5. Quoted in Nissim Rejwan, "Discord in Israel," *Dissent* (New York), Spring 1972, 319.

6. Jakob J. Petuchowski, *Zion Reconsidered* (New York, 1967), 117–18.

7. Henry Bamberger, "The Nature of the Jew," *The Jewish Spectator* (New York), June 1968, 11–13.

8. Salo W. Baron, *Modern Nationalism and Religion* (New York, 1947), 248. For a resumé of the views of various Jewish scholars on "Who is a Jew?" see Meir Ben-Horin, "Interpretations of Judaism," in *Studies and Essays in Honour of Abraham A. Neuman* (Leiden, 1962), 49–87.

9. Salomon Schechter, *Aspects of Rabbinic Theology* (New York, 1909), 105–6.

10. David Ben-Gurion in an interview in *Maariv* (Tel Aviv), May 12, 1967.

11. Bamberger, "Nature of the Jew," 12–13.

12. Petuchowski, *Zion Reconsidered*, 30.

13. Ibid., 30–31, 118–21, 123.

14. Joseph L. Blau, *Modern Varieties of Judaism* (New York, 1966), 119–20, 123.

15. Jacob Katz, *Exclusiveness and Tolerance* (Oxford, 1961), 183–84.

16. Max Margolis and Alexander Marx, *History of the Jewish People* (Philadelphia, 1927), 686–87.

17. Ibid., 703.

18. Freundlich, *Peretz Smolenskin*, 55.

19. Hannah Arendt, "The Jewish State Fifty Years After: Where Have Herzl's Politics Led?," in *The Jew as Pariah*, 165–66.

20. Israel Cohen, *The Zionist Movement* (London, 1945), 78.

21. Leon Simon, *Ahad Ha-Am: A Biography* (London, 1960), 184.

22. Arthur Hertzberg, *The Zionist Idea: A Historical Analysis and Reader* (New York, 1960), 52.

23. Simon, *Ahad Ha-Am*, 266.

24. Blau, *Modern Varieties*, 161.

25. Hertzberg, *Zionist Idea*, 55.

26. Kedourie, *Nationalism*, 81.

27. Simon, *Ahad Ha-Am*, 229.

28. Ibid., 207.

29. Leon Roth, *Judaism: A Portrait* (New York, 1961), 224–26.

30. Ibid., 111.

31. Ibid., 225.

32. Simon, *Ahad Ha-Am*, 207.

33. Roth, *Judaism*, 226.

Chapter 4: In Search of Identity

1. Eliezer Livneh, "The Test of Israel," in *Confrontations with Judaism*, ed. Philip Longworth (London, 1967), 146–47.

2. Abba Eban, *The Jewish Observer and Middle East Review* (London), September 11, 1964.

3. Raphael Loewe, "Unifying and Diversifying Forces in Jewish Culture," *Kol Sepharad* (London), July–August 1967, 9–10.

4. Ibid., 12.

5. Ibid., 13.

6. Louis Ginsberg, *Students, Scholars and Saints* (Philadelphia, 1928), 35–36.

7. Ibid., 37.

8. Hugh Trevor-Roper, *Historical Essays* (London, 1958), 5.

9. *Jerusalem Post*, August 17, 1951.

10. Reported in *The Jewish Chronicle* (London), May 26, 1971.

11. Mimeographed statement, p. 1.

12. Louis Wirth, *The Ghetto* (Chicago, 1956), 5–6.

13. Ibid., 130–31.

Chapter 5: Israel as an Open Society

1. Robert Lynd, *Knowledge for What? The Place of Social Science in American Culture* (Princeton, 1939), 203–4.

2. Pinhas Sapir, *Le Monde* (Paris), March 9, 1966.

3. Irving Horowitz and Maurice Zeitlin, "Israeli Imperatives and Jewish Agonies," *Judaism* (New York), Fall 1967, 387, 389.

4. Charles Malik, "The Middle East: The Search for Truth," *Foreign Affairs* (New York), July 1955, 189–224.

5. Zvi Kurzweil, *Modern Trends in Jewish Education* (New York, 1964), 57.

6. Ibid., 58.

7. Isaiah Berlin, "The Origins of Israel," in *The Middle East in Transition*, ed. W. Z. Laqueur (London, 1958), 208.

8. Ibid., 209.

9. Joseph Bentwich, *Education in Israel* (London, 1965), 44.

Chapter 6: Arab Nationalism and Pan-Arabism

1. H. A. R. Gibb, *The Arabs* (London, 1940), 3.

2. Quoted in Charles F. Gallagher, "Culture, Language and Ideology: The Arab World," in *Expectant Peoples*, ed. K. H. Silvert (New York, 1963), 202.

3. Bernard Lewis, *The Arabs in History* (London, 1951), 9–10.

4. Faris's remarks are quoted in *Arab Nationalism: An Anthology,* ed. Sylvia G. Haim (Berkeley, 1962), 62.

5. Abd al-Rahman 'Azzam, *The Arab Nation: Paths and Obstacles to Fulfillment* (Washington, 1960), 5–14.

6. Abdel Rahman al-Bazzaz, "Islam and Arab Nationalism," in *Arab Nationalism*, ed. Haim, 172–88.

7. S. D. Goitein, *Jews and Arabs: Their Contacts through the Ages* (New York, 1964), 215.

8. Bernard Lewis, *The Middle East and the West* (London, 1964), 70–71.

9. Ibid., 81–82.

10. George Antonius, *The Arab Awakening* (New York, 1946), 15–16, 18.

11. Nabih Amin Faris and M. T. Husayn, *The Crescent in Crisis* (Lawrence, Kans., 1955), 11.

12. Gallagher, "Culture, Language and Ideology," 2.

13. W. B. Fisher, *The Middle East* (London, 1950), 91.

14. Hazem Z. Nuseibeh, *The Ideas of Arab Nationalism* (Ithaca, N.Y., 1956), 46–54.

15. Sati' al-Husri, "The Myth of Separate Arab Entities" [Arabic], *Al-Hayat* (Beirut), August 12, 1951.

16. Albert Hourani, *Arabic Thought in the Liberal Age* (London, 1964), 313.

17. Al-Husri, "Myth of Separate Arab Entities."

18. Kedourie, *Nationalism*, 73.

19. Cecil Hourani, "The Arab League in Perspective," in *Middle East Reader*, ed. Gendzier, 282–83.

20. Boutros Boutros-Ghali, Mahmoud K. 'Isa, and Abdel Malik 'Oda, *Al-Qawmiyya al-'Arabiyya* [Arab nationalism] (Cairo, 1960), 26–29.

21. The text of Nasser's speech is printed in Arabic in *Al-Ahram* (Cairo), May 21, 1964.

22. Ihsan Abdel Quddous, "Socialism and Nationalism" [Arabic], *Rose el-Yusuf* (Cairo), May 25, 1964.

23. Quoted in Hans Kohn, *Pan-Slavism: Its History and Ideology* (New York, 1960), 24–25.

24. Jalal al-Sayyid, *Al-Katib* (Cairo), February 1970, 61–63.

25. 'Ismat Seif el-Dawla, "Resistance from the Nationalist Point of View" [Arabic], *Al-Adab* (Beirut), January 1970, 2–10.

26. Muta' Safadi, in *Al-Adab* (Beirut), February 1970.

27. Lewis, *Middle East and the West*, 70.

Chapter 7: East, West, and Other Vanities

1. Saul Friedlander, *When Memory Comes* (New York, 1978).

2. Ibid., 1–2.

3. Yoram Bronowski, "Barbarians in the Garden," *Haaretz* (Tel Aviv), July 16, 23, 1982.

4. George Kneller, *Educational Anthropology* (New York, 1966), 9.

5. Ibid., 10.

6. A. L. Kroeber and Clyde Kluckhohn, *Culture: A Critical Review of Concepts and Definitions* (New York, 1966), 11.

7. Alfred G. Meyer, "Historical Notes on Ideological Aspects of the Concept of Culture in Germany and Russia," in *Culture*, ed. Kroeber and Kluckhohn, 404–5 (italics added).

8. Kroeber and Kluckhohn, *Culture*, 3.

9. George Kneller, *Educational Anthropology*, 45.

10. Arnold Toynbee, *A Study of History* (London, 1942), 2:256.

11. Ibid., 2:257.

12. Erik Cohen, "Ethnicity and Legitimation in Present-Day Israel," *Jerusalem Quarterly*, no 28 (Summer 1983): 120.

13. Ibid., 113–15.

14. Ibid., 116.

15. Cited in C. Northcote Parkinson, *East and West* (London, 1963), 262.

16. Ibid., 262.

17. Ibid., 262.

18. Ibid., 262–63.

19. Ibid., 263.

20. Robert E. Speer, *Race and Race Relations* (New York, 1924), 126, cited in P. Kodanda Rao, *East versus West: A Denial of Contrast* (London, 1939), 29.

21. C. Wissler, *Man and Culture* (New York, 1923), 232, cited in Rao, *East versus West*, 21.

22. Hans Kohn, *Orient and Occident*, 76, cited in Rao, *East versus West*, 21.

23. Taha Hussein's views are summarized from Nissim Rejwan, *Arabs Face the Modern World: Religious, Cultural, and Political Responses to the West* (Gainesville, Fla., 1998), 43–53.

24. Gilbert Murray and R. Tagore, *East and West* (London, 1935), 12–14.

Afterword: A Bold Look Ahead

1. Lionel Kochan, *Acton on History* (London, 1954), 63–64.

2. E. H. Carr, *What Is History?* (London, 1961), 24.

INDEX